Dynamics of Interorganisational Collaborative Relationships

Dynamics of Interorganisational Collaborative Relationships

Editor

Sandra G. L. Schruijer

MDPI • Basel • Beijing • Wuhan • Barcelona • Belgrade • Manchester • Tokyo • Cluj • Tianjin

Editor
Sandra G. L. Schruijer
Utrecht University; Tilburg University.
The Netherlands

Editorial Office
MDPI
St. Alban-Anlage 66
4052 Basel, Switzerland

This is a reprint of articles from the Special Issue published online in the open access journal *Administrative Sciences* (ISSN 2076-3387) (available at: https://www.mdpi.com/journal/admsci/special_issues/Collaborative_Relationships).

For citation purposes, cite each article independently as indicated on the article page online and as indicated below:

LastName, A.A.; LastName, B.B.; LastName, C.C. Article Title. *Journal Name* **Year**, *Article Number, Page Range.*

ISBN 978-3-03943-420-6 (Hbk)
ISBN 978-3-03943-421-3 (PDF)

Contents

About the Editor

Sandra G. L. Schruijer is Professor of Organization Sciences at the Utrecht University School of Governance and Professor of Organizational Psychology at Tias School for Business and Society, Tilburg University, both in The Netherlands. Her research involves the psychological dynamics of conflict and collaboration within groups and between organizations. Sandra further heads Professional Development International, an institute that organizes professional development programs and consults organizations and managers with respect to interorganizational collaboration and large-scale change.

administrative sciences

Editorial

The Dynamics of Interorganizational Collaborative Relationships: Introduction

Sandra Schruijer [1,2]

[1] Utrecht University School of Governance, Utrecht University, 3511 ZC Utrecht, The Netherlands; S.G.L.Schruijer@uu.nl

[2] Tias School for Business and Society, Tilburg University, 5037 AB Tilburg, The Netherlands

Received: 3 August 2020; Accepted: 5 August 2020; Published: 11 August 2020

1. Introduction

In all spheres of life, relationships among public and private organizations are built in order to deal with complex societal problems and to address economic challenges that cannot be dealt with by single organizations. The world has become interconnected, and many new organizational forms, such as strategic alliances, public–private partnerships, and networks have seen the light of day (e.g., Castells 2009). Because of the interdependencies, interorganizational collaboration is essential, yet working across organizational boundaries is far from simple. It involves a multitude of different organizations, each having its own interests, perspectives, and identities while also varying in power and size. Further, the societal problems that are dealt with often are wicked. The complexities are of a strategic, informational, procedural, yet also of a relational nature as in the end collaborating is a social activity that involves social systems.

The social and relational side of collaborating across organizational boundaries has been addressed by authors such as Barbara Gray (Gray 1989; Gray and Purdy 2018), Chris Huxham, and Siv Vangen (Huxham 1996; Huxham and Vangen 2005). Gray was among the first to introduce the term "collaboration" in this context, describing the conditions for engaging in collaboration and formulating which phases can be discerned in interorganizational work and what tasks need to be dealt with in each of these. Huxham and Vangen wrote about "collaborative advantage" (a very apt term in the world of management and organization where "competitive advantage" dominates the thinking) and "collaborative inertia" (making tangible that collaboration can be painfully slow and can even get stuck). They also described, among other themes, the dynamics of trust building as well as the meaning and nature of leadership where positional authority is absent (Vangen and Huxham 2003; Huxham and Vangen 2000).

The innovative research by Gray and Huxham on the social and relational aspects of collaboration has inspired a lot of research, affecting domains such as public administration, organization theory, project management, regional development studies, and supply chain management, to name but a few. Studies are nowadays being conducted on, for example, trust and its development (e.g., Swärd 2016), on the social and discursive practices in complex collaboration (Van Marrewijk et al. 2016), on joint sense making (Merkus et al. 2016), on action learning in collaboration (Coghlan and Coughlan 2015), on the social dynamics during interorganizational gatherings (for example Sharma and Kearins 2011; Solansky et al. 2014), on the deeper emotional dynamics of such multiparty encounters (Prins 2010), on collective and collaborative leadership (Ospina and Foldy 2010; Ospina and Saz-Carranza 2010), and on the effect of intra-organizational dynamics on interorganizational dynamics (Brattström and Faems 2019). Still, attention to the human and relational side of interorganizational collaboration is not overwhelming, while a deeper understanding of the relational dynamics seems crucial. A well-developed psychological perspective seems especially absent.

This special issue focuses on the relational complexities of interorganizational collaboration, captured by the term dynamics. Dynamics in this context refers to: (a) the social and psychological processes (and their emotional foundations) that occur when organizations and their representatives interact to engage in cross-boundary or collaborative work (e.g., trust and distrust, intergroup stereotyping and conflict, conflict avoidance, inclusion and exclusion of stakeholders, power dynamics, leadership emergence)—occurring both within the participating organizations and between these organizations, as well as (b) the development of these processes over time, in view of external and internal events and/or as a consequence of deliberate interventions to enhance collaborative success. Thus, the emphasis is on the quality of experienced human interactions in interorganizational collaborative processes and the development thereof. The perspective put forward is largely (social and organizational) psychological and sociological, both in terms of understanding the group and intergroup processes as well as efforts to intervene to develop collaborative relationships, based on action research and an organizational development (OD, e.g., Cummings and Worley 1993) approach.

2. Interorganizational Collaboration and Its Dynamics

Interorganizational collaboration refers to the relational processes that emerge when two or more legally independent organizations engage in when coming together to deal with their interdependencies regarding a certain problem domain. They (ideally) jointly define the problem and from there arrive at a joint goal that also serves the interests of the participating organizations. In order to define and realize such a joint goal, the parties need to work with and capitalize on the diversities that are constituted by the organizations' different interests, perspectives, identities, power positions, sectors, and other differences that are relevant to their jointly defined task (Gray 1989; Gray and Purdy 2018; Huxham and Vangen 2005; Bouwen and Taillieu 2004; Vansina et al. 1998; Schruijer and Vansina 2008).

Thus, interorganizational collaboration:

- Involves two or more legally independent parties;
- Is a multilevel process, simultaneously taking place at various system levels, namely, among individuals with their idiosyncratic make-ups and experiences (individual and interindividual level), individuals who also act as representatives of their respective organizations, having their own organizational interests (intra-organizational and interorganizational level), who during their interorganizational meetings make up a temporary group (group level), and all this in a larger context that influences the interorganizational system and is influenced by it;
- Consists of participating organizations that are interdependent with respect to a particular problem domain (while all interdependencies are generally not known fully from the start, and neither is it known from the very beginning who all the stakeholders are, thus participation may shift over time);
- Implies jointly defining a problem domain and from there developing a joint goal—a goal that also is expected to serve the stakeholders' individual interests;
- Is a developmental process where relationships are built, identities and interdependencies are explored, trust is developed, and a collaborative climate is jointly shaped;
- Occurs without positional authority as the interorganizational system jointly defines and works towards the collaborative agenda and thus governs itself (while of course roles may be taken up, such as being a chairperson, yet such roles serve the common purpose);

Organizes itself as it moves from an underorganized state towards a commonly defined goal, jointly developed collaborative climate, self-governance, mutually explored and accepted roles, and validated difference.

These characteristics of successfully collaborating across organizational boundaries are difficult to realize. Collaboration is a complex endeavor, considering the often wicked nature of the issues at hand, the multiple interdependencies, the number of parties and their differences, and the underorganized nature of the setting. Working with difference, a key element of collaboration, is far from simple—and neither is being able to tolerate the complexities and ambiguities involved. The tensions may be very difficult to contain or to address, and can get played out relationally. Rather than realizing that the complexity of the task gives rise to relational tensions, and giving space to ventilate emotions and jointly working these through, the tensions have a tendency to go underground and from there undermine the necessary relationship building. Collaboration, although genuinely wanted by stakeholders, simultaneously invokes conscious and unconscious emotional, relational, and political processes that pose various challenges to the social system (Gray 1989; Huxham and Vangen 2005; Gould et al. 1999; Prins 2010; Schruijer and Vansina 2008; Schruijer 2008).

Stresses and concerns that are experienced (although they may not be attended to at the time) evolve around a number of questions and uncertainties. For example: How can diversity be acknowledged or embraced when people fear "the other" and seem to universally value commonality? Is it safe to bring in one's uniqueness without being rejected or excluded? How can interdependence be accepted when trust between parties has not been built yet? How can trust be built where it is absent or even when distrust dominates? How can one be collaborative while also addressing one's own needs? How can one become part of the whole while keeping one's identity? How can one's role be taken up without knowing whether one's point of view will be accepted by the others? Who is the first party to make a move in a trust building process? Given the ambiguity and complexity, how should one cope with the unknown, uncertainty, and tentativeness, without feeling lost or overwhelmed and without succumbing to overorganizing or oversimplifying? How can the felt need or persistent call for a "strong leader" be resisted? How should one behave when one has little power vis-a-vis the other parties—be visible with the risk of being rejected, or, stay quiet and risk being overlooked?

These challenges, concerns, and fears come together at the collaboration table, where representatives meet so as to explore their possibilities to work together. Such representatives face a difficult task; on the one hand, they need to strike up relationships with the other representatives and build mutual trust (and manage their own tensions as a result of facing diversity), while on the other hand they are simultaneously monitored by their constituencies who want to make sure that the organizational interests are served (and who are not part of trust building or relational development and thus may not be able to correct the distorted images they have of the other organization(s)). Such dual conflicts enhance the pressure and anxieties that are felt by the representatives, who have to work with the complexity and ambiguity, as well as develop a shared goal and a shared strategy. Thus, collaboration takes place in relation to the other representatives, yet also in relation to one's own constituency. The difficulties entailed by working across organizational boundaries become clear in frequently observed phenomena such as premature closure, dissatisfaction with the process and outcomes, suboptimal performance, a climate of distrust, stereotyping, scapegoating, win–lose behavior, positional bargaining, collusion (where any conflict, even constructive conflict, is avoided (Gray and Schruijer 2010; Schruijer 2018)), and power games (Gray 1989; Schruijer and Vansina 2008).

An illustration of the relational complexities of working across organizational boundaries is provided by the observations of what happens during a simulation, that has been played for approximately a hundred times over the last 25 years, as part of open professional development programs and in-company workshops (Vansina et al. 1998; Schruijer and Vansina 2008; see also Curşeu and Schruijer 2018, this issue). It is based on real events concerning economic, social, and ecological challenges in a particular region and involves seven stakeholders. The participants (around 20 to 25 in number), experienced managers and consultants, are eager to learn experientially about the relational dynamics of working across organizational boundaries. They are distributed over the seven stakeholders according to their preference and are asked to identify as much as possible with the interests of the assigned party and try to be themselves (rather than play a role). No assignment is given—it is up to the participants how they want to spend their time (compete, collaborate, self-isolate, come to an agreement or not, etc.). The set program caters for two type of meetings: so-called "visiting", during which they are allowed to meet but never more than three parties simultaneously, and "town hall meetings" where all parties can, if they want to, come together in one room where one representative per party can take a place at a table while the constituency can sit behind him or her. The simulation lasts for more than a full day, while the second day is spent jointly reviewing the dynamics so as to come to an understanding what happened and why.

The group and system dynamics that emerge are generally quite intense and provide for some, as it is called, "unhappy learning" (Ketchum and Trist 1992). While at the beginning of the review the participants generally are fairly happy with the outcome and their own performance, these impressions give way for different and sometimes more confrontational understandings as the joint review progresses. The joint review, after having stepped out of the "heat", helps participants to slowly see the whole system dynamics and their own role in it, to which they seemed blinded during the simulation.

Some frequent dynamics that can be observed (for more information see Vansina et al. 1998; Schruijer and Vansina 2008; Schruijer 2015; Curşeu and Schruijer 2020) are the following:

- A win–lose and distrustful climate develops quickly from the start, even before parties have a chance to meet one another;
- This climate may be played out openly or covertly;
- If this climate is not overcome, it can end in a confrontational power game;
- Alternatively, another (unconscious) dynamic seems to take over, namely one of "pussyfooting", in which conflict avoidance seems to have become the overall purpose, providing for a shared illusion that the participants are collaborating well.
- An interesting dynamic between the public authorities, one of the stakeholders and the other (private) parties, is that the public authorities almost immediately proclaim themselves to be the facilitating and chairing party. The other parties almost never question this, or even call for the public authorities to take a lead. The public authorities mostly truly intend to facilitate the process, yet halfway, mostly too late, realize they are not interest-free, thus not neutral, and have transformed into a manager or director of the process.

Other common observations pertain to:

- The failure to come to a joint problem definition;
- Working with vague shared goals only, that seem to resist any attempt at concretization;
- That hardly any process interventions are made during the simulation;
- That if adequate process interventions are made, the dynamics can change.

Comparable dynamics can also be observed in real-life cross-boundary work, as testified by the many participants of the simulation but also by (action) research conducted in ongoing multiparty projects (e.g., Gray 1989; Huxham and Vangen 2005; Sharma and Kearins 2011; Solansky et al. 2014; Gray and Purdy 2018; Schruijer 2020). It is striking that, despite genuine intentions to collaborate as well as obvious possibilities for parties to add value to one another by collaborating, relational dynamics are triggered anyhow, which jeopardizes the development of truly collaborative relationships. If these dynamics are unacknowledged, remain unaddressed, and are ineffectively handled, it will be very hard for collaboration to be successful. It is therefore necessary, in our networked world, to gain more understanding of the relational dynamics of interorganizational collaboration and to find ways to intervene for the better.

Interventions that are carried out from an OD or a systems-psychodynamic perspective have been developed and are used to stimulate interorganizational collaboration (e.g., Prins 2010; Schruijer 2020). This literature points to the importance of installing the appropriate conditions that are conducive for collaboration (such as creating a holding and containing environment and establishing a minimal structure (Vansina and Vansina-Cobbaert 2008). It also suggests the design and implementation of various interventions such as creating a transitional space (Amado and Ambrose 2001) during which stakeholders can become aware of their relational tensions and their behaviors and through joint review can bring about change (making use for example of multi-stakeholder working conferences), adopting practices to learn from the collaborative experiences (through joint reflection (Vansina 2005)) and helping protagonists work with the diversity, complexity, and ambiguity (for example through process consultation (Schein 1988)).

3. The Special Issue

This special issue consists of seven articles that address the dynamics of collaborating across organizational boundaries. The authors present research on group and intergroup processes while collaborating and on dynamics as they evolve over time, whereas one paper reports on interventions to develop collaborative relationships. The contributions come from Belgium, England, Scotland, Finland, Romania, and The Netherlands, demonstrating that the dynamics of interorganizational relationships have captured the (research) interests across Europe. Some deal with cross-sector relationships, while three papers focus on the care sector. Three articles are written from an action research perspective, where the researchers engage in research with organizations rather than on organizations (see also Huzzard et al. 2000). Two papers are based on questionnaire data collected during simulations. The research approach in these papers is quantitative and seems more "traditional", yet the simulations are embedded in a context where there is ample time created for joint sense-making of the experienced dynamics (and are reported elsewhere). The special issue furthermore contains one theoretical paper that presents a conceptual framework, developed for empirical and practical ends, and finally, as mentioned, one paper is written from the perspective of practitioners. The individual contributions are the following.

The theoretical contribution by Dewulf and Elbers (2018) is a conceptual analysis of power dynamics in cross-sector partnerships. They argue that partnerships are not a panacea for solving complex issues as power imbalances are very likely to exist, and as a consequence, low-power parties are likely to be excluded or not have their interests served. A conceptual framework is developed on power and power asymmetries and how these affect the processes and outcomes of cross-sector partnerships, using various disciplinary perspectives (organizational psychology, business and management, governance literature). A central tenet is that context, namely the interplay of institutional fields and issue fields, determines what type of power can be exercised in and over cross-sector partnerships. Direct power is exercised in cross-sector partnerships through the deployment or withholding of resources, drawing on discursive legitimacy and (subtly) claiming authority, while power is exercised indirectly over cross-sector partnerships through setting the rules of the game (e.g., with respect to participation, defining the agenda, decision-making) and thus determining the latitude for within-partnership outcomes and dynamics (the power to set these rules are determined, again, by resources, discursive legitimacy, and authority). Dewulf and Elbers hope that their framework is used in empirical research, as well as by actors to decide whether or not to participate in partnerships.

Craps et al. (2019) present a relational approach to leadership in the context of multi-actor governance. Their work is based on a relational approach to organizational life (e.g., Hosking 2006) and on complexity leadership theory that has been developed understanding leadership within organizations (e.g., Uhl-Bien et al. 2007), leaving the focus on individual leaders and leadership positions aside. Uhl-Bien's ideas are worked with to comprehend leadership processes and practices between organizations. The case presented involves a landfill mining initiative in Belgium, with actors from government, civil society, business, and the university. The authors focus on the interactions during meetings and explore how group developmental processes and trust building are aided by relational leadership practices. They describe how administrative, adaptive, and enabling leadership practices help shape the developmental process. They argue that enabling leadership is central in coming to a joint understanding and common purpose and point to their own role as action researchers as they engage in enabling practices (bringing the diverse parties and their viewpoints together, facilitating an open dialogue, and creating space for reflection).

Cropper and Bor (2018) present a case study of an association of organizations providing pediatric services in the United Kingdom (general hospitals, specialist hospitals, community service, and primary care trusts). The authors draw on meta-organization theory (Ahrne and Brunsson 2005) to explore the evolution of the membership composition and its effects on the "character" of the association (phrased as the "compositional dynamics"). The association's compositional dynamics and their relation to the institutional environment over the course of 17 years are described, based on the reading of annual reports. A meta-organization is an association of organizations, different from a network as members are similar rather than different and hierarchy and boundedness are stronger than in networks. Moreover, changes of the association are, according to the theory, less a consequence of external events than of the internal relationships between the member organizations and the meta-organization. The authors' findings pose some challenges for meta-organization theory as it appears that the composition, at least in this case, is more diverse (in identity and in activity) than meta-organization theory would expect. Further, the institutional environment and the association's internal dynamics were more closely intertwined than the theory states; the boundaries of the association are more fluid than assumed. The findings thus contribute to a further development of meta-organization theory.

Hujala and Oksman (2018) report on the emotional dimensions of integrated care, based on the experiences of care professionals and care managers, working in cross-boundary teams, when delivering services to clients with multiple complex health and social care problems. Servicing the latter clients requires collaboration between services in primary health care, specialized health care, and social care as well as between professions (nurses, doctors, social workers). The article is based on a large action research project in Finland where complete integration of health and social care is to be realized in 2021. Adopting an emotional labor perspective (e.g., Mann 2005), the authors reanalyzed interviews conducted with managers and professionals, as well as problem analyses conducted by the cross-boundary teams. The main findings are that being a multiple problem client and being a care professional working with these clients give rise to various emotions and that the emotional burden increases as a consequence of ineffective cross-boundary collaboration. Further, care professionals experience difficulties in handling the diverse emotions, leading to avoiding emotions, which can hinder a deeper engagement with the client so that needed services remain unknown or may lead to quickly passing the client on to someone else. While the emotional burden may be shared, rules with respect to how to engage with emotions differ between professions. Finally, the authors noted the occurrence of power dynamics, stereotyping, and territorial behavior.

Kennedy et al. (2019) also write about the integration of health and social care, but now as it happens in Scotland and from the perspective of practitioners, who were contracted to support the process of learning to collaborate across organizational boundaries. The authors describe the principles underlying their approach, couched in organization development, action research thinking, and system psychodynamics. Working with 10 health and social care partnerships across Scotland, they aimed at helping the participants (care professionals and managers) understand how the development of interorganizational relations affected themselves and their teams and, in turn, how they affected the wider organizational system. To illustrate their actual way of working in this project, the events and dynamics within one partnership are described in more detail. Six practices are formulated that in the authors' view are helpful in creating the conditions for successful collaboration: suspending disbelief that "it will not work", having experienced so many earlier organizational changes; coming to a shared purpose; developing a sense of accountability to the shared purpose; exploring diversity, developing relationships, and building trust; designing structures that fit the purpose; leadership that is courageous and willing to work with the whole system.

Fodor et al. (2018) studied the effect of trust enhancement (creating a positive distinction between expected trust in one's own party, compared to expected trust in the other parties) on the expected and actually experienced stakeholder's centrality in a multiparty system, using a social network perspective. To test their prediction (that trust enhancement has a positive effect on centrality) the authors developed a multiparty task, simulating the decision making of six stakeholders that had one day to reach a consensus decision on Romanian educational policy. Altogether 239 students participated (54 groups, distributed over nine runs of the simulation), who took part in a course on learning about group and intergroup dynamics (these dynamics were reflected upon after the simulation ended). Data were collected at four points in time (at the first point perceptions on trustworthiness were tapped, while in the all other rounds data were collected that allowed for the computation of network centrality). Analyses show that, indeed, trust enhancement, based on expectations of trustworthiness, predicts the evolution of network centrality, in a particular sequence. Thus, the authors claim, networks "originate in minds" and after that are shaped by the emerging relational dynamics.

Curşeu and Schruijer (2018), finally, investigate how relational phenomena within stakeholders have an impact on the whole multiparty system (consisting of all stakeholders) and vice versa, namely, how relational phenomena at the whole system level influence the stakeholder level. Predictions were formulated based on social interdependence theory (Deutsch 1949) and on notions regarding emotional contagion. They used the very same simulation that was described earlier in this article as the research context. During the simulation, questionnaires were distributed at various times assessing participants' perceptions of each stakeholder (their collaborativeness and conflictuality) and their perceptions of the within-stakeholder relational climate (task conflict and relational conflict). These questionnaire data were fed back during the review of each simulation so as to aid the joint sense-making. For this study the questionnaire data of five runs were combined. The occurrence of bottom-up processes was more strongly supported than of top-down; changes in within-stakeholder task conflict were positively related to changes in perceived collaborativeness at the multiparty system level, while changes in within-stakeholder relationship conflict were positively associated with conflictuality at the multiparty system level. In the reverse direction, relationship conflict at the multiparty level went together with changes in relationship conflict at the stakeholder level.

These seven articles, despite their differences, also have various elements in common. This introduction to the special issue started with citing the work of Barbara Gray, Chris Huxham, and colleagues, who have done pioneering work when it concerns fathoming and developing the social and relational dynamics of interorganizational relations. Now, having briefly presented the seven articles that are included, it may already be obvious that they are all indebted to and build on the ideas developed by Gray and Huxham. All articles, furthermore, address multiple system levels as the relational dynamics are created and are played out at multiple levels. Disciplinary boundaries are transcended in most of them, through working with diverse bodies of literature. The importance of creating "actionable knowledge" (Argyris 1996) transpires through the special issue, given the role of action research and the importance of reflection, learning and development, even in the more "traditional" research articles. This special issue shows the complexity and multidimensionality of the relational dynamics of interorganizational collaboration. It is hoped that it will stimulate further research and help shape the praxis.

Funding: This research received no external funding.

Conflicts of Interest: The authors declare no conflict of interest.

References

Ahrne, Göran, and Nils Brunsson. 2005. Organizations and Meta-Organizations. *Scandinavian Journal of Management* 21: 429–49. [CrossRef]

Amado, Gilles, and Tony Ambrose, eds. 2001. *The Transitional Approach to Change*. London: Karnac.

Argyris, Chris. 1996. Actionable Knowledge: Design Causality in the Service of Consequential Theory. *The Journal of Applied Behavioral Science* 32: 390–408. [CrossRef]

Bouwen, Rene, and Tharsi Taillieu. 2004. Multi-Party Collaboration as Social Learning for Interdependence: Developing Relational Knowing for Sustainable Natural Resource Management. *Journal of Community and Applied Social Psychology* 14: 137–53. [CrossRef]

Brattström, Anna, and Dries Faems. 2019. Inter-Organizational Relationships as Political Battlefields: How Fragmentation within Organizations Shapes Relational Dynamics between Organizations. *Academy of Management Journal*. [CrossRef]

Castells, Manuel. 2009. *The Rise of the Network Society*. London: Wiley.

Coghlan, David, and Paul Coughlan. 2015. Effecting Change and Learning in Networks through Network Action Learning. *The Journal of Applied Behavioral Science* 51: 375–400. [CrossRef]

Craps, Marc, Inge Vermeersch, Art Dewulf, Koen Sips, Katrien Termeer, and René Bouwen. 2019. Relational Approach to Leadership for Multi-Actor Governance. *Administrative Sciences* 9: 12. [CrossRef]

Cropper, Steve, and Sanne Bor. 2018. (Un)bounding the Meta-Organization: Co-Evolution and Compositional Dynamics of a Health Partnership. *Administrative Sciences* 8: 42. [CrossRef]

Cummings, Thomas, and Christopher Worley. 1993. *Organization Development and Change*. Minneapolis and West Paul: West Publishing Company.

Curşeu, Petru, and Sandra Schruijer. 2018. Cross-Level Dynamics of Collaboration and Conflict in Multi-Party Systems: An Empirical Investigation Using a Behavioural Simulation. *Administrative Sciences* 8: 26. [CrossRef]

Curşeu, Petru, and Sandra Schruijer. 2020. Participation and Goal Achievement of Multiparty Collaborative Systems Dealing with Complex Problems: A Natural Experiment. *Sustainability* 12: 987. [CrossRef]

Deutsch, Morton. 1949. A theory of co-operation and competition. *Human Relations* 2: 129–52. [CrossRef]

Dewulf, Art, and Willem Elbers. 2018. Power in and over Cross-Sector Partnerships: Actor Strategies for Shaping Collective Decisions. *Administrative Sciences* 8: 43. [CrossRef]

Fodor, Oana, Alina Fleştea, Iulian Onija, and Petru Curşeu. 2018. Networks Originate in Minds: An Exploration of Trust Self-Enhancement and Network Centrality in Multiparty Systems. *Administrative Sciences* 8: 60. [CrossRef]

Gould, Larry, Robert Ebers, and Ross Clinchy. 1999. The Systems Psychodynamics of a Joint Venture: Anxiety, Social Defenses and the Management of Mutual Dependence. *Human Relations* 52: 697–722. [CrossRef]

Gray, Barbara. 1989. *Collaborating: Finding Common Ground for Multiparty Problems*. San Francisco: Jossey-Bass.

Gray, Barbara, and Jill Purdy. 2018. *Collaborating for our Future: Multistakeholder Partnerships for Solving Complex Problems*. Oxford: Oxford University Press.

Gray, Barbara, and Sandra Schruijer. 2010. Integrating Multiple Voices: Working with Collusion. In *Relational Practices, Participative Organizing*. Edited by Chris Steyaert and Bart van Looy. Emerald: Bingley, pp. 121–35.

Hosking, Dian-Marie. 2006. Not Leaders, Not Followers: A Post-Modern Discourse of Leadership Processes. In *Follower-Centered Perspectives on Leadership: A Tribute to the Memory of James R. Meindl*. Edited by Boas Shamir, Rajnandini Pillai, Michelle C. Bligh and Mary Uhl-Bien. Greenwich: Information Age Publishing.

Hujala, Anneli, and Erja Oksman. 2018. Emotional Dimensions in Integrated Care for People with Multiple Complex Problems. *Administrative Sciences* 8: 59. [CrossRef]

Huxham, Chris, ed. 1996. *Creating Collaborative Advantage*. London: Sage.

Huxham, Chris, and Siv Vangen. 2000. Leadership in the Shaping and Implementation of Collaboration Agendas: How Things Happen in a (not quite) Joined-Up World. *Academy of Management Journal* 43: 1159–75.

Huxham, Chris, and Siv Vangen. 2005. *Managing to Collaborate: The Theory and Practice of Collaborative Advantage*. London and New York: Routledge.

Huzzard, Tony, Beth Maina Ahlberg, and Marianne Ekman. 2000. Constructing Interorganizational Collaboration: The Action Researcher as Boundary Subject. *Action Research* 8: 293–314. [CrossRef]

Kennedy, Jo, Ian McKenzie, and Joette Thomas. 2019. Developing Effective Collaborations: Learning from Our Practice. *Administrative Sciences* 9: 68. [CrossRef]

Ketchum, Lyman, and Eric Trist. 1992. *All Teams are not Created Equal: How Employee Empowerment Really Works*. London: Sage.

Mann, Sandi. 2005. A health-care model of emotional labour. An evaluation of the literature and development of a model. *Journal of Health Organization and Management* 19: 304–17. [CrossRef]

Merkus, Sander, Thijs Willems, Danny Schipper, Alfons van Marrewijk, Joop Koppenjan, Marcel Veenswijk, and Hans Bakker. 2016. A Storm is Coming? Collective Sensemaking and Ambiguity in an Inter-Organizational Team Managing Railway System Disruptions. *Journal of Change Management* 17: 228–48. [CrossRef]

Ospina, Sonia, and Erica Foldy. 2010. Building Bridges from the Margins: The Work of Leadership in Social Change Organizations. *The Leadership Quarterly* 21: 292–307. [CrossRef]

Ospina, Sonia, and Angel Saz-Carranza. 2010. Paradox and Collaboration in Network Management. *Administration & Society* 42: 404–40.

Prins, Silvia. 2010. From Competition to Collaboration: Critical Challenges and Dynamics in Multiparty Collaboration. *The Journal of Applied Behavioral Science* 46: 281–312. [CrossRef]

Schein, Edgar. 1988. *Process Consultation: Its Role in Organization Development*. Reading: Addison-Wesley.

Schruijer, Sandra. 2008. The Psychology of Interorganizational Relations. In *The Oxford Handbook of Interorganizational Relations*. Edited by Steve Cropper, Mark Ebers, Chris Huxham and Peter Smith Ring. New York and Oxford: Oxford University Press, pp. 417–40.

Schruijer, Sandra. 2015. The Narcissistic Group Dynamics of Multiparty Systems. *Team Performance Management* 21: 310–19. [CrossRef]

Schruijer, Sandra. 2018. The Role of Collusive Dynamics in the Occurrence of Organizational Crime: A Psychoanalytically Informed Social Psychological Perspective. *Administrative Sciences* 8: 1–5.

Schruijer, Sandra. 2020. Developing Collaborative Interorganizational Relationships: An Action Research Approach. *Team Performance Management* 26: 17–28. [CrossRef]

Schruijer, Sandra, and Leopold Vansina. 2008. Working across Organizational Boundaries: Understanding and Working with the Psychological Dynamics. In *Psychodynamics for Consultants and Managers: From Understanding to Leading Meaningful Change*. Edited by Leopold Vansina and Marie-Jeanne Vansina-Cobbaert. London: Wiley, pp. 390–410.

Sharma, Aarti, and Kate Kearins. 2011. Interorganizational Collaboration for Regional Sustainability: What Happens when Organizational Representatives Come Together? *The Journal of Applied Behavioral Science* 47: 168–203. [CrossRef]

Solansky, Stephanie, Tammy Beck, and Deandra Travis. 2014. A Complexity Perspective of a Meta-Organization Team: The Role of Destabilizing and Stabilizing Tensions. *Human Relations* 67: 1007–33. [CrossRef]

Swärd, Anna. 2016. Trust, Reciprocity, and Actions: The Development of Trust in Temporary Inter-Organizational Relations. *Organization Studies* 37: 1841–60. [CrossRef]

Uhl-Bien, Mary, Russ Marion, and Bill McKelvey. 2007. Complexity Leadership Theory: Shifting Leadership from the Industrial Age to the Knowledge Era. *Leadership Quarterly* 18: 298–318. [CrossRef]

Van Marrewijk, Alfons, Sierk Ybema, Karen Smits, Stewart Clegg, and Tyrone Pitsis. 2016. Clash of the Titans: Temporal Organizing and Collaborative Dynamics in the Panama Canal Megaproject. *Organization Studies* 37: 1745–69. [CrossRef]

Vangen, Siv, and Chris Huxham. 2003. Nurturing Collaborative Relations: Building Trust in Interorganizational Collaboration. *The Journal of Applied Behavioral Science* 39: 5–31. [CrossRef]

Vansina, Leopold. 2005. The Art of Reviewing. In *The Transitional Approach in Action*. Edited by Gilles Amado and Leopold Vansina. London: Karnac, pp. 227–54.

Vansina, Leopold, Tharsi Taillieu, and Sandra Schruijer. 1998. 'Managing' Multiparty Issues: Learning from Experience. In *Research in Organizational Change and Development (Vol. 11)*. Edited by William Pasmore and Richard Woodman. Greenwich: JAI Press, pp. 159–83.

Vansina, Leopold, and Marie-Jeanne Vansina-Cobbaert. 2008. *Psychodynamics for Consultants and Managers: From Understanding to Leading Meaningful Change*. London: Wiley.

Article

Power in and over Cross-Sector Partnerships: Actor Strategies for Shaping Collective Decisions

Art Dewulf [1,*] **and Willem Elbers** [2]

1   Public Administration and Policy Group, Wageningen University and Research, 6708 PB Wageningen,
    The Netherlands
2   African Studies Centre Leiden, Leiden University, 2300 RB Leiden, The Netherlands;
    w.j.elbers@asc.leidenuniv.nl
*   Correspondence: art.dewulf@wur.nl

Received: 15 February 2018; Accepted: 8 August 2018; Published: 12 August 2018

Abstract: While cross-sector partnerships are sometimes depicted as a pragmatic problem solving arrangements devoid of politics and power, they are often characterized by power dynamics. Asymmetries in power can have a range of undesirable consequences as low-power actors may be co-opted, ignored, over-ruled, or excluded by dominant parties. As of yet, there has been relatively little conceptual work on the power strategies that actors in cross-sector partnerships deploy to shape collective decisions to their own advantage. Insights from across the literatures on multiparty collaboration, cross-sector partnerships, interactive governance, collaborative governance, and network governance, are integrated into a theoretical framework for empirically analyzing power sources (resources, discursive legitimacy, authority) and power strategies (power over and power in cross-sector partnerships). Three inter-related claims are central to our argument: (1) the intersection between the issue field addressed in the partnership and an actor's institutional field shape the power sources available to an actor; (2) an actor can mobilize these power sources directly in strategies to achieve power in cross-sector partnerships; and, (3) an actor can also mobilize these power sources indirectly, through setting the rules of the game, to achieve power over partnerships. The framework analytically connects power dynamics to their broader institutional setting and allows for spelling out how sources of power are used in direct and indirect power strategies that steer the course of cross-sector partnerships. The resulting conceptual framework provides the groundwork for pursuing new lines of empirical inquiry into power dynamics in cross-sector partnerships.

Keywords: cross-sector partnerships; institutional fields; issue field; collaboration; power sources; power strategies

---

1. Introduction

Processes of globalization have resulted in a wide range of societal problems, which, due to their complexity, can no longer be solved by one actor alone. This new reality requires different kinds of actors, such as governmental agencies, businesses, and NGOs to work together in what is variously referred to as cross-sector partnerships (Van Huijstee and Glasbergen 2010; Selsky and Parker 2005), multiparty collaboration (Gray 1985, 2011; Vangen et al. 2015; Vansina et al. 1998), collaborative governance (Ansell and Gash 2007; Emerson et al. 2012; Huxham et al. 2000), interactive governance (Edelenbos 2005; Torfing et al. 2012a), or network governance (Hajer and Versteeg 2005; Koppenjan and Klijn 2016; Klijn et al. 1995; Provan and Kenis 2007; Sørensen and Torfing 2007).

Cross-sector partnerships have become common practice over the last decades (Gray and Purdy 2018) and range from formal roundtables aiming for certification processes at the global level (e.g., Schouten et al. 2012), to informal coordination mechanisms to manage natural resources at the local level (e.g., Visseren-Hamakers et al. 2010). While cross-sector partnerships are highly diverse in terms of design and objectives, they are characterized by collective decision-making in which a plurality of government, business, and civil society actors are involved (Gray 2007; Selsky and Parker 2005).

Despite evidence that cross-sector partnerships are quite challenging and demanding, once summarized in the principle "don't do it unless you have to" (Huxham and Vangen 2005), they are promoted globally as a 'magic bullet' to deal with complex societal problems. Cross-sector collaboration is often viewed as a straightforward way 'to get things done' through consensus-seeking interaction among relevant and affected actors who share information, authority, and legitimacy (Torfing et al. 2012a, p. 51). The misguided assumption that by merely putting the right people in one room, a workable solution for everybody will emerge, leads people to believe that cross-sector partnerships are power-free processes, in which technical or consensual solutions can be found without dissent or opposition (Torfing et al. 2012a, p. 68). When promoting the concept, partnership enthusiasts often argue that, because of the interdependence of actors in solving the complex issue at stake, cross-sector partnerships will automatically create trust-based relations that result in synergy and enable the active participation of all. In addition, they are associated with flexibility, innovation, low transaction costs, and cross-sectoral learning. The call for cross-sector partnerships is strongly voiced and endorsed by world leaders, governments, and international organizations.

While cross-sector partnerships are sometimes depicted as a pragmatic 'problem solving' arrangements devoid of politics and power, they are characterized by power dynamics (Elbers and Schulpen 2013; Hardy and Phillips 1998; Hendriks 2009; Purdy 2012). Actors in partnerships tend to differ in terms of their control over resources while their interests are diverse and the stakes are high. When power relations are so asymmetric that one of the actors can basically impose its will on the others, one could argue that a partnership approach simply does not apply, and that trying to set up a partnership in those conditions would be ill-advised because the interdependencies linking the actors are missing (Gray and Purdy 2018). However, even when interdependencies between all actors form a good starting point for a cross-sector partnership, dependencies are unlikely to be balanced in all directions, so power imbalances are almost unavoidable (Purdy 2012). Even in situations with clear interdependencies between all actors, partnerships run the risk of becoming arenas for conflict and power struggles (Gray 2004; Purdy 2012).

The power imbalances within cross-sector partnerships are potentially problematic as less powerful actors run the risk of being ignored, overruled, or excluded. There is a growing concern that cross-sector partnerships, as instruments for solving complex societal problems, will not live up to their expectation if power asymmetries are not managed (Purdy 2012). Such asymmetries are said to undermine effectiveness and reduce the likelihood of synergy, trust, and creativity (Hardy and Phillips 1998, p. 218). If the voices of some parties are left out, important pieces of information may be missing from the discussion. More importantly, less powerful actors may be co-opted or excluded from the decision-making table, while decisions may be biased to those with greater resources (Gray 2004; Phillips et al. 2000; Purdy 2012). In such cases, the outcomes of the cross-sector partnerships will not reflect the interests and needs of less powerful actors. Moreover, actors, such as NGOs or community organizations, risk losing their credibility, as they will be held accountable for the cross-sector partnership's outcomes by other actors and by their constituency. Finally, power asymmetries contrast with the normative ideal of collaborative decision-making where all parties involved have equal opportunity to voice their concerns.

While power imbalances play a crucial role in shaping the processes and outcomes of cross-sector partnerships, these issues are often overlooked and they remain generally poorly understood in the literature (Gray 2004; Hardy and Phillips 1998; Purdy 2012; Torfing et al. 2012b). To our understanding, the current theoretical literature dealing with cross-sector partnerships is characterized by at least three limitations: (1) existing frameworks that are proposed for analyzing power within cross-sector partnerships remain at a high level of abstraction making them less useful for empirical research; (2) existing studies do not systematically distinguish between direct power strategies (which produce effects immediately) and indirect power strategies (setting the rules that regulate cross-sector partnerships); and, (3) power dynamics tend to be analyzed without considering the institutional environment in which cross-sector partnerships are embedded. Yet, actors draw upon the institutional context while exercising power within inter-organizational relations (Phillips et al. 2000, p. 30).

This paper seeks to address the above limitations and aims to contribute to the literature by offering a theoretical framework for empirically analyzing how power shapes the outcomes of cross-sector partnerships. Our framework clarifies (1) the nature of the power dynamics within partnerships (through the lens of actor-based, or episodic power), and (2) how these dynamics are influenced by the broader institutional environment of institutional fields and issue fields (using a structural, or systemic, power perspective). Our framework connects the so-called pluralist tradition of the political sciences, which views the exercise of power as a strategic act initiated by actors to advance certain interests, with a view of power that resonates with (post-)structuralist theorists (Foucault 1977; Laclau and Mouffe 1985). The latter tradition emphasizes the power of social structures as opposed to that of actors through self-regulation and internalized constraints.

Our framework bridges disciplinary boundaries and draws on theoretical work on power from different disciplines, including organizational psychology, public administration, organizational science, international relations, and political science. We have built our framework by bringing together insights from the following related, but parallel, literatures: (1) multiparty collaboration, originating in organisational psychology studies of conflict and negotiation in inter-organisational relations; (2) cross-sector partnerships, originating in the business and management literature, with a particular interest in business-NGO partnerships; and, (3) the governance literature originating in public administration and political science, emphasizing how governments engage with non-state actors in interactive, networked, and/or collaborative modes of governance. In building the framework, we rely on insights on power dynamics from each of these three literatures. The framework results in a number of guiding analytical questions that are essential for understanding power in cross-sector partnerships.

2. Conceptualizing Power in Cross-Sector Partnerships

Power is a contested concept and in the literature a variety of definitions and approaches can be found (Bachrach and Baratz 1962; Bourdieu 1989; Castells 2011; Clegg 1989; Dahl 1957; Emerson 1962; Fairclough 1992; Hayward and Lukes 2008; Pettit 2010). Some define power in terms of having resources; others focus on the effects it produces. For some theorists, power is intentional, while others emphasize that power also works unintentionally. For some power is always against the will of others, while others emphasize the power of persuasion, arguing and the possibility of granting power. Some theorists situate power at the level of the actor, while others situate power at the level of structure. Some view power as a zero-sum game (A achieves something at the expense of B), while others relate to achieving collective outcomes. Overall, there is no agreement in the literature on what power is or what dimensions it has.

The complexity of the power concept means that any framework that is designed for empirical analysis must start by situating itself in the literature and offering conceptual clarity. Our starting point is an understanding of power as "the ability to shape and secure particular outcomes" (Torfing et al. 2012b, p. 48). Because collective decision-making is at the core of cross-sector partnerships, power can here be understood more specifically as the ability of individual actors to influence collective decisions of the partnership to their own advantage, in a variety of different ways. The addition of "to their own advantage" signals that our focus is on "power over" others, rather than the more general capacity of "power to" achieve things (Anthony 1984; Gray and Purdy 2018), the power of working together expressed as "power with" others (Gaventa 2006), or the "power for" others that goes beyond self-interest, by aiming for balancing power relations or empowering actors (Huxham and Vangen 2005). In focusing on the ability of individual actors to influence collective decisions of the partnership to their own advantage, we make a distinction between having power and exercising power (Nye 1990). Having power refers to the ability that an actor has to get others to act in line with one's preferences or interests (Dahl 1957, pp. 202–3). Thus, having power is about being able to enforce one's own intentions, interests, preferences, or will, over those of others, in this case, in the context of cross-sector partnerships. Exercising power, also referred to as influence, refers to actors' actual use of their capacity to get others to change their behavior and thus generate an effect. This distinction is relevant because there is no one-to-one relationship between having and exercising power. An actor with a lot of capacity may still have little political influence, while an actor with seemingly little resources may still be very influential, depending on when and how actors decide to use their capacities.

Within cross-sector partnerships that are characterized by some degree of institutionalization (Gray 2004), power refers to the capacity of individuals and groups to influence the outcomes of collective decision-making processes and to benefit from those decisions (Phillips et al. 2000). It is not hard to see that power lies at the basis of political inequality within cross-sector partnerships: by being able to dominate the outcomes of decision-making processes in partnerships, resulting policies and practices may end up favoring the needs and interests of certain actors at the expense of others. We will see below that political inequality in cross-sector partnerships also means that not all actors have equal opportunities to participate in the decision-making in the first place (Nye 1990).

The ability of individual actors to influence collective decisions of the partnership to their own advantage can take a variety of forms. While emphasis in the partnership literature is often on direct power that is based on resource dependencies (Emerson 1962; Emery and Trist 1965; Pfeffer and Salancik 2003; Scharpf 1978), indirect and ideological forms of power are equally important. In the power literature, a distinction is often made between three different faces of power (Bachrach and Baratz 1962; Hayward and Lukes 2008; Torfing et al. 2012b), which can be summarized, as follows: (1) direct power: the ability of actor A, in open conflict with actor B, to make actor B do something that B would otherwise not have done; (2) indirect power: the ability of actor A to regulate and control the decision-making agenda, suppressing issues and proposals promoted by actor B; and, (3) ideological power: the ability of actor A to manipulate actor B's subjective perception of his or her interests, thereby avoiding conflicts altogether. The three faces of power are forms of 'episodic power' and capture the ways actors exercise power over other actors (Gray and Purdy 2018; Lawrence 2008). In this paper, we also take into account the 'systemic power' that is 'exercised' by structures, which is sometimes referred to as a fourth face of power (Torfing et al. 2012b) This form of power is embedded in on-going, taken-for-granted practices and understandings that advantage some groups over others (Gray and Purdy 2018; Lawrence 2008). The framework that we outline below clarifies how episodic forms of power are enabled or constrained by systemic power, embedded in institutional fields and issue fields (Gray and Purdy 2018).

Fundamental to our argument is the conceptualization of power and interactive governance (Torfing et al. 2012b) that analyzes the relations between interactive governance and the broader governance context in terms of power *in*, *of*, *over*, and *as* interactive governance. This relation can be analyzed in terms of "power *in* interactive governance" (multi-actor view of power struggles between actors within an interactive governance arena), but also in terms of "power *of* interactive governance" (ability of interactive governance arenas to influence the social and political environment), "power *over* interactive governance" (ability of governments and other actors to shape and regulate interactive governance arenas"), and "power *as* interactive governance" (interactive forms of governance as a particular historical form of power in advanced liberal societies, through the mobilization of autonomous actors in self-regulating governance arenas).

Given our focus on the ability of individual actors to influence collective decisions of the partnership to their own advantage, and translating these concepts to cross-sector partnerships, our interest is mainly in "power in cross-sector partnerships" (*power in CSPs*) and "power over cross-sector partnerships" (*power over CSPs*). While most attention has been payed to *power in CSPs*, the perspective of *power over CSPs* brings different mechanisms into the picture through which actors can influence collective decisions to their own advantage. These include initiating and terminating partnerships, regulating access to partnerships, framing the type of interaction, or assessing the performance of partnerships (Torfing et al. 2012b).

The ability of actors to exercise *power in* and *over CSPs* depends on the sources of power they have at their disposal. Three sources of power have been consistently mentioned in the collaboration literature and constitute another important foundation for our framework: resources, discursive legitimacy, and authority (Gray and Purdy 2018; Hardy and Phillips 1998; Phillips et al. 2000; Purdy 2012). Resource-based power builds on the dependencies among actors and their access to resources like finance, technology, knowledge, or human resources. Each actor brings in its own set of resources, yet not all resources are of equal value. In those cases where actors depend on others for critical resources, the resource-rich party has a strong source of power at its disposal. Discursive legitimacy refers to the ability of an actor to represent a particular view, or speak on behalf of an issue in the cross-sector partnership. For example, actors can be in the position to speak legitimately on behalf of economic rationality, ecological conservation, or the respect for diverse cultures. Authority is the socially acknowledged right to take action or make decisions based on position within hierarchical settings, and it relates to the relative status of actors in the institutional field in which the participating parties are embedded. While actors may have a variety of power sources at their disposal this does not mean they will actually deploy them to create an effect. Cross-sector partnerships will often try to ask more powerful actors not to use all of the power sources at their disposal during the course of the cross-sector partnership, or to strengthen the power position of less powerful actors through providing funding or capacity building.

3. Institutional Fields, Issue Fields and Systemic Power

To understand how power dynamics in cross-sector partnerships are shaped by the broader environment in which they are positioned, we draw upon the related concepts of issue fields and institutional fields (Gray and Purdy 2018).

An issue field, also known as an inter-organizational problem domain (Gray and Purdy 2018; Trist 1983), refers to a meta-problem that requires inter-organizational response capability. It is comprised of a set of issues that are related to the meta-problem, and a set of actors who have an interest in these issues. Meta-problems are not clearly defined individual problems, but rather 'messes' of interrelated problems that are hard to pin down or delineate (Trist 1983). Examples of meta-problems could be urban homelessness (involving issues of poverty, housing, health care, etc.) or water pollution (involving issues of industry emissions, agricultural practices, biodiversity, etc.). Interdependencies between actors in an issue field provide the potential for collaboration as well as for conflict.

Actors in partnerships have different backgrounds and represent different types of organizations, even more so in the case of cross-sectoral partnerships. The concept of institutional field, coming from organisational institutionalism (DiMaggio and Powell 1983), provides a way of capturing those different backgrounds and their effects on cross-sector collaboration. An institutional field can be defined as a 'recognized area of institutional life' (DiMaggio and Powell 1983, p. 83) in which there is 'a community of organizations that partakes of a common meaning system and whose participants interact more frequently and fatefully with one another than with actors outside the field' (Scott 2008, p. 84). The underlying assumption here is that organisations understand themselves and the world based on shared, and often taken for granted and internalized, belief systems that are learned and maintained through the membership of a given institutional field.

Institutional fields develop through the process of structuration (Anthony 1984), which refers to the interaction between actors that produce and reproduce, the belief systems and practices that constitute the field (DiMaggio and Powell 1983; Lawrence et al. 2002; Scott 2008). Through repeated interactions, groups of organizations develop common understandings and practices that define the field. Actors draw upon the belief systems and accepted practices of their respective institutional field for guidance, meaning, and legitimacy (Phillips et al. 2000, p. 29). The institutional field provides organisations with collective identities, motives, and vocabularies while offering guidance with regard to which problems get attended to, which solutions get considered, what outcomes are to be achieved, and what practices are considered (Townley 1997, p. 263; Thornton and Ocasio 2008, pp. 111–14; Greenwood et al. 2002, p. 59). This implies that the preferences and interests of organisations are seen as socially constructed and varying by institutional context.

Actors in cross-sector partnerships bring with them sets of ideas and languages and practices that are institutionalized with their respective fields (Meyer and Rowan 1977). This means that the range of institutional fields from which actors originate has a major impact on the collaboration (Phillips et al. 2000, p. 28). The more different fields are brought together within a cross-sector partnership, the more values, languages, and working practices enter the cross-sector partnership and the more complex cooperation becomes. This can be a cause for friction as multiple belief systems and standards may be in conflict with each other.

In our view, the concepts of issue field and organizational fields need to be better distinguished, and analyzed in combination, in order to understand how the systemic power embedded in these fields shapes the sources of power that actors have at their disposal for episodic power strategies (see Figure 1). In combination, the concepts of issue field and institutional field help to understand how the broader institutional environment carries systemic power that shapes the power dynamics within cross-sector partnerships. It is at the intersection of institutional fields and a particular issue field that systemic power shapes the power sources that actors can mobilize in episodic power strategies. The starting situation for a cross-sector partnership is usually a weakly institutionalized issue field, with its patterns of dependencies, power relations, and conflicts of interest between actors. The partnership then engages a set of actors of this issue field into direct interaction and collective decision-making, thereby confronting multiple institutional fields that shape the identities, motives, and vocabularies of these multiple actors, *in relation to this particular issue field*. It makes a difference whether the issue field constitutes the core business versus a secondary concern for an individual actor. The power sources (resources, authority, discursive legitimacy) that are available to an actor in a particular partnership are shaped by this intersection. For example, a large food corporation may have huge amounts of financial resources available, e.g., for investing in new product development, but prevailing norms, rules and meanings from its institutional field may limit the amount of resources the organization can actually invest when the partnership addresses an issue field like improving the local education infrastructure in overseas producer communities. Similarly, the authority that a Ministry of Environment is granted within its own institutional field does not necessarily constitute a strong source of power in a partnership that addresses an issue field, like innovating agricultural technology, although it may have a clear interest in the issue field. As another example, the discursive legitimacy of a nature conservation organization to speak on behalf of the natural environment will likely be higher than when it speaks on behalf of poor communities. It depends on the nature of the issue that a partnership seeks to address whether power sources can actually be 'converted' to real influence. Actors draw upon the power sources (e.g., resources, discursive legitimacy, authority) from their respective institutional fields to achieve their goals within cross-sector partnerships. How much power different sources provide, however, is always context-dependent (Clegg 1989). Consequently, the power that certain resources provide in a given institutional field may not translate to the same extent in a cross-sector collaboration. The more the institutional field and the issue are aligned, the greater the likelihood that resources translate to actual power within a partnership.

The above implies a more pervasive and less tangible form of power that cannot be attributed to the strategic acts of self-interested actors. This form of power, which in the literature is often referred to as systemic power, is inherent in the structures of signification pertaining to an institutional field, and shape the identity, motives, and interests of actors in relation to a particular issue field (Lawrence 2008, p. 174), leading to a specific set of power sources (resources, authority, discursive legitimacy) available to each of the actors in a cross-sector partnership.

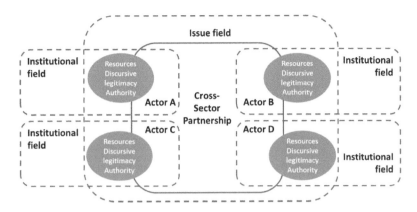

Figure 1. Power sources at the intersection of issue field and institutional fields.

4. Sources of Power and Episodic Power Strategies

The outcomes of cross-sector partnerships for an important part are determined by power games in which actors try to influence collective decisions. Starting from the intersection of issue field and institutional fields, Figure 2 gives an overview of how available power sources can be mobilized for episodic power strategies of two different types: *power over CSPs* and *power in CSPs*.

When actors exercise power, the resources, discursive legitimacy, and/or authority they dispose of are used in episodic power strategies in an effort to steer the behavior of other actors and as such the course of the cross-sector partnership. There are two levels at which these efforts can be oriented: (1) *power in CSPs* and (2) *power over CSPs* (Torfing et al. 2012b). At the level of *power in CSPs*, actors use direct power strategies to influence each other and the outcomes of the cross-sector partnership directly. At the level of *power over CSPs*, actors use indirect power strategies to set or change the rules of the game. Once these rules have been set, they continue to influence the actors within the cross-sector partnership and its course and outcomes (Klijn 2001).

Power in CSPs. Direct power strategies mobilize resources, discursive legitimacy, and/or authority to shape and secure collective decisions in the cross-sector partnership. Resources can be mobilized and exchanged for achieving agreements about outcomes, giving the actors disposing of better resources an advantage in the partnership game. The meaning and implications of partnership goals, knowledge, or problem definitions can be shaped and reshaped in processes of interactive and strategic framing, giving the actors disposing of greater discursive legitimacy or persuasive skills an advantage. Finally, authority deriving from one's position in the partnership (e.g., convener) or in the broader institutional field (e.g., policy maker or CEO) can be mobilized to push claims, preferences, or proposals through.

Power over CSPs. Rules allow for power to be exercised indirectly in the sense that they influence behavior beyond the current moment (Clegg 1989, p. 213). Once established, rules continue to shape the future choices of actors. Indirect power strategies mobilize resources, discursive legitimacy, and/or authority to shape and secure the rules of the game, thereby indirectly influencing the cross-sector partnership actors and outcomes. Starting or continuing a partnership in itself requires resources, and actors who are able to invest these resources can take advantage of this to set the rules of the game for the cross-sector partnership. Actors that have access to high discursive legitimacy in the broader institutional field can obtain easier access to the partnership or can influence how the scope of the problem to be addressed gets framed. Authority can also be mobilized to set the rules for the partnership in terms of access (who is in and who is out) and decision-making (e.g., decision by consensus or majority).

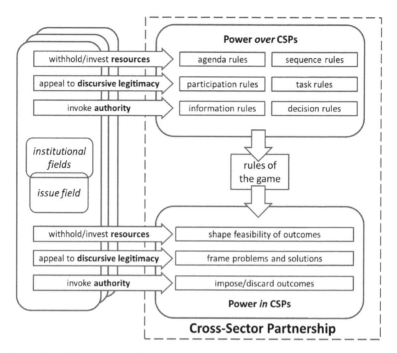

Figure 2. Mobilizing sources of power in strategies for exercising power in and over CSPs.

5. Strategies for Exercising *Power in CSPs*

In the context of cross-sector partnerships, actors use a variety of strategies to directly exercise power over each other to influence collective agreements. Three strategies are prominent, which are directly linked to the power sources actors have at their disposal: (1) withholding/investing resources; (2) appealing to discursive legitimacy; and (3) invoking authority.

5.1. Withold/Invest Resources to Shape Feasibility of Collective Decisions

Within the context of partnerships, actors' influence is strongly based on relations of resource (inter)dependence (Pfeffer and Salancik 2003). In inter-organizational domains, actors depend upon each other for material and immaterial resources, such as money, expertise, information, or contacts to achieve their goals and ensure their survival. Within these relations, each actor brings in its own set of resources, depending on the institutional field in which the actor is embedded. Yet, not all resources are of equal value, leading to relations of autonomy and dependence between actors. When the control of critical resources is diffused among actors and a lot of interdependencies are at play, the collaboration will likely involve greater levels of negotiation, compromise, and pooling of resources (Bouwen and Taillieu 2004; Hardy and Phillips 1998).

In those cases where actors depend on others for critical resources, the resource-rich party is in a strong position to influence collective decisions by withholding resources versus committing to invest resources—assuming that the availability of those resources determines the feasibility of the involved decisions. This way, the desire for resources or the fear of having them withheld ensures the obedience of those being influenced. Pfeffer and Salancik (2003, pp. 45–51) identify three crucial factors for determining the dependence of one actor on another: (1) resource importance—the extent to which a resource is needed by an actor for organizational survival; (2) discretion over resource allocation and use—the degree to which an actor can control how the resource received from another actor is allocated and used; and, (3) concentration of resource control—the extent to which alternative sources of a resource are available and accessible.

5.2. Appeal to Discursive Legitimacy to Frame Collective Decisions

Another important source of power in playing the partnership game is discursive legitimacy (Hardy and Phillips 1998; Purdy 2012). This refers to an actors' ability to speak legitimately for issues or other organizations to influence what situations, issues, or solutions are taken to mean. We try to grasp this aspect through the concept of interactional framing (Dewulf et al. 2009) and collective sense-making (Van Buuren et al. 2014; Vink 2015). From a framing perspective (Schön and Rein 1994; Stone 2002; Van Hulst and Yanow 2014), decision-making in partnerships is shaped by the 'contest over the framing of ideas' through 'selecting, organising, interpreting and making sense of a complex reality to provide guideposts for knowing, analysing, persuading and acting' (Schön and Rein 1994, p. 146). These frames often take shape as short storylines or metaphors, explicitly or implicitly saying something about the cause of the often problematic reality, taking a normative standpoint towards this reality and pointing towards possible solutions.

Taking an interactional framing approach, playing the partnership game involves the interactive alignment of meaning in a process of sensemaking (Weick 1995). In this paradigm, framing refers to a highly dynamic process of actors continuously negotiating over meaning through language. Since each participant co-develops the discussion, they negotiate the relevant framing on the spot, relying on different frame interaction strategies to include or exclude particular ways of framing the issue (Dewulf and Bouwen 2012). Whoever is able to get his or her frame adopted by other actors is setting the terms for the further debate and thereby influencing collective decisions. Interactional framing can therefore be understood as the interplay between puzzling over ideas and powering over interests, through mobilizing power sources, such as discursive legitimacy from the broader institutional field.

5.3. Invoking Authority to Impose/Discard Collective Decisions

Authority as the socially acknowledged right to exercise judgment, make a decision, or take action (Purdy 2012) can derive from one's position in the cross-sector partnership (e.g., convener) or one's position in the broader institutional field (e.g., policy maker, CEO or scientist). Furthermore, within cross-sector partnerships, it is common to have designated 'lead organizations' specified, for example, by an external funder or government policy. By assuming the position of designated lead organization status, actors are in a privileged position to influence collective decisions process.

Invoking authority often sits uncomfortably with the assumption of many partnerships that all actors should have an equal say in the cross-sector deliberations. Open and explicit appeals to authority are therefore not very likely to occur publicly in cross-sector partnerships, but more implicit references to one's position and its accompanying authority are commonly observed. Statements on substantive issues but clearly referencing one's position are good examples, e.g., "as conveners of this partnership, we propose..." or "given our responsibility for the national policy framework, we want to put forward..." (Dewulf et al. 2005). While away from the negotiation table and outside of public scrutiny, more direct appeals to authority can be made in e.g., bilateral talks, e.g., when government actors try to overrule others by stating that a certain proposal will not stand a chance in the current policy framework.

6. Strategies for Exercising *Power over CSPs*

Power games in cross-sector partnerships take place within sets of rules that provide a framework within which concrete interactions can take place (Klijn 2001). These rules both enable and constrain behavior by defining what actors are allowed, required, and not allowed to do. They bring stability and predictability to the partnership game by regulating interactions. Rules can be formal and informal. While formal rules are fixed and authorized in legal texts (e.g., laws, MoUs, contracts), informal rules have a more tacit character and often achieve a 'taken for granted' status (Anthony 1984; Klijn 2001;

Koppenjan and Klijn 2016). Once established, rules have a profound impact on what actors do and do not do in the cross-sector partnership.

Exercising *power over CSPs* is possible through setting the rules of the game for a partnership, e.g., by defining the substantive scope, by selecting the actors, or by setting decision-making rules (Elbers and Schulpen 2013). As such, an important part of the power game relates to actors' efforts to manipulate the rules to their advantage and thereby indirectly influencing the partnership game. These strategies for achieving *power over CSPs*, which aim at shaping the game through setting the rules, are of crucial relevance at the start of a partnership, but can, given the often fluid and ambiguous nature of cross-sector partnerships (Huxham and Vangen 2000), actually be deployed at any stage of a cross-sector collaboration. When compared to the direct exercise of power associated with episodic power, such indirect power strategies can considered to be equally effective and probably less visible. Barnett and Duvall (2005, p. 52) refer to rules as 'frozen configurations of privilege and bias', which continue to shape the future actions of actors long after they have been established.

Which rules are of relevance to cross-sector partnerships? Different authors have proposed rule typologies (e.g., Burns and Flam 1987; Ostrom 2011). The set of rules that was proposed by Koppenjan and Klijn (2016) are particularly useful for the purpose of this paper as they explicitly deal with interactions and processes within cross-sector collaboration:

- *Participation rules* define who can participate, under what conditions, and in which roles. Inclusion and exclusion is an important mechanism of power. Through influencing participation rules, actors can try to get their preferred partners on board, or to keep their adversaries out of the partnership. Participation rules also define in what capacity actors participate: as key actors, as beneficiaries, as experts, as implementers, etc., shaping their power relations within the partnership.

- *Agenda rules* relate to the scope and objectives of the partnership. They define the mission and identity of the joint undertaking and the issues that will and will not be addressed. Through influencing agenda rules, actors can secure sufficient attention for they key issues in the partnership, or conversely, keep important issues off the negotiation table such that no collective decisions are made regarding these issues. Keeping issues of the table is a form of "nondecision-making" (Bachrach and Baratz 1962) that can advantage actors who benefit more from the current situation than from a major change.

- *Sequence rules* define the steps to be taken in the interaction process, for example, which steps to take for mapping the problem, how soon or how late in the process are specific solutions discussed, how much time to reserve for representatives to consult with their constituencies, etc. Setting deadlines is an important way of putting pressure on the process and pushing reluctant actors to commit to a collective decision.

- *Task rules* define the structuring of activities within the partnership. They may concern the division of labor between the parties, for example through installing a steering group or working groups for particular issues. Task rules can also define practical things, like work methods or which information and communication systems to use to work together. Through setting task rules, actors can try to position their priority issues or decision proposals as the key topic of a working group, for example, or to propose an sophisticated on-line collaboration environment in which only certain actors are proficient, giving them an advantage in directing the flow of information.

- *Information rules* define how to use information and whether and how information will be shared with others. Actors may have different interests regarding transparency versus confidentiality of information towards to outside world. Media attention can advantage some actors and disadvantage other actors in their negotiation positions. Influencing information rules therefore exercises *power over CSPs*.

- *Decision-making rules* define how decisions are going to be made in the partnership. Specifying what will be considered as a decision (verbal agreement during a meeting, action point mentioned in the minutes of meeting, or only an officially signed agreement), how decisions are to be made (e.g., by consensus or majority), or what is allowed or required in terms of consulting with constituencies (e.g., no major decisions are taken without consulting constituencies) all shape the relative influence actors have on the collective decisions resulting from the partnership.

These rules can be implicitly adopted, unilaterally determined, or collectively negotiated and validated. Because each of these rules shape the decision-making process and indirectly the collective decisions resulting from the partnership, influencing these rules becomes a viable strategy for exercising *power over CSPs*.

Similar to *power in CSPs*, actor can mobilize available sources of power to achieve *power over CSPs*. Strategies to exercise *power over CSPs* involve influencing the rules of the game for the partnership, including participation rules, agenda rules, sequence rules, task rules, information rules, and decision-making rules. As discussed above, these episodic power strategies rely on the mobilization of resources, discursive legitimacy, and authority as sources of power, differentially available to actors because of their position in the relevant issue field and institutional fields. Although some connections are more obvious than others—e.g., invoking authority to set decision-making rules, or appealing to discursive legitimacy to set agenda rules—each of the three sources of power can potentially be mobilized to shape any of the six type of rules. Particularly at the moment of initiating a partnership, a variety of different rules are implicitly or explicitly set. Substantial financial and human resources are usually necessary to invest in the laborious start of a partnership. But, resources are not all that matters in being involved early on in partnership formation. An actor's discursive legitimacy may be so high that starting a partnership without them affects the legitimacy of the entire partnership. Or an actor's authority position in e.g., the governmental system may so crucial for the partnership's success that they are effectively unavoidable. Each of these mechanisms puts some actors in the position to be there when these rules are set, while others join only at a later stage, when a set of rules are already in use.

Being able to set or at least influence the rules that guide cross-sector partnerships is therefore a desirable goal for most actors. The rules that guide partnerships are usually set in two different ways. First, actors may decide upon the nature of the rules during the collective decision-making process. For example, actors may decide on the roles of the different members in the collaboration (participation rules) or the type of information that is shared (information rules). Second, certain actors, typically those that are in control of critical resources, may set the rules unilaterally without the involvement of others. The reality of many cross-sector partnerships, however, is that not all participants can equally participate in decision-making processes. With many cross-sector partnerships, it is common to have designated 'lead organizations' specified, for example, by an external funder or government policy. By assuming the position of designated lead organization actors are in a privileged position to set the terms of the partnerships from the onset.

7. Discussion and Conclusions

Power is only one dimension of cross-sector partnerships but it is a relatively understudied one. Our aim was to create a better conceptual understanding of power strategies in these partnerships, specifically of the ability of actors to influence collective decisions of the partnership to their own advantage. The result is an integrated framework on how actors can exercise *power in* and *over CSPs*. We built the framework by bridging different literatures (multiparty collaboration, cross-sector partnerships and interactive, network, and collaborative governance) and power traditions (systemic and episodic power), capturing the layered power dynamics in partnerships. We explain that actors can mobilize sources of power (by withholding/investing resources, appealing to discursive legitimacy and invoking authority) in order to exercise power directly (*power in CSPs*) and indirectly by setting the rules that govern the partnership (*power over CSPs*). Furthermore, we demonstrate that these episodic power strategies are fundamentally shaped by the intersection of the institutional fields from which actors originate and the issue field, which connects the actors in the partnership.

The novelty of the framework itself is threefold: unlike existing frameworks it (1) offers guidance for empirical research, (2) it distinguishes between direct and indirect power strategies, and (3) it clarifies how power dynamics within cross-sector partnerships are linked to the institutional context. The relevance of our framework also lies in the guidance it offers for pursuing new lines of empirical inquiry. Based on the different analytical dimensions of the framework and the connections between them, important questions for future empirical research emerge. With respect to the power sources that are available to actors, an important question concerns the relative importance of institutional fields and issue fields in shaping the availability of power sources. For example, does a strong and stable institutional field make for a stronger impact on the available power sources relative to the issue field? Does an established issue field, rooted in a history of interactions between actors, make for a stronger impact on the available power sources relative to the institutional field an actor comes from? We have mostly considered sources of power separately, but to what extent and how the different sources of power reinforce each other or are mobilized in conjunction is another relevant question. Finally, one could test the implication of our theoretical framework that actors from similar institutional fields engaging in the same issue field should look more alike in terms of available power sources, than actors from different institutional fields. With respect to strategies for exercising *power in CSPs*, one could investigate whether certain types of actors exercise power predominantly through particular strategies, e.g., business actors through withholding/investing resources, government actors through invoking authority, and civil society actors through appealing to discursive legitimacy. With respect to strategies exercising *power over CSPs*, the relative importance of the different types of rules can be questioned: are certain types of rules more important than others in shaping ability of actors to influence collective decisions of the partnership to their own advantage? Also, the relation between the different sources of power and the different types of rules can be empirically investigated: are certain sources of power mobilized more often for setting certain types of rules. For example, are decision rules more strongly influenced by invoking authority, are agenda rules more strongly influenced by appealing to discursive legitimacy, and are sequence rules more strongly influenced by withholding/investing resources in joint activities? Finally, our framework is limited to identifying the menu of strategies available to actors. An important question that would require in-depth study of interactions in partnerships is how other actors recognize, accept, contest, or respond to these power strategies in a strategic game of moves and counter-moves.

When a cross-sector partnership is successful, it leads to concrete outcomes, generally in the form of implemented agreements among the involved actors. The question to what extent this agreement, or the cross-sector platform itself, can and should be institutionalized is an important one at that point (Gray 2007). Related to this is the question whether the cross-sector partnership effects an enduring change in the issue field and respective institutional fields, e.g., by introducing new practices or changing the relations between actors—this is the question whether institutional change has occurred. A more specific question that is related to our exploration of power in cross-sector partnerships concerns the degree to which the distribution of access to power sources has changed. Or, if one wants to ask this question in terms of empowerment, the degree to which less powerful or marginalized actors have obtained more access to power sources as a result of the partnership (Woodhill and van Vugt 2011). These questions are clearly relevant in a broader analysis of the *power of* cross-sector partnerships over their social and political environment (Torfing et al. 2012b), but are beyond the scope of our current analysis, and thus constitute an interesting opportunity for further elaborating the current framework.

While analyzing power dynamics in partnerships is a valid topic of inquiry in its own right, the starting-point of this paper is our concern with the inequality that characterizes many cross-sector partnerships. Inequality can only exist in situations where power is exercised, making the study of power dynamics within cross-sector partnerships an important topic for further research. Although the paper mainly has a theoretical focus, we believe that it also has practical relevance. By shedding light on the power dynamics in partnerships and clarifying why certain actors are more powerful than others through identifying concrete power strategies, it offers starting-points for addressing power imbalances. In addition, the framework can be used by less powerful actors to understand the opportunities, limitations, and risks that cross-sector partnerships offer. This way they can make informed decisions about whether or not to participate in particular partnerships.

Author Contributions: Both authors contributed to the theoretical thinking, literature review and writing up for each of the sections of the paper. Elbers' contribution was relatively stronger on the institutional aspects of partnerships, while Dewulf's contribution was relatively stronger on the interactional aspects of partnerships. Dewulf led the final writing up of the manuscript and its revision in response to the reviewers' comments.

Funding: This research received no external funding.

Conflicts of Interest: The authors declare no conflicts of interest.

References

Ansell, Chris, and Alison Gash. 2007. Collaborative Governance in Theory and Practice. *Journal of Public Administration Research and Theory* 18: 543–71. [CrossRef]

Anthony, Giddens. 1984. *The Constitution of Society: Outline of the Theory of Structuration. Critique.* Cambridge: Polity Press.

Bachrach, Peter, and Morton S. Baratz. 1962. Two Faces of Power. *American Political Science Review* 56: 947–52. [CrossRef]

Barnett, M., and R. Duvall. 2005. Power in International Politics. *International Organization* 59: 39–75. [CrossRef]

Bourdieu, Pierre. 1989. Social space and symbolic power. *Sociological Theory* 7: 14–25. [CrossRef]

Bouwen, Rene, and Tharsi Taillieu. 2004. Multi-party collaboration as social learning for interdependence: Developing relational knowing for sustainable natural resource management. *Journal of Community & Applied Social Psychology* 14: 137–53. [CrossRef]

Burns, Tom R., and H. Flam. 1987. *The Shaping of Social Organization: Social Rule System Theory with Applications.* London: Sage.

Castells, Manuel. 2011. A network theory of power. *International Journal of Communication* 5: 773–87.

Clegg, Stewart R. 1989. *Frameworks of Power.* London: Sage.

Dahl, Robert A. 1957. The concept of power. *Behavioral Science* 2: 201–15. [CrossRef]

Dewulf, Art, and René Bouwen. 2012. Issue Framing in Conversations for Change: Discursive Interaction Strategies for "Doing Differences". *The Journal of Applied Behavioral Science* 48: 168–93. [CrossRef]

Dewulf, Art, Marc Craps, René Bouwen, Tharsi Taillieu, and C. Pahl-Wostl. 2005. Integrated management of natural resources: Dealing with ambiguous issues, multiple actors and diverging frames. *Water Science and Technology* 52: 115–24. [CrossRef] [PubMed]

Dewulf, Art, Barbara Gray, Linda Putnam, Roy Lewicki, Noelle Aarts, Rene Bouwen, and Cees Van Woerkum. 2009. Disentangling approaches to framing in conflict and negotiation research: A meta-paradigmatic perspective. *Human Relations* 62: 155–93. [CrossRef]

DiMaggio, Paul J., and Walter W. Powell. 1983. The iron cage revisited: Institutional isomorphism and collective rationality in organizational fields. *American Sociological Review* 48: 147–60. [CrossRef]

Edelenbos, Jurian. 2005. Institutional Implications of Interactive Governance: Insights from Dutch Practice. *Governance* 18: 111–34. [CrossRef]

Elbers, Willem, and Lau Schulpen. 2013. Corridors of Power: The Institutional Design of North–South NGO Partnerships. *VOLUNTAS: International Journal of Voluntary and Nonprofit Organizations* 24: 48–67. [CrossRef]

Emerson, Kirk, Tina Nabatchi, and Stephen Balogh. 2012. An Integrative Framework for Collaborative Governance. *Journal of Public Administration Research and Theory* 22: 1–29. [CrossRef]

Emerson, Richard M. 1962. Power-Dependence Relations. *American Sociological Review* 27: 31–41. [CrossRef]

Emery, Fred E., and Eric L. Trist. 1965. The causal texture of organizational environments. *Human Relations* 18: 21–32. [CrossRef]

Fairclough, Norman. 1992. Discourse and Power. In *Language and Power.* London: Sage, pp. 43–76.

Foucault, Michel. 1977. *Discipline and Punish.* New York: Pantheon.

Gaventa, John. 2006. Finding the Spaces for Change: A Power Analysis. *IDS Bulletin* 37: 23–33. [CrossRef]

Gray, Barbara. 1985. Conditions facilitating inter-organizational collaboration. *Human Relations* 38: 173–84. [CrossRef]

Gray, Barbara. 2004. Strong opposition: Frame-based resistance to collaboration. *Journal of Community & Applied Social Psychology* 14: 166–76. [CrossRef]

Gray, Barbara. 2007. The process of partnership construction: Anticipating obstacles and enhancing the likelihood of successful partnerships for sustainable development. In *Partnerships, Governance and Sustainable Development*. Edited by P. Glasbergen, F. Biermann and A. P. J. Mol. Cheltenham: Edward Elgar.

Gray, Barbara. 2011. The Complexity of Multiparty Negotiations: Wading into the Muck. *Negotiation and Conflict Management Research* 4: 169–77. [CrossRef]

Gray, Barbara, and Jill Purdy. 2018. *Collaborating for Our Future. Multi-Stakeholder Partnerships for Solving Complex Problems*. Oxford: University Press.

Greenwood, R., R. Suddaby, and C. R. Hinings. 2002. Theorizing change: The role of professional associations in the transformation of institutionalized fields. *Academy of Management Journal* 45: 58–80.

Hajer, Maarten, and Wytske Versteeg. 2005. Performing Governance through Networks. *European Political Science* 4: 340–47. [CrossRef]

Hardy, Cynthia, and Nelson Phillips. 1998. Strategies of engagement: Lessons from the critical examination of collaboration and conflict in an interorganizational domain. *Organization* 9: 217–30. [CrossRef]

Hayward, Clarissa, and Steven Lukes. 2008. Nobody to shoot? Power, structure, and agency: A dialogue. *Journal of Power* 1: 5–20. [CrossRef]

Hendriks, Carolyn M. 2009. Deliberative governance in the context of power. *Policy and Society* 28: 173–84. [CrossRef]

Huxham, Chris, and Siv Vangen. 2000. Ambiguity, complexity and dynamics in the membership of collaboration. *Human Relations* 53: 771–806. [CrossRef]

Huxham, Chris, and Siv Vangen. 2005. The principles of the theory of collaborative advantage. In *Managing to Collaborate. The Theory and Practice of Collaborative Advantage*. Abingdon: Routledge, pp. 30–42.

Huxham, Chris, Siv Vangen, Christine Huxham, and Colin Eden. 2000. The Challenge of Collaborative Governance. *Public Management: An International Journal of Research and Theory* 2: 337–58. [CrossRef]

Klijn, Erik-Hans. 2001. Rules as Institutional Context for Decision Making in Networks: The Approach to Postwar Housing Districts in Two Cities. *Administration & Society* 33: 133–64. [CrossRef]

Klijn, Erik-Hans, Joop Koppenjan, and Katrien Termeer. 1995. Managing networks in the public sector: A theoretical study of management strategies in policy networks. *Public Administration* 73: 437–54. [CrossRef]

Koppenjan, Joop, and Erik Hans Klijn. 2016. *Governance Networks in the Public Sector*. London: Routledge.

Laclau, Ernesto, and Chantal Mouffe. 1985. *Hegemony and Socialist Strategy: Towards a Radical Democratic Politics*. London: Verso.

Lawrence, Thomas B. 2008. Power, institutions and organizations. In *Sage Handbook of Organizational Institutionalism*. Edited by R. C. Greenwood, C. Oliver, K. Sahlin and R. Suddaby. London: Sage, pp. 170–97.

Lawrence, Thomas B., Cynthia Hardy, and Nelson Phillips. 2002. Institutional effects of interorganizational collaboration: The emergence of proto-institutions. *Academy of Management Journal* 45: 281–90.

Meyer, John W., and Brian Rowan. 1977. Institutionalized Organizations: Formal Structure as Myth and Ceremony. *American Journal of Sociology* 83: 340–63. [CrossRef]

Nye, Joseph S. 1990. Soft Power. *Foreign Policy* 80: 153–71. [CrossRef]

Ostrom, E. 2011. Background on the Institutional Analysis and Development Framework. *Policy Studies Journal* 39: 7–27. [CrossRef]

Pettit, Jethro. 2010. Multiple Faces of Power and Learning. *IDS Bulletin* 41: 25–35. [CrossRef]

Pfeffer, Jeffrey, and Gerald R. Salancik. 2003. *The External Control of Organizations: A Resource Dependence Perspective*. Stanford: Stanford University Press.

Phillips, Nelson, Thomas B. Lawrence, and Cynthia Hardy. 2000. Inter-organizational Collaboration and the Dynamics of Institutional Fields. *Journal of Management Studies* 37. [CrossRef]

Provan, Keith G., and Patrick Kenis. 2007. Modes of Network Governance: Structure, Management, and Effectiveness. *Journal of Public Administration Research and Theory* 18: 229–52. [CrossRef]

Purdy, Jill M. 2012. A Framework for Assessing Power in Collaborative Governance Processes. *Public Administration Review* 72: 409–17. [CrossRef]

Scharpf, Fritz W. 1978. Interorganizational Policy Studies: Issues, Concepts and Perspectives. In *Interorganizational Policy Making. Limits to Coordination and Central Control*. London: Sage.

Schön, Donald A., and Martin Rein. 1994. *Frame Reflection: Towards the Resolution of Intractable Policy Controversies*. New York: Basic Books.

Schouten, Greetje, Pieter Leroy, and Pieter Glasbergen. 2012. On the deliberative capacity of private multi-stakeholder governance: The Roundtables on Responsible Soy and Sustainable Palm Oil. *Ecological Economics* 83: 42–50. [CrossRef]

Scott, W. Richard. 2008. *Institutions and Organizations: Ideas, Interests, and Identities*. London: Sage.

Selsky, John W., and Barbara Parker. 2005. Cross-Sector Partnerships to Address Social Issues: Challenges to Theory and Practice. *Journal of Management* 31: 849–73. [CrossRef]

Sørensen, Eva, and Jacob Torfing. 2007. Theories of Democratic Network Governance. *Regulation* XIV: 356S. [CrossRef]

Stone, Deborah A. 2002. Decisions. In *Policy Paradox. The Art of Political Decision-Making*. Glenview: Scott, pp. 232–57.

Thornton, P., and W. Ocasio. 2008. Institutional logics. In *Handbook of Organizational Institutionalism*. Edited by R. Greenwood, C. Oliver, K. Sahlin-Andersson and R. Suddaby. Thousand Oaks: Sage, pp. 99–129.

Torfing, Jacob, B. Guy Peters, Jon Pierre, and Eva Sørensen. 2012a. *Interactive Governance. Advancing the Paradigm*. Oxford: Oxford University Press.

Torfing, Jacob, B. Guy Peters, Jon Pierre, and Eva Sørensen. 2012b. Power and politics in interactive governance. In *Interactive Governance: Advancing the Paradigm*. Oxford: Oxford University Press.

Townley, B. 1997. The institutional logic of performance appraisal. *Organization Studies* 18: 261–85. [CrossRef]

Trist, Eric. 1983. Referent Organizations and the Development of Inter-Organizational Domains. *Human Relations* 36: 269–84. [CrossRef]

Van Buuren, Arwin, Martinus Vink, and Jeroen Warner. 2014. Constructing Authoritative Answers to a Latent Crisis? Strategies of Puzzling, Powering and Framing in Dutch Climate Adaptation Practices Compared. *Journal of Comparative Policy Analysis: Research and Practice* 18: 70–87. [CrossRef]

Van Huijstee, Mariette, and Pieter Glasbergen. 2010. Business–NGO Interactions in a Multi-Stakeholder Context. *Business and Society Review* 115: 249–84. [CrossRef]

Van Hulst, Merlijn, and Dvora Yanow. 2014. From policy "frames" to "framing": Theorizing a more dynamic, political approach. *The American Review of Public Administration* 46: 92–112. [CrossRef]

Vangen, Siv, John Paul Hayes, and Chris Cornforth. 2015. Governing Cross-Sector, Inter-Organizational Collaborations. *Public Management Review* 17: 1237–60. [CrossRef]

Vansina, Leopold, T. C. B. Taillieu, S. G. L. Schruijer, W. Pasmore, and R. Woodman. 1998. "Managing" multiparty issues: Learning from experience. *Research in Organizational Change and Development* 11: 159–81.

Vink, Martinus Janszoon. 2015. *Navigating Frames: A Study of the Interplay between Meaning and Power in Policy Deliberations over Adaptation to Climate Change*. Wageningen: Wageningen University.

Visseren-Hamakers, Ingrid Jacoba, Pieter Leroy, and Pieter Glasbergen. 2010. Conservation partnerships and biodiversity governance: Fulfilling governance functions through interaction. *Sustainable Development* 20: 264–75. [CrossRef]

Weick, Karl E. 1995. *Sensemaking in Organizations*. Thousand Oaks: Sage.

Woodhill, A. J., and S. M. van Vugt. 2011. Facilitating MSPs—A Sustainable Way of Changing Power Relations? In *Guidebook for MSP Facilitation*. Edited by GIZ South Africa. Eschborn: Deutsche Gesellschaft für Internationale Zusammenarbeit (GIZ), pp. 36–46.

Article

A Relational Approach to Leadership for Multi-Actor Governance

Marc Craps [1,4,*], **Inge Vermeersch** [1,2], **Art Dewulf** [2,4], **Koen Sips** [3,4], **Katrien Termeer** [2] **and René Bouwen** [5]

1   Centre for Corporate Sustainability, KU Leuven, 3000 Leuven, Belgium; Inge.Vermeesch@telenet.be
2   Public Administration and Policy Group, Wageningen University and Research, 6708 PB Wageningen,
    The Netherlands; Art.Dewulf@wur.nl (A.D.); Katrien.Termeer@wur.nl (K.T.)
3   Point Consulting Group, 2800 Mechelen, Belgium; Koen.Sips@point-consulting.be
4   Cycloop, Network for Action Research on Multi-actor Collaboration, 2800 Mechelen, Belgium
5   Centre for Organizational Psychology, KU Leuven, 3000 Leuven, Belgium; Rene.Bouwen@kuleuven.be
*   Correspondence: Marc.Craps@kuleuven.be; Tel.: +32-2-6081411

Received: 22 April 2018; Accepted: 28 January 2019; Published: 1 February 2019

Abstract: Multi-actor governance, in which a broad mix of actors collaborates to deal with complex societal problems, requires a leadership approach that can take into account the dynamic interdependencies between the involved actors. A relational approach to leadership, focusing on processes and practices, is more adequate for that purpose than approaches focusing on individuals and positions. Complexity leadership theory offers such a relational approach to leadership *within* organizations. In this article, we use complexity leadership theory to capture the emergent leadership processes *between* organizations. We focus on the characteristics of the informal relations between representatives of different organizations that enable dealing with the often-conflicting goals and values in multi-actor governance. The case of a landfill mining initiative for sustainable materials governance is used as an illustration to clarify the main concepts and arguments.

Keywords: relational approach; inter-organizational collaboration; multi-actor governance; complexity leadership theory; landfill mining

---

1. Introduction: Complexity and Multi-Actor Governance

Because of the increasing complexity of contemporary society and the erosion of existing institutions, the attention of policy makers has turned to participatory modes of governance (Rhodes 1996; Osborne 2006). They increasingly try to address complex societal issues with a collaborative multi-actor approach (Gray and Purdy 2018; Ansell and Gash 2007; Lowndes and Skelcher 1998; Vangen et al. 2015). A multi-actor governance (MAG) approach accepts non-governmental actors taking diverse steering initiatives through formal and informal interactions to find innovative solutions for complex societal problems and to develop policies collaboratively (Huxham 2000b; Johnson and Wilson 2000). The approach stimulates processes of self-regulation and reduces government control; hence, new roles for private and public actors and new forms of leadership are required (Vangen and Huxham 2003; Sydow et al. 2011; Sullivan et al. 2012).

The complexity of the task, the network configurations, and the dynamic interdependencies between actors produce specific leadership challenges. While the huge volume of research on leadership in management and organization studies is still focused on individual characteristics of hierarchical leaders in single organizations (Bass 1999; Harding et al. 2011), research on leadership in MAG is less developed. The very idea of collaborative processes, in which stakeholders jointly take key decisions in non-hierarchical networks, seems to have side-tracked leadership as a topic in the research on multi-actor collaboration (Huxham and Vangen 2005). A strong performance management culture continues to attribute leadership to a limited number of people who are perceived to be accountable for outcomes and results. However, the complexity of the task and the dynamic interdependencies between different types of actors involved in multi-actor governance present specific leadership challenges, including the presence of multiple leaders (Sydow et al. 2011). We therefore advocate in this article a relational approach to leadership for collaborative governance, with a focus on processes and relational practices instead of on individuals. A relational approach to leadership replaces the idea that leadership results out of the actions of an individual leader with the view that leadership emerges from the interactions between persons, groups, and organizations (Cunliffe and Eriksen 2011). Complexity leadership theory (CLT) offers such a relational approach to leadership and identifies different types of leadership within organizations (Uhl-Bien 2006; Fairhurst and Uhl-Bien 2012). We demonstrate in this article that CLT is as well highly relevant to analyze emergent leadership and collaboration between organizations by focusing on the relational characteristics of the interactions between representatives of these organizations.

Relational leadership has been the subject of multi-paradigmatic approaches. Some approaches can be considered as "entitative" (post-positivist) and others as "constructionist" (Uhl-Bien and Ospina 2012). Entitative approaches describe traits, patterns, and characteristics of leadership interactions, while constructionist approaches document relational leadership practices in ongoing interactions. Especially for the multi-voiced and varied work contexts of multi-actor governance, a paradigm interplay approach may be very contributive to new discoveries. This article has the intention to contribute to relational leadership research that transforms the aspiration for methodological pluralism from a philosophical longing to a pragmatic concern: The need to advance the theoretical and practical understandings of the complex social realities of leadership.

In what follows, we first indicate the specific relational challenges for group development in MAG. Then, we explain the relational action logics of leadership to deal with these challenges and demonstrate the relevance of the different leadership functions, identified by CLT, for MAG. The integration of the former parts in the final section results in suggestions for further research about leadership for MAG. We clarify our arguments with illustrations from a real life case of landfill mining for sustainable materials governance (Craps and Sips 2010; Sips et al. 2013).

2. Group Development in Multi-Actor Governance

The field of leadership research has traditionally been leader-centric, focusing on individuals, their activities, characteristics, and competences (Dachler and Hosking 1995; Sullivan et al. 2012). By contrast, a relational approach to leadership does not look at individual leaders but at how leadership is enacted in emergent or existing leadership relations. It is primarily concerned with where, how, and why leadership work is being organized and accomplished, rather than with who is offering visions for others to do the work (Raelin 2011; Cunliffe and Eriksen 2011; Crevani et al. 2010; Uhl-Bien 2006). The term 'relational' refers to a view on leadership "that emanates from the rich connections and interdependencies of organizations and their members" (Hosking 2006). Without denying the importance for MAG of the structural characteristics of interactions between organizations at macro-level, the relational approach that we advocate here is focused on micro-level practices in concrete settings of inter-organizational relations. It is indeed in these micro-contexts that meanings are generated by interacting individuals that may possibly change conditions at the macro-level (Sullivan et al. 2012).

A group development process unfolds among MAG participants in these micro-meetings as they try to solve the problems at hand (Bouwen and Taillieu 2004). They are confronted with the challenges of dependence, counter-dependence, and interdependence, similar to the phases described in group dynamics (Srivastva et al. 1977; Delbecq and Ven 1971). Participants in MAG need as well to develop learning and task performance to be effective. However, in MAG, they are not participating in fixed small groups such as those studied by the aforementioned scholars of group development, but in highly dynamic and changing constellations. MAG often functions in sub-groups and commissions that have limited direct contacts among them. New members tend to join or leave at any moment, and they are replaced due to internal changes in their constituent organizations. Group development theories advocate interdependency between the participants as a development goal to be reached (Srivastva et al. 1977; Bouwen 1998). However, this is very challenging for MAG, which is often functioning through several loosely coupled sub-groups, passing periods of intense collaboration alternated with languid activity that might result in different levels of group development at a given moment.

To be relevant for complex societal issues, MAG brings together people with diverging, often conflicting perspectives on problems, possible solutions, and suitable courses of action. Exclusively focusing on the task content can accentuate these differences and hamper the necessary group development. The concept of relational practices, 'task-oriented actions with relational qualities of reciprocity and some kind of reflexivity' (Bouwen and Taillieu 2004), draws attention to the potential of shared practices. Argyris and Schön (1978) were the first authors to describe the process of learning within organizations as the result of complex interactive episodes, in which the mutually open quality of the communication makes development towards innovative outcomes possible. By engaging in relational practices, MAG participants explore in a similar way differences of opinion, interdependencies, roles, and positions between organizations. As a result, they go through a learning process that helps them to collectively discover how they create their reality and how they can change it.

Group Development and MAG in the Landfill Mining Case

The landfill mining initiative that we present as an illustrative case is part of a paradigm shift to sustainable materials governance: Instead of dumping waste in landfills, the idea is to keep materials in closed loops. The aim is to reopen old landfills to mine the stored waste, to recover valuable materials, and to generate energy. Behind this simple idea lies a complex reality that asks for the involvement of many actors from the government, civil society, business, and academia. Indeed, the initiative raises questions related to economic feasibility, nature conservation, health concerns, public acceptability, technological challenges, and legal and policy issues.

In this case, the initiative for landfill mining was taken by a medium-sized, family-run company. The company ran a large landfill for a couple of decades, accumulating 16 million tons of household and industrial waste on the site. Landfill mining fits within the business strategy to reposition the company as a technology innovator with a 'green' image. Because of the technical and social complexity of the initiative, the company was in contact with various research centers. A research consortium was set up, with an academic engineering scientist as coordinator. The Consortium assembled researchers from many disciplines—hard and applied sciences as well as human and social sciences—with scholars coming from various research institutes. They were selected by the coordinator based on their expertise, their interest in sustainability, their open-mindedness to consider various interests, and their possible access to funding channels. The regional Waste Agency and an investment fund for the regional development were also invited to be part of the Consortium. However, the Waste Agency opted after a while for a special status of "observing member" because of their conflicting interests as member of the Consortium propagating landfill mining and controller of the legal and environmental conditions of the concerned landfill. After a few meetings, a member of the local city council was also invited to be part of the Consortium. This person was the representative of an active local citizen group, as the initiative triggered a lot of questions, worries, distrust, and resistance in the local population.

At the start, there were frequent plenary Consortium meetings. After a while, various new initiatives originated that were loosely coupled with the Consortium. The company decided to set up a joint venture with a UK company because the advanced technology it offers was judged as the best available technology by the Consortium. The Consortium organized various international symposia, inviting interested academics and policy makers. These symposia lay the ground for a European network dedicated to the promotion of landfill mining for sustainable materials governance through research and lobbying. In the same period, the Waste Agency organized a couple of broad stakeholder meetings, with representatives of different governmental agencies and private companies related to waste and materials management. The local citizen group played an important role in transmitting the worries of the local community to the consortium and translating scientific information to the community.

Activities with the qualities of relational practices, as described above, turned out to be very helpful to bridge differences and enable learning between the different kinds of public and types of knowledge in the broadening network around the landfill mining Consortium. Examples are the joint site visit of researchers and local citizen representatives to the technical installations of the company in the UK and the active participation of the local citizen group in the preparation of the symposia. In these symposia, the local community representatives had ample opportunities for expressing their ideas and entering in an open dialogue with researchers, corporate officers, and policy makers.

3. Relational Action Logics for Multi-Actor Governance

An interesting debate is that on the suitability of different leadership styles for complex network leadership (Osborn and Marion 2009; DeRue 2011). A leadership style characterizes one specific person as the individual leader of a group or organization. However, as the term 'style' refers to an individual attribute, we propose the concept 'relational action logic' to characterize concrete relational practices among actors involved in mutual exchanges, in the sense that leadership interventions are enacted between different actors that engage in an interaction process. A relational action logic describes the—often implicit—strategic reasoning and the tactical interventions to secure the involvement of the adequate stakeholders and the necessary high quality of their interrelatedness in a joint initiative (Argyris and Schön 1978; Bouwen and Taillieu 2004).

In MAG, different relational action logics that have similarities with the transactional and transformational style in leadership studies (Bass 1999) seem necessary simultaneously. Transactional leadership takes place by keeping track of what attracts and motivates the partners to be part of the joint initiative and by assigning incentives (project funding, responsibilities, business opportunities, shared expertise, public credibility, etc.) to the partners according to their specific interests. This type of leadership tends to satisfy the actual needs and interests of the parties around the table by distributing the possible benefits of the MAG initiative among them. Indeed, each of the participants has to justify their involvement in MAG by demonstrating the benefits of participation to their constituency. There is little space for long-term concerns, other stakeholders, and innovative thinking.

Transformational leadership, by contrast, steers the initiative by stimulating identification with overarching long-term values that go beyond the interests of the joint members, and for which a profound systemic transformation is necessary, with unclear consequences for the participating organizations. Both types of leadership are necessary because without transactional leadership, the network may lack the necessary support from constituencies to introduce change. But without transformational leadership, MAG risks being limited to the vested interests of the participants and undermining its transformational potential for the broader society (Craps and Sips 2010).

Transactional and Transformational Leadership in the Landfill Mining Case

In the landfill mining case, the main participants were well aware of the benefits each one expected in return for the invested time and energy in the joint initiative. The Company hoped to advance its new 'green' business strategy thanks to the results of the Consortium. Its position and reputation as an innovative and trustworthy environmental services company was at stake. The interactions between the Company and the researchers of the Consortium were thus informed by a mutual transactional logic. The business partner provided funding and access to a real-life industrial project with unique opportunities for scientific experimentation in return for research contributions to its landfill mining project. Through the Consortium, the research coordinator was able to set up other related initiatives on a regional and international level and strengthen his academic position. The strategic partnership with the Waste Agency provided access to extensive data and information on landfills, while in return, its representative got a front-row seat in the discussions about innovative waste management solutions. These examples illustrate how transactional leadership is enacted by managerial actions that secure resources, promote the project, and shape decisions.

Although in the first meetings of the initiative, the conversations between the participants expressed clearly their concern about securing the institutional agenda of their constituency, according to a transactional logic, these conversations soon shifted to innovative thinking about solutions for waste and materials governance. The research coordinator and the representative of the Company selected and invited participants for the Consortium, based on their supposed personal interest in sustainability-related research, and in the transdisciplinary setting (interacting with other disciplines and non-academic stakeholders). Informal gatherings and intense conversations beyond the formal workshops of the Consortium reflected the positive excitement of the participants to develop together a new landfill mining concept for sustainable materials governance.

4. Developing Complexity Leadership Theory for Multi-Actor Governance

Complexity leadership theory (CLT) (Uhl-Bien 2006; Uhl-Bien and Marion 2009; Fairhurst and Uhl-Bien 2012) offers an interesting relational approach to leadership by viewing leadership as an emergent dynamic of different leadership functions that exceed the attempts of individual position holders. In what follows, we demonstrate the relevance of CLT, developed in business contexts, to understand leadership in MAG.

CLT is rooted in complexity science, searching for a leadership paradigm that would better fit today's post-industrial knowledge-creating organizations (Richardson et al. 2005; Uhl-Bien et al. 2007). An increasingly fast changing environment expects organizations to process larger amounts of increasingly complex information at a rapid pace. Today's organizations must learn, innovate, and adapt quickly to remain competitive. The law of requisite complexity demands that organizations become as complex internally as their external environment, to guarantee the necessary information processing, learning, innovative, and adaptive capacities to this environment. Over the past few decades, organizations have progressively done so by adopting network-like formations, characterized by rather loose and informal relations. Such 'loosely coupled' network structures defy the logic of formal, hierarchical leaders and models of leadership based on centralized planning and control. Problem solving happens in emerging, ad hoc, self-steering, flexible, and changing networks; instead of in imposed, fixed, controlled, stable, and permanent teams. However, research suggests that informal dynamics may jeopardize organizational goal achievement if they lack sufficient coordination (Uhl-Bien et al. 2007). For that reason, CLT aims at a leadership model for complex networks of informally linked actors within a bureaucratically coordinated organizational context. CLT thus combines the leadership potential of informal network dynamics that foster learning, innovation, and adaptability in complex contexts with the leadership of central structures for coordination and the production of outcomes in line with the vision and mission of the organization

Whereas Uhl-Bien and colleagues developed CLT to conceptualize and study leadership dynamics within organizations in a business context, Nooteboom and Termeer (2013) showed that CLT also has an important potential for complex governance systems including multiple actors. On the basis of two case studies, Nooteboom and Termeer (2013) revealed leadership strategies creating conditions that are favorable for the emergence of innovations. They concluded that embedding leadership in informal networks, where people have personal relationships, is important. However, they have not further elaborated on this relational dimension and have not related it to literature.

In MAG, leadership results from a process that takes place among the participants who belong to different organizations and societal sectors. Order in MAG is not pre-determined but emergent, and its future is unpredictable. MAG networks are capable of solving problems creatively and able to learn and to adapt quickly, although they do not always or necessarily achieve their problem-solving potential. According to Huxham and Vangen (2005), it is often unclear in multi-actor networks who is in or out at a given moment, who is linked to whom and in which capacity, or who is dependent of whom for other goals than those pursued by the network.

Complexity leadership theory has been applied to public sector leadership, to study the relationship between the complexity of urban regeneration projects (low to high) and the role and importance of administrative, adaptive, and enabling leadership (Murphy et al. 2017). While these projects sample a relevant range of complexity, including public and private actors, the focus is predominantly on the public sector leadership in these cases. Our interest is in multi-actor governance and how leadership plays out in governance networks that link up public, private, and civil society actors. Complexity leadership, or the emergent dynamic of different leadership functions, plays out between these different actors, sometime with and other times without a prominent role of the public sector. Complexity leadership in multi-actor governance networks is therefore broader than public sector leadership.

According to CLT, the combination of three leadership functions allows for the integration of the apparently contradictory demands of adaptability and structure for leadership in complex contexts: Administrative leadership, adaptive leadership, and enabling leadership. Crevani et al. (2010) conceived interactions resulting in direction as administrative leadership practices, interactions resulting in action-spacing as adaptive leadership practices, and interactions resulting in co-orientation as enabling leadership practice. Direction refers to managerial and decision-making actions of those who plan and coordinate activities to effectively and efficiently achieve set goals, as part of a MAG process. Action-spacing refers to creating possibilities, opportunities, and limitations for individual and collective action within the local–cultural context. Co-orientation refers to enhancing the understanding of possibly diverging arguments, interpretations and decisions (Crevani et al. 2010).

While addressing large societal issues, a MAG network cannot be guided by a single vision and mission, because society is characterized by ideological plurality and policies have to take into account the values and goals of different groups. In the following paragraphs, we clarify the specific relational challenges of MAG for administrative, adaptive, and enabling leadership, with illustrations of the landfill mining case.

4.1. Administrative Leadership for MAG in the Landfill Mining Case

Administrative leadership refers to the traditional top–down relations, based on authority and position. As the implementation of innovative solutions is often hampered by a risk-averse or outdated regulation, these situations require some 'bureaucratic entrepreneurship' (Termeer and Kranendonk 2008). Moreover, formal leaders can sometimes guarantee necessary resources or useful alliances to clear the path for innovative ideas. Although one might expect governmental actors as the traditional steering agent in societal issues, they are not the only ones fulfilling administrative leadership functions. According to the power of the actors, based on their competencies and resources, and to their legitimacy for the concerned issues, different constellations of public, private, and civil actors can fulfill administrative leadership functions.

Various of the above-recounted events in the case of landfill mining for sustainable materials governance can be considered as actions of administrative leadership, through acts of controlling, planning, structuring, and coordinating between people in managerial positions. The administrative function was primarily taken up at the Board of Directors of the Company. The Director of Environmental Projects engaged in the administrative leadership process by internally exploring with his colleagues the possibility for this innovative business case and by building a vision around it. Then, resources were allocated, and external contacts were established with governmental agencies, investors, and researchers. The Company representative together with a well-positioned research engineer, publicly known for his dedication to sustainability, set up a research Consortium and joint forces to work it out. The first contacts were based on both their position and authority in their own business and academic domain, not yet on a close personal relationship. They built together a team of researchers and scientists with a clear vision and specific strategy in mind. They included people that shared a common interest in sustainable materials management, acknowledged the company's business interests, and provided possible access to further research funding. People that could present a threat to the growing consensus in the Consortium on the convenience of landfill mining and the business case were avoided at that stage.

In a similar way, a formal network was set up with official representatives of the city council, provincial political structures, the Waste Agency, the investment fund, etc. The Waste Agency, although a bit reluctant to participate at first, soon realized it lagged behind on these newly-developing visions on waste and materials management, so it used its position as official waste regulator to convene large scale workshops with interested actors from the public, private, and civil sector and in this way promoted and supported the idea. Later on, the Waste Agency integrated landfill mining in its strategic plan for sustainable materials governance.

International symposia disseminated the built-up knowledge in academic circles. By organizing them close to the location of the project case, the link with the Company was underscored. These symposia also allowed local and national political actors to put the area on the map as a welcoming region for sustainable development initiatives, a core asset of landfill mining according to its defenders.

4.2. Adaptive Leadership for MAG in the Landfill Mining Case

Adaptive leadership is possible thanks to emerging mechanisms of resonance, information patterning, and dealing with tension. It takes place throughout the organization but adopts different forms according to the involved hierarchical levels. The upper levels can secure strategic relations with the organization's environment, safeguard niches, and anchor new strategic insights for innovations in their own organization. The middle levels can allocate specific resources and focused planning. However, adaptive leadership is most active and visible at the 'work floor' level, where new insights and products are conceived interactively. Adaptive leadership allows groups to 'learn their way out' of adaptive challenges (Uhl-Bien et al. 2007). Its primary outputs are learning, creativity, and adaptability. This dynamic can properly be considered as 'leadership', as it is fundamental for the direction of a change process. The participants in adaptive leadership settings stimulate and trigger each other in their meetings to come up with effective innovations for the challenges of the environment (Uhl-Bien et al. 2007; DeRue 2011; Uhl-Bien and Marion 2009).

The larger societal issues that MAG wants to tackle often demand changes that remain unknown until they manifest themselves as a result of paradigmatic shifts in thought or behavior patterns. Adaptive leadership is an interactive and generative dynamic that emerges out of the clash and connection between the discordant ideas and conflicting interests of people belonging to different social groups, engaged in MAG. Building on the resulting tension, adaptive leadership produces complex outcomes, integrating innovative ideas or technologies with new social alliances and cooperative efforts.

In the landfill mining case, adaptive leadership was mainly enacted by the researchers in the Consortium while exchanging knowledge and expertise between different scientific disciplines, including social sciences, in this highly technical endeavor. The Consortium counted in its starting phase with a relatively limited number of active members, 15 approximately. The first year, they met frequently in an informal way. This helped the exchange and elaboration of ideas and information and resulted in a shared vision on landfill mining for sustainable materials governance. Simultaneously, adaptive leadership was also enacted in other change alliances, around the business joint venture and around the participation of the local communities. In the joint venture, business partners and scientists were looking for ways to upgrade and commercialize the materials resulting from the application of new technologies. A group of local inhabitants living in the neighborhood of the targeted landfill site enacted also adaptive leadership, related to local community concerns about the project. They expanded the dominant technical perspective of the Consortium by asking critical questions about public health and safety aspects.

4.3. Enabling Leadership for MAG in the Landfill Mining Case

According to Uhl-Bien et al. (2007), enabling leadership fulfills two important functions: It catalyzes adaptive leadership, by encouraging the necessary interaction and information exchange in adaptive leadership groups, and it entangles this adaptive leadership with administrative leadership. Brokering and boundary spanning activities are essential for this type of leadership. In MAG, this implies stimulating an awareness of interdependency between the participants, managing productive interfaces between administrative and adaptive leadership, and taking care of the dissemination of innovation towards external parties that are not directly involved. Enabling leadership also has to protect the initiative against top–down politics imposed by external parties that prefer continuity, competition, and defensive strategies, instead of the innovative and interdependent–collaborative strategies proposed by MAG.

Enabling leadership is hard to study, as it often takes place through confidential contacts in personal relationships. In our case, the research coordinator of the Consortium had an active role in different networks related to sustainable materials governance, linking the worlds of engineering scientists, research managers, green activists, and political and public debate, even long before the start of the project. After the start of the Consortium, the representative of the Company became also involved in these networks. Numerous personal conversations about the project took place with "trusted" people. The location and setting for these conversations were adapted dependent on the type of conversation and of the participants. Sometimes, the meetings were more formal, in an office at the university, at the Company or even at the Waste Agency, but often these conversations also took place in an informal get-together in a pub before or after work time. As the research coordinator was active in various networks, he was often part of the brokering and boundary spanning activities.

As a consequence of these activities, higher officials of the universities and research centers, members of the Company family and their board of directors, and officers at the Waste Agency and political power holders were gradually willing to challenge their traditional roles and the boundaries between their organizations. Scientists became interested parts of a shared Consortium with private and civil partners instead of distant researchers of an external project. The Waste Agency found itself in a position of considering policy adaptations to make the project possible.

In addition to brokering and boundary spanning between different organizations and societal sectors, enabling leadership was also necessary to facilitate adaptive leadership practices inside the research Consortium. Indeed, researchers with different disciplinary backgrounds and belonging to different research institutes had to discover how to connect their interests and insights with those of their colleagues. This challenge became even bigger after incorporating public health scientists—originally not conceived as relevant for the initiative—and a representative of the local population. The social scientists in the Consortium enacted this function of enabling leadership by critically reflecting with the researchers about the constellation of the Consortium, by carefully preparing the meetings of the Consortium together with the research coordinator and the Company representative, to make these meetings as interactive as possible, and by stimulating active listening and open dialogue among the participants in the meetings of the Consortium.

5. Discussion and Conclusions

MAG generates multiple relations between the involved public, private, and civil actors. A relational approach is appropriate to analyze leadership because relations and connections matter more than individuals and positions in networks. Relational scholars put conversation and dialogue in the center as essential relationship building and sense-making tools. According to this relational approach, leadership is enacted in 'relational practices' that are able to connect discordant ideas through the qualities of reflexivity and reciprocity in shared activities. As leadership develops out of and through the relations and interactions in the network, it is an emergent construction within the MAG process and not a given top–down or outside–in facilitating force. It is definitely not a well-defined position or function assigned to an individual person who could then simply be considered the leader of a MAG network.

We described the case of landfill mining for sustainable materials governance to demonstrate a relational approach to leadership in MAG. This relational approach draws the attention to the specific characteristics of group development in MAG. Actors become increasingly aware of their different perspectives, values, goals, and interdependencies as the process unfolds. The interpersonal relationships gradually develop as a result of a group development process with specific challenges because of the loose coupling between different sub-groups and because of the plural values and interests of its participant (Bouwen and Taillieu 2004). Meetings often count with new members and generate a lot of ambiguity because of the different back grounds of the participants. As a consequence, the opportunities to go through a group development process are more limited and meetings are more demanding than in intra-organizational teams. Nevertheless, trust building is equally required before participants involved in MAG can engage in exploring the diversity of opinions, interests and values, and in cultivating transboundary relationships and common identities. The actors involved in MAG not only have to cultivate interdependence and connectedness among them, but they also have to take care of the broader society, and they have to be sensitive for the voices and interests of people that are not directly participating, as an outcome of this group process.

A relational approach also draws the attention to the relational action logics—rather than on the style of individual leaders. We observed in our case a gradual shift from a predominantly transactional action logic, paying attention to the direct benefits for the participants in the joint landfill mining initiative, to a transformational action logic, based on identification with the value of sustainable materials governance for the broader society. Not only governmental actors, but other actors as well, belonging to the private and civil sector, can become part of this transformational action logic. Leadership for MAG consists then of favoring the conditions that stimulate the development of a group process leading to this outcome.

CLT, developed within organizations, offers a valuable relational approach to grasp the variety of leadership tasks that are needed in the MAG setting of loosely coupled interorganizational networks. Administrative leadership practices are characterized by engaging in planning, structuring and controlling activities, while remaining receptive for the rapid changes in the outside world. Adaptive leadership practices are triggered by societal challenges for which participants want to co-create social and technological innovative solutions. Enabling leadership is key in MAG by managing the interface between administrative and adaptive leadership and by fostering the catalyzing conditions for adaptive leadership. It is enacted in brokering and boundary spanning activities among persons belonging to different organizations and social sectors that have a trust relationship with the administrative leadership in their own constituent organizations and that are acquainted with the social and technological novelties generated by adaptive leadership. They create opportunities by activating contacts 'behind the scene' and by establishing close personal relationships within the network.

Different types of leadership practices and relational action logics may not only co-exist in MAG; they also need each other and have to function in synergy to enhance the innovative capacities needed for the collective. Strengthening and promoting leadership practices according to the needs of the situation, thus, requires participants developing together contextual sensitivity, dialogical capacities, and reflexivity. Our case suggests that administrative leadership is predominantly characterized by a transactional action logic, that adaptive leadership thrives on a transformational logic, while the bridging function of enabling leadership is possible thanks to an ambidextrous combination or balancing of transactional and transformational action logics.

Further research is needed to analyze more in-depth the relational action logics of the leadership functions that can take into account the specific challenges for group development in MAG. Collaborative action–research is consistent with the relational approach to leadership argued for in this article (Eden and Huxham 1994; Bradbury and Lichtenstein 2000; Huxham 2000a). Theorizing and intervening are then conceived as interconnected, and research is conceived as a joint enactment of the worlds it wants to help to co-create. Doing research in this way raises however important new questions about the relational action logics of the researchers and how their research practices may contribute to a desirable group development for MAG.

Author Contributions: Conceptualization: M.C., A.D., K.T., R.B.; Methodology: M.C., I.V., A.D., K.T.; Investigation: M.C., I.V., K.S.; Analysis: M.C., I.V.; Writing original draft: M.C., I.V.; Writing—review and editing: M.C., A.D., K.T., R.B.; Funding acquisition: M.C., K.S., A.D.

Funding: This research was funded by the Flemish government as part of the policy support research center on Sustainable Materials Management SuMMa (2012–2016).

Acknowledgments: We are grateful to the inspiring persons engaged in the leadership practices described in this publication, for sharing their experience and insights with us.

Conflicts of Interest: The authors declare no conflict of interest.

References

Ansell, Chris, and Alison Gash. 2007. Collaborative Governance in Theory and Practice. *Journal of Public Administration Research and Theory* 18: 543–71. [CrossRef]

Argyris, Chris, and Donald A. Schön. 1978. *Organizational Learning II*. Reading: Addisson-Wesley.

Bass, Bernard M. 1999. Two Decades of Research and Development in Transformational Leadership. *European Journal of Work and Organizational Psychology* 8: 9–32. [CrossRef]

Bouwen, Rene. 1998. Relational Construction of Meaning in Emerging Organization Contexts. *European Journal of Work and Organizational Psychology* 7: 299–319. [CrossRef]

Bouwen, Rene, and Tharsi Taillieu. 2004. Multi-Party Collaboration as Social Learning for Interdependence: Developing Relational Knowing for Sustainable Natural Resource Management. *Journal of Community & Applied Social Psychology* 14: 137–53.

Bradbury, Hilary, and Benyamin B. Lichtenstein. 2000. Relationality in Organizational Research: Exploring the Space Between. *Organization Science* 11: 551–64. [CrossRef]

Craps, Marc, and Koen Sips. 2010. Enhanced Landfill Mining as a Governance Challenge: Managing Multiple Actors, Interests and Perspectives. In *Enhanced Landfill Mining and the Transition to Sustainable Materials Management*. Edited by Peter Tom Jones and Yves Tielemans. Houthalen-Helchteren: Haletra, pp. 265–77.

Crevani, Lucia, Monica Lindgren, and Johann Packendorff. 2010. Leadership, Not Leaders: On the Study of Leadership as Practices and Interactions. *Scandinavian Journal of Management* 26: 77–86. [CrossRef]

Cunliffe, Ann L., and Matthew Eriksen. 2011. Relational Leadership. *Human Relations* 64: 1425–49. [CrossRef]

Dachler, H. P., and D. Hosking. 1995. The Primacy of Relations in Socially Constructing Organizational Realities. In *Management and Organizations: Relationship Alternatives to Individualism*. Edited by Dian Marie Hosking, H. P. Dachler and Kenneth J Gergen. Farnham: Ashgate/Avebury, pp. 1–28. [CrossRef]

Delbecq, André, and Andrew Van De Ven. 1971. A Group Process Model for Problem Identification and Program Planning. *Journal of Applied Behavioral Science* 7: 466–92. [CrossRef]

DeRue, D. Scott. 2011. Adaptive Leadership Theory: Leading and Following as a Complex Adaptive Process. *Research in Organizational Behavior* 31: 125–50. [CrossRef]

Eden, Colin, and Chris Huxham. 1994. Action Research for the Study of Organizations. In *Handbook of Organization Studies*. Sage: Beverly Hills, pp. 526–42.

Fairhurst, Gail T., and Mary Uhl-Bien. 2012. Organizational Discourse Analysis (ODA): Examining Leadership as a Relational Process. *The Leadership Quarterly* 23: 1043–62. [CrossRef]

Gray, Barbara, and Jill Purdy. 2018. *Collaborating for Our Future. Multistakeholder Partnerships for Solving Complex Problems*. Oxford: Oxford University Press.

Harding, Nancy, Hugh Lee, Jackie Ford, and Mark Learmonth. 2011. Leadership and Charisma: A Desire That Cannot Speak Its Name? *Human Relations* 64: 927–49. [CrossRef]

Hosking, D. M. 2006. Not Leaders, Not Followers: A Post-Modern Discourse of Leadership Processes. In *Follower-Centered Perspectives on Leadership: A Tribute to the Memory of James R. Meindl*. Edited by Boas Shamir, Rajnandini Pillai, Michelle C. Bligh and Mary Uhl-Bien. Greenwich: Information Age Publishing.

Huxham, Chris. 2000a. *Working Paper Series The New Public Management: An Action Research Approach*. Glasgow: Strathclyde University.

Huxham, Chris. 2000b. The Challenge of Collaborative Governance. *Public Management* 2: 337–57. [CrossRef]

Huxham, Chris, and Siv Vangen. 2005. *Managing to Collaborate.* London: Routledge.

Johnson, Hazel, and Gordon Wilson. 2000. Biting the Bullet: Civil Society, Social Learning and the Transformation of Local Governance. *World Development* 28: 1891–906. [CrossRef]

Lowndes, Vivien, and Chris Skelcher. 1998. Multi-Organizational Partnerships: An Analysis of Changing Modes of Governance. *Public Administration* 76: 313–33. [CrossRef]

Murphy, Joanne, Mary Lee Rhodes, Jack W. Meek, and David Denyer. 2017. Managing the Entanglement: Complexity Leadership in Public Sector Systems. *Public Administration Review*, 692–704. [CrossRef]

Nooteboom, Sibout G., and Catrien J. Termeer. 2013. Strategies of Complexity Leadership in Governance Systems. *International Review of Public Administration* 18: 1–16. [CrossRef]

Osborn, Richard N., and Russ Marion. 2009. Contextual Leadership, Transformational Leadership and the Performance of International Innovation Seeking Alliances. *Leadership Quarterly* 20: 191–206. [CrossRef]

Osborne, Stephen P. 2006. The New Public Governance? *Public Management Review* 8: 377–87. [CrossRef]

Raelin, Joe. 2011. From Leadership-as-Practice to Leaderful Practice. *Leadership* 7: 195–211. [CrossRef]

Rhodes, R. A. W. 1996. The New Governance: Governing without Government. *Political Studies* XLIV: 652–67. [CrossRef]

Richardson, Kurt A., Jeffrey A. Goldstein, Peter M. Allen, and David Snowden. 2005. *Emergence, Complexity and Organization. E: CO ANNUAL Volume 6.* Mansfield: ISCE Publishing.

Sips, Koen, Marc Craps, and Art Dewulf. 2013. Local Participation in Complex Technological Projects as Bridging between Different Communities in Belgium. *Knowledge Management for Development Journal* 9: 95–115.

Srivastva, Suresh, S. L. Obert, and E. Neilsen. 1977. Organizational Analysis through Group Processes: A Theoretical Perspective for Organizational Development. In *Organizational Development in the UK and USA.* Edited by Cary Cooper. London: MacMillan, pp. 83–111.

Sullivan, Helen, Paul Williams, and Stephen Jeffares. 2012. Leadership for Collaboration: Situated Agency in Practice. *Public Management Review* 14: 41–66. [CrossRef]

Sydow, Jörg, Frank Lerch, Chris Huxham, and Paul Hibbert. 2011. A Silent Cry for Leadership: Organizing for Leading (in) Clusters. *Leadership Quarterly* 22: 328–43. [CrossRef]

Termeer, Catrien J. A. M., and Remco Kranendonk. 2008. Governance of Regional Innovations towards Sustainability. Paper presented at EGPA Conference, Wageningen, The Netherlands, September 3–6.

Uhl-Bien, Mary. 2006. Relational Leadership Theory: Exploring the Social Processes of Leadership and Organizing. *The Leadership Quarterly* 17: 654–76. [CrossRef]

Uhl-Bien, Mary, and Russ Marion. 2009. Complexity Leadership in Bureaucratic Forms of Organizing: A Meso Model. *The Leadership Quarterly* 20: 631–50. [CrossRef]

Uhl-Bien, Mary, Russ Marion, and Bill McKelvey. 2007. Complexity Leadership Theory: Shifting Leadership from the Industrial Age to the Knowledge Era. *Leadership Quarterly* 18: 298–318. [CrossRef]

Uhl-Bien, Mary, and Sonia Ospina, eds. 2012. *Advancing Relational Leadership Research. A Dialogue Among Perspectives.* New York: Information Age Publishing.

Vangen, Siv, John Paul Hayes, and Chris Cornforth. 2015. Governing Cross-Sector, Inter-Organizational Collaborations. *Public Management Review* 17: 1237–60. [CrossRef]

Vangen, Siv, and Chris Huxham. 2003. Enacting Leadership for Collaborative Advantage: Dilemmas of Ideology and Pragmatism in the Activities of Partnership Managers. *British Journal of Management* 14. [CrossRef]

Article

(Un)bounding the Meta-Organization: Co-Evolution and Compositional Dynamics of a Health Partnership

Steve Cropper [1,*] and Sanne Bor [2]

[1] Research Office, Faculty of Humanities and Social Sciences, Keele University, Newcastle ST5 5BG, UK
[2] Department of Marketing, Hanken School of Economics, P.O. Box 479, 00100 Helsinki, Finland;
   bor@hanken.fi
* Correspondence: s.a.cropper@keele.ac.uk; Tel.: +44-7901-760256

Received: 16 May 2018; Accepted: 24 July 2018; Published: 3 August 2018

Abstract: In their treatise on meta-organization, Ahrne and Brunsson theorize a distinctive organizational form, the association of organizations. Meta-organizations have the properties of formal organizations—boundaries set by determinations of membership, goals, a centre of authority, and ways of monitoring and sanctioning member behaviors. The theory draws a strong distinction between meta-organizations and networks, suggesting that similarity among members is the primary characteristic of meta-organizations, whereas networks signify complementarity and difference. Meta-organizations serve and are governed by their members, though the meta-organization itself may develop its own agency and may regulate its members. It is on this basis that Ahrne and Brunsson develop an account of the dynamics of meta-organizations, placing less emphasis on external sources of change than on the internal relationships between members and the meta-organization itself. This paper appraises the theory of meta-organizations, using a case study of Partners in Paediatrics, a subscription association of health care organizations, as the empirical reference point. Data about this partnership's membership and its activities are drawn from 12 'annual reports' covering a 17-year period. Focusing, particularly, on the membership composition of the Partnership and its relationship to the changing environment, the case analysis traces the changing character and circumstances of the Partnership, identifying four distinct phases, and raising questions for meta-organization theory and its account of meta-organization dynamics.

Keywords: dynamics; boundaries; change; co-evolution; meta-organization; partnership; institutional environment; composition; membership; healthcare

---

1. Introduction

There is a growing literature on the dynamics of cooperation among organizations (see Cropper and Palmer 2008), though Bell, den Ouden, and Ziggers (Bell et al. 2006) argue that the field is *"fragmented, lacks coherence, and has produced non-comparable research"*. In their review of 22 longitudinal cases of inter-organizational collaborations, Majchrzak et al. (2015) start to draw together insights into dynamics, conceived as changes in the characteristics of inter-organizational collaborations and as patterns of relationships between sources and characteristics of inter-organizational collaborations. Most studies of dynamics focus on alliances between two firms, often taking the perspective of one side of the alliance (Bell et al. 2006). In this paper, by comparison, we focus on associations composed of multiple organizations, drawing on, and appraising, aspects of the theory of meta-organization (Ahrne and Brunsson 2005, 2008). Majchrzak et al. (2015) include only one study on the dynamics of meta-organizations, the study of Sematech by Browning et al. (1995), and no specific attention is given to the difference in dynamics. The (relatively limited) literature on organizational federations and associations does contain some studies of importance (e.g., Lowndes and Skelcher 1998; Selsky 1998;

Traxler 2002). However, insights into the specific character of meta-organizations remain limited and fragmentary (Berkowitz and Bor 2018; Berkowitz and Dumez 2016).

This paper presents changes in the membership composition of a meta-organization over a 17-year period and discusses the significance of these changes for the character of the meta-organization. In the case study, we draw on the annual reports of Partners in Paediatrics (PiP), from its initiation in 1997 until 2014, to capture what we term the 'compositional dynamics' of this formalized association of organizations (Cropper 2001), which meta-organization theory suggests will have distinctive characteristics. We understand 'character' in institutional terms. As Selznick (1957) observed, *"This patterning [character] is historical, in that it reflects the specific experiences of the particular organization; it is functional in that it aids the organization to adapt itself to its internal and external social environment; and it is dynamic, in that it generates new and active forces, especially internal interest-groups . . . .the emergence of organizational character reflects the irreversible element in experience and choice"*. In this paper, we ask whether closer attention to the institutional environment, to change over time, and to changes in membership composition would both indicate and explain changes to meta-organizational character and strengthen the core claims of the theory of meta-organization.

The paper is organized as follows. We start by discussing the characteristics of meta-organizations and review the literature on dynamics relevant to this associational form of organization. We describe our methodology and the data included in the study. This is followed by an account and discussion of the dynamics of the case against the terms of meta-organization theory.

2. Characteristics of Meta-Organizations and Key Sites of Dynamics

In a recent series of publications, Ahrne and Brunsson (2005, 2008, 2011) have proposed that meta-organizations are a distinct type of inter-organizational entity (Cropper et al. 2008). They stipulate some characteristics of the form: *"meta-organizations are all associations; membership is voluntary and members can withdraw at will. The purpose of a meta-organization is to work in the interests of all its members, with all members being equally valuable and membership being based on some form of similarity"* (Ahrne and Brunsson 2008, p. 11). Although, in these senses, meta-organizations may be likened to other associations, Ahrne and Brunsson (2008) emphasize the significance of the composition of meta-organizations: Members are organizations not individuals.

Ahrne and Brunsson (2008) also stipulate a formality of character. A meta-organization *"is not the same as a network, class, or society. For people to believe that something is an organization, it must have members, a hierarchy, autonomy, and a constitution."* (Ahrne and Brunsson 2008, p. 45). Such formalization, seen as a process and an outcome (Vlaar et al. 2006), creates the conditions for a 'decided order' (Ahrne and Brunsson 2011; Ahrne et al. 2016). Decisions concerning members specify who are in, and who are out and so set the boundary. The hierarchy exists as a center of authority: Though this may be no more than a mechanism for making decisions, it may equally hold the right to issue commands and rules prescribing members' actions. Such rights and rules are laid down in constitutions, which may also describe the goals or tasks of the organization. Ahrne and Brunsson (2008) observe that a meta-organization can gain a degree of autonomy, and become recognized as an organization in their own right. Formalization can have positive effects in terms of a meta-organization's presence and agency; however, it may also provide false impressions of comprehensibility and controllability (Vlaar et al. 2006).

In their account of dynamics, Ahrne and Brunsson (2008) focus substantially on the composition and order of the meta-organization, arguing that *"meta-organizations can best be understood as being in a transitional phase between a weak organization with strong members and a strong organization with weak members"* (p. 132). Like other accounts that focus on inherent instabilities (Das and Teng 2000), tensions (Huxham and Vangen 2000), or dialectics (De Rond and Bouchikhi 2004) in inter-organizational entities, meta-organization dynamics are held to arise from the interplay between members, the meta-organization, and their collective activities. Although Ahrne and Brunsson (2008) explain the formation of a meta-organization as a move on the environment, they say less about the way the meta-organization might continue to respond to field influences as a source of change. The boundary between organizations and their environment is moved, but a new boundary and set of relationships both within the meta-organization and between the meta-organization and its environment are produced. Other accounts of organizational change, including the co-evolutionary perspective, recently reexamined by Rodrigues and Child (2003, 2008), frame dynamics essentially in terms of the mutual and reciprocal influence between an organization as a collective effort or strategy and its environment (see also Barnett et al. 2000; Selsky 1998). We move on to discuss institutional environment and membership composition as sources of dynamics using a third lens—that of patterned transitions through time, i.e., history.

2.1. Institutional Environment

The environment of organizations is unpredictable and meta-organizations are an attempt at organizing salient parts of the environment (Ahrne and Brunsson 2008). As Ahrne and Brunsson (2008, p. 56) note, "*Creating meta-organizations entails the reduction of environment and an increase in organization—transforming part of what was once the members' environment into organization. Instead of constituting each other's environment, the organization's members become members in the same organization.*" A new and additional organization is formed while no organization is 'lost' (unlike in a merger or acquisition). Members, thus, "*retain their organizational boundaries, but a new boundary is placed around them all.*" (p. 64). While the meta-organization organizes part of the environment, the environment does not disappear. Ahrne and Brunsson note, "*To a great extent, organizations must accept the environment as it is and adapt to it rather than attempt to control it.*" (Ahrne and Brunsson 2008, p. 56). However, the meta-organization still needs to deal with its environment and so do the members. Frequently, meta-organizations seek deliberately to influence and to change their environments (and that of the members) for the benefit of the members. Meta-organization theory says little about this ongoing work. In his analysis of the developmental dynamics in non-profit federations, Selsky (1998) observes that the federation's dynamics include both forms of adaptation and efforts at construction. Adaptation consists in the federated referent organization's (FRO; Selsky's term is conceptually close to meta-organizations) responses to "*influences and pressures from constituent member organizations, domain elites, and the wider context of resource and policy environments in which they operate.*" (p. 298). Construction is where the FRO seeks to shape the context through its own presence and actions. This can be understood in terms of co-evolution (Rodrigues and Child 2003), whereby the environment influences the meta-organization, but, at the same time, the meta-organization influences the environment. Rodrigues and Child (2003) recognize three system levels, that of the macro (the general environment), the meso (the immediate environment), and the micro (the organization internal), which interact. Preempting Rodrigues and Child (2008) work, Selsky concludes that the developmental dynamics of the FRO are characterized by a continuous interplay between the FRO and its context, in which it seeks to maintain effective alignment between its strategy and the significant elements of the field within which it is set. However, becoming an actor that can influence its environment requires a high degree of coordination and a strengthened common identity, according to Ahrne and Brunsson, and may increase the need for similarity among members. In addition, one of the issues with meta-organizations is that the member organizations as individual organizations also remain embedded within their environment; they can act and attempt to influence their environment as well. We expect much more of an active and complex relationship to the remaining environment than simple acceptance.

2.2. Membership Composition

Membership of a meta-organization is a voluntary decision by organizations: "*As members, they keep most of their autonomy and identity as independent organizations*" (Ahrne and Brunsson 2008, p. 3). Organizations need a reason for becoming and remaining a member, and many organizations may choose to stay outside meta-organizations they would be eligible to join. This is particularly the case for those with the ability to influence their environment successfully on their own, or where they expect status, identity, or operating flexibility to be maintained outside the meta-organization. Staying outside a meta-organization can, however, *"reduce the possibility of interacting with its members or worsen the conditions for interaction"* (Ahrne and Brunsson 2008, pp. 87–88) and it can raise questions and speculations from the environment about why it is not a member.

Ahrne and Brunsson (2008) assume that the decision by organizations to become a member and the decision to accept members is based on some form of similarity, belonging to a group of organizations. Yet they also note *"many of the conflicts that exist in meta-organizations are about the extent to which the members should be similar to each other"* (Ahrne and Brunsson 2008, p. 100). A lack of similarity may lead to difficulties as it may make it difficult to identify meaningful interaction or collective action for all members. They suggest that meta-organizations can create a different category of members, associate members, to allow non-similar members to engage, while preserving the similarity among main members. The nature of the required similarity among members remains, however, somewhat unclear. Their specification is that members *"perform similar tasks and strive for similar things"* (Ahrne and Brunsson 2008, p. 60). Berkowitz and Dumez (2016) found that the membership of oil and gas organizations in meta-organizations shows significant variety with membership commonly from different sectors and hence different types of organizations (public, private, non-governmental organizations, etc.). Similarity, may then be found more in identification with the purpose of the meta-organization than in performing similar tasks or, as Ahrne and Brunsson suggest, some other 'family resemblance'. The focus of Ahrne and Brunsson, as well as other scholars writing about meta-organizations, has primarily been on the relation between the members and the meta-organization. Because they stipulate the criterion of similarity so strongly, they say less about the composition, about the limits to variety or difference, or the ways of handling difference and change in composition over time.

In what follows, we consider the dynamics that arise at the external boundary—those between the meta-organization and the environment—and those generated by the composition of the meta-organization as seen in terms of its membership and the activity that is decided and pursued on their behalf by the meta-organization.

3. Method & Data

Using a single-case study design, we explore aspects of a significant phenomenon under rare circumstances (Eisenhardt and Graebner 2007), a partnership's life from its inception in 1997 to its position in the healthcare sector in the UK 17 years later. We draw on the series of publicly available reports, published annually or biennially (they are referred to as Annual Reports or Partnership Reports) that offer narrative accounts of the work of 'Partners in Paediatrics' (the Partnership). The twelve reports published during this period give a rich, cumulative, and reflective account of the purpose, membership, and activities of the Partnership. Typically, the reports profile the activity of the Partnership during the reporting period and discuss its significance in relation to the Partnership's purpose and context. The Reports do not give a clear sense of the relationship between the meta-organization itself and its members, except in the discussions of what has been achieved or not achieved, by the Partnership on behalf of the membership. They say little about members' motives in joining or leaving the Partnership. Nevertheless, they offer a sense of pattern through time. We have summarized the Reports, year-by-year and section-by-section, tracking the changes in Partnership structure, membership, work streams/activity, resourcing, and claims about achievement and impact. There are clear continuities in each of these, but there is also disjuncture. As well as exploring the internal bases of change, we have also noted where the Reports comment on how it is connected to its environment, both through the member organizations, but also directly as an actor in its own right. Duriau et al. (2007) note the value of annual reports as a source of data for longitudinal analysis, they also caution that there are limitations, e.g., such reports tend to be strongly biased to positive accounts of the organization, and they present, essentially, a singular view. We recognize this and the potential for a lack of chronological precision given the irregular production of the reports and the movement between the Partnership age and calendar date across the reports. Nevertheless, the content of the reports allows for checks on sequence, period, and date, and the tone of these twelve reports is not wholly self-satisfied: As much as reporting success, they identify and explain tensions and frustrations, not least in the Partnership's capacity to produce change. Several of the reports take 'change' as the central theme and offer reflective comments in which connections are made between the Partnership, its ambitions and capacities, the receptiveness, or otherwise of the Partnership's environment, and the degree of alignment between these.

Analysis of this data allows us to explore both the question of the character of the Partnership, in terms of the formal characteristics of meta-organizations, and to track certain forms of dynamics that have been significant in the evolution of the Partnership. This will also allow us to offer an empirically informed appraisal of important arguments within meta-organization theory.

We start with a brief account of four phases in the life of the Partnership:

(i)   Initiation and formalization of the Partnership;
(ii)   a period focused on the promotion and organized exploration of 'wide area managed clinical networks' as a means of organizing pediatric services;
(iii)   a stalling of energy and progress on wide area managed clinical networks; and
(iv)   competition for wide area network leadership, and a split agenda within the Partnership.

These phases are a temporal bracketing (Langley 2010) in which we identify continuities within phases and discontinuities in character at the frontiers. Between phase (i) and (ii), the discontinuity concerns changes in the constitution of the Partnership, and, particularly, its formalization. Between phase (ii) and (iii), the discontinuity concerns the change in membership composition and a stable programme of collectively organized activity. In addition, between phase (iii) and (iv), the discontinuity concerns institutional pressures (conducive or adverse/disrupted policy and influence from powerful actors, both within the Partnership and from outside). This next section serves to introduce the partnership, its evolution through 17 years, and events that have affected its character. The section that then follows comments specifically on the compositional dynamics of the Partnership, a consequence of internal tensions that arise from the meta-organizational form, but also from the circumstances that shape its membership, and from the patterns of membership themselves. The paper concludes with a brief response to Ahrne and Brunsson (2008) specification of the character of meta-organizations, and some suggestions for future research.

4. *Partners in Paediatrics*: **Environment and Partnership (Co-)Evolution**

In this section, we draw out two sets of observations about Partners in Paediatrics (PiP) as it has evolved over time and about the sources of this change. First, we comment on the effects of the changing environment on the Partnership. Like recent studies of co-evolution (Rodrigues and Child 2003, 2008), the UK health sector—the National Health Service (NHS)—is rich with institutions, and is highly politicised. The professions have influence and the administrative hierarchy remains a significant factor in institutional and ideological forces, which are seen as the process of translating the most significant of influences, policy—or rather myriad policies, often ambiguous, and contradictory—into effect. We also map the changing composition of the Partnership, and the effects that a changing membership mix has on the character of the Partnership.

4.1. Partnership (Co-)Evolution: Four Phases of the Meta-Organisation in Its (Changing) Environment

4.1.1. Phase 1: Initiation, Formation, and Formalization

Ahrne and Brunsson (2008, p. 79) observe that the meta-organizations they studied *"typically started at conferences to which all relevant parties were invited."* The Partnership was, indeed, initiated by representatives (pediatricians and managers) of nine general hospitals (NHS provider organizations are constitutionally designated as 'Trusts') who met in November 1997 to *"discuss the opportunities for developing greater collaborative links between providers of paediatrics in this geographical area ... There are already signs that collaborations are developing in an informal way ... "* .... (Letter of Invitation, 6 October 1997).

Behind the invitation and the list of invitees was concern about the effects of the internal market established within the NHS from 1991 on the planning and resourcing of pediatric hospital services. The internal market separated provider organizations from commissioners of services, the latter being charged with defining and securing services to meet the health care needs of their local population. Commissioners hold authority over the organization of services and access to services through their decisions about the services they specify and fund. As Ahrne and Brunsson (2008, p. 65) observe, *"If a field already has a high degree of order, one might think the need for a meta-organization is less; yet another type of order may be desired."* The call for greater collaboration was in the face of incentives towards competition between provider organizations, a lack of meaningful dialogue between commissioners and provider organizations about services required, especially more specialized services, and how best to secure them. At a second meeting of this group one month later, the group agreed on a Statement of Purpose, outlining the rationale and proposed activity of a Partnership:

> *"The driving purpose of the collaboration is to improve the quality and accessibility of services for children across the area served by the participating hospitals.".* (AR1: p. 3)

Three objectives were also specified:

- Balancing local needs and provision of high quality specialist services;
- managing manpower, training, and research; and
- Advising commissioning agencies and groups re. paediatric services. (AR1: p. 3)

The three objectives can be seen consistently to have guided the activities of the Partnership.

The initiating group of hospitals could be said to have two similarities—identity and interest. In terms of similarity of identity, the nine hospitals invited to the first exploratory meetings were all general hospitals providing secondary care services for their local populations (250–400,000): All had pediatric divisions, generally small compared to other divisions, e.g., medical or surgical, within the hospital. In addition, all served communities in the triangle set between three major cities and their Children's Hospitals. The Children's Hospitals provide specialist, tertiary services to the wider region and its population (usually several million), and potentially very specialist services for still larger populations. However, they also provide general secondary services for the children within their city hinterlands. In part, because of difficulties of access to the tertiary services in the Children's Hospitals, but also because Pediatrics was following the tendency within medicine towards greater specialization of training and practice, the larger general hospitals were starting to develop specialist services within their general pediatric offer. Nearby, smaller, general hospital units were then referring patients to them as well as, or instead of, to Children's Hospitals for specialist opinions and treatment. Among the nine general hospitals that formed the Partnership, there were shared interests and concerns about a) the quality and range of healthcare provision in the general hospitals, even the larger ones, could, themselves, viably provide, and b) whether access to specialist services that the Children's Hospitals were funded to provide was fair or adequate. They agreed it was not.

From the discussions and the statement of the purpose that was fashioned by this group came a decision, relatively rapidly, to formalize arrangements. The first annual report notes:

> *"The group is suggesting strengthening the organizational basis ... as a means of identifying and pursuing shared agendas where joint action could bring benefit. This would also mean some formalisation of the Partnership itself: its boundaries, so far open, might be more visible and the terms of membership more defined and conditional on appropriate contribution to the work of the group."* (AR1: p. 13)

By September 1998, as the Partnership moved towards a more formal constitution, representatives of 14 Trusts were actively involved. At the [second] Conference, there was a report:

> *"to the Chief Executives of the participating Trusts on the progress made to date and to seek a mandate to continue with this work . . . . the Chief Executives requested a written summary report before agreeing to a financial contribution to support the further work of the Partnership . . . . A further 'Open' meeting was held in January 1999, to conclude the work of Year 1, to agree the programme of work for Year 2, establish the formation of the Steering Group and appoint its 'officers' . . . "* (AR1: pp. 1–2)

The agreement of the Chief Executives signaled, it was understood, the commitment of each member organization to the Partnership. Subscription fee levels varied depending on size of hospital, but, in all other respects, it was a 'partnership of equals' represented on the Partnership Steering Group. (AR1, p. 5). There is a reminder of the governance arrangements in each Annual Report and many more detailed explanations in the early years (AR1, pp. 4, 12–19; AR2, p. 7; AR3, pp. 5–6) and in later Reports from the Chair of the Partnership (AR7, p. 3; AR12, pp. 1–2).

Not all Trusts involved in the formation joined: Four community health trusts, responsible for providing health care outside hospitals to local communities, did not continue into Year 2. However, another community health trust did join the general hospitals in founding the Partnership, and there is evidence in an evaluation reported in AR3 that the issue was one of the relevance of the agenda and priorities, which focused on secondary and tertiary care rather than the community- and home-based care that was the main business of this other type of health care provider organization.

Appointed officers of the Partnership formed a core group, a management and coordinating center for the Partnership. Ahrne and Brunsson (2008) stipulate a 'center of authority', responsible for decision-making within the meta-organization, which we take, in this instance, to refer to the Steering Group: They also note that the meta-organization may be allowed, or may develop, a certain degree of agency independent of the members, and that the dynamics of governance between members and the meta-organization itself are a matter of central interest in understanding the character of any meta-organization. Early in the Partnership's development, the sense of collective and mutual responsibility was promoted. For example, a coordinated action to map the availability of specialist practitioners in the member Trusts reported that:

> *"The Partnership members have all agreed to adopt a protocol to share information and accept influence from the Partnership concerning the appointment of consultants and this, together with the development of a strategy and service plan, will be the foundation stones for provider collaboration in service delivery in the future."* (AR2, p. 13)

Attention to governance, as a means of deciding on its programme of activity, as a means of rendering account, and as a source of legitimacy with members (Human and Provan 2000), reveals the careful development of the (internal) relationship between the Partnership and its members. However, it is equally clear from the Reports that the Partnership was also developing its connections to the wider scene.

4.1.2. Phase 2: Wide Area Managed Clinical Networks

The formalization of the Partnership coincided almost with a significant change in the policy environment. First, a trenchant critique of policy attention to children and young people (Aynsley-Green et al. 2000) meant that the government was urgently issuing new national guidance. The first tranche (Department of Health 2003) focused attention on the quality of care within the hospital setting. AR5 (pp. 5–6), issued at the end of 2003, provides a detailed comparison of the policy mandate, with the work of the Partnership boosting the legitimacy of the Partnership, and strengthening the hand of those stakeholders who would recognize the Partnership's value. The policy also asks for closer partnership among organizations. In this second phase of the Partnership, an idea becomes central to the work of the Partnership. A 'managed clinical network' is defined as *"linked groups of health professionals and organisations from primary, secondary and tertiary care working in a co-ordinated manner, unconstrained by existing professional and existing [organisational] boundaries to ensure equitable provision of high quality services.*" (Baker and Lorimer 2000, p. 1152) This idea captures exactly the task set by the Partnership. It was also starting to receive significant attention nationally (e.g., NHS Confederation 2001). In both respects, the Partnership was ahead of the crowd.

The (long) second phase of development of the Partnership involved a series of projects, several running at any time, to apply the idea of the managed clinical network to the services identified as priorities for improvement. This work evidently took the Partnership beyond its membership. Thus, we observe a distinction drawn between the members of the Partnership (listed in each Report) and the full range of participants that are reported to be contributing. Members have attendance and voting rights at the Steering Group/Board of the Partnership. Moreover, they are mentioned as privileged beneficiaries of the Partnership. However, participants are also important. The following appears in a number of the Annual Reports:

> "*We are an open organization and as such are keen to work with anyone to help further our aims. Please get in touch if you are interested in getting involved in any of our projects.*". (AR4, p. 2)

Participants, from non-member organizations help to populate the Partnership's Working Groups. They bring reputation, expertise, and energy, and act as ambassadors to their own organizations and to other significant stakeholders. This cast of agents at, or just beyond, the boundary of the Partnership, but who also are invited into, or encroach on, the Partnership, has clear significance in making and sustaining the Partnership. The Partnership's boundaries are in place, but they are low and porous, and the presence and actions of non-members shape the character of the Partnership.

Within this period, there was also significant interchange between the Partnership and other stakeholders. Learning is shared widely among a range of beneficiaries rather than restricted to membership as 'club goods' would be. At the macro level, the Partnership was recognized nationally, and internationally, for its work in exploring how managed networks could work for pediatric services, even if market practices and a strong sense of hierarchical control remained central to the NHS. At the meso-level, the Reports suggest that its most important external relations are at the regional or strategic levels, where the scale of the geographical responsibility of NHS organizations matched that of the Partnership and its focus on wide-area managed clinical networks for specialist services. There are references to strong links to the Strategic Health Authority and to projects supported and funded by that influential external organization. The Annual Reports start, after five years, to suggest that the more localized, commissioning organizations that purchase health services from providers for their populations are also engaging with the Partnership: "*Commissioners are well-represented as advisers* ... " (AR5, p. 5), and "*PiP has a lot of knowledge about services that could assist the commissioners* ... " (p. 6). AR6 then reports that the Partnership has been able to establish a means of conducting relations with the commissioners, at a scale that would potentially enable coordinated action: "*This year, PiP and commissioners have formed the Paediatric Specialised Services Steering Group. The group's overall objective is to develop strategic planning advice with commissioners for development and deployment of paediatric services across* ... *.the PiP area. This is a huge step in taking PiP's service projects forward*" (AR6, p. 3).

4.1.3. Phase 3: Wide Area Networks Stalling

However, ARs 5 and 6 also suggest a turning point, in part as a consequence of continuing changes to the organizational structure of the NHS. AR5 notes a 'whole new set of challenges': "*It had always been an issue for PiP how most effectively to engage with multiple commissioners.* ... *With the advent* ... *.of Primary Care Trusts (PCT), PiP now has a significantly altered landscape within which to plan and develop services. On the one hand, the environment is more complex; fourteen PCTs as opposed to five Health Authorities* ... *On the other hand, PCTs are not solely commissioners but also significant providers of services to children. This latter point represents an opportunity for PiP.*" (AR5, p. 3). The membership now includes three PCTs, which have both commissioner and provider responsibilities—the internal market structure had been compromised by the latest NHS reorganisation. The commissioning arm was responsible for securing all children's secondary care services and access to tertiary care. That these organizations are members is therefore significant. We note, however, that it is likely that PCTs became members because community services for children have been transferred from what were member organizations, now reorganized, into their newly-mandated provider 'arms'.

The Partnership also notes that *"...ultimately PiP is only as strong as its member commitments will allow."* (AR5, p8) and, most tellingly: *"Where members have been most frustrated is in implementing proposals for collaborative service change and development. As a partnership, PiP has no power or authority to effect change: authority lies with individual members and through the commissioning systems. Where issues require a view across services, or across health localities, there has often been uncertainty about whose responsibility it is to mandate, lead, or take action. PiP has been able to help in coordinating action where there is commitment from interested parties."* (AR6, p. 6). Subsequent Annual Reports, therefore, reflect on the limits to the Partnership's ability to effect planned change. Initial steps to implement plans for networks in pediatric gastroenterology and in surgery are reported, with investments by groups of members on behalf of the Partnership. However, these do not pay off as planned, in part, because supporting investments from other members, needed to develop and sustain the new planned patterns of service delivery, do not materialize in time. The Partnership is not alone in this, but it has evidently understood that Baker and Lorimer's (2000) warning that managed clinical networks are difficult to implement and sustain is well-founded. Second, the serial reorganization of the local NHS not only affects the membership composition of the Partnership, but also disrupts its immediate environment, with repeated change to commissioning organizations and to the regional/strategic tier at which scale the managed clinical networks would have had a natural alignment. (see Paton 2014).

4.1.4. Phase 4: Split Agenda and Competition for Field (Meta-) Organization

Column 5 of Table 1, as shown below, shows that membership of the Partnership had incrementally become more varied. The general hospital trusts were no longer the dominant majority: A substantial minority of members are community service trusts, and yet the activities of the Partnership have only marginally met the interests of these organizations. AR5 explores different future programmes of activity: One of these involved *"drawing away from PiP's focus on care for the acutely ill child."* Then, AR6 reports that a project had been initiated to address issues in Child Protection. As it had done for the specialist acute services, the Partnership had seen, earlier than other agencies, problems with the quality and accessibility of services. It assertively pursued this problem. A project group both incorporated and supported Police and Social Services organizations and health service commissioners. Its work was covered in each subsequent Annual Report, including, ultimately, a note reporting tangible improvements to services.

By 2009, a split in activity and in the Partnership is apparent, reflecting different member interests and a changing relationship between the Partnership and one powerful member, the Children's Hospital, responsible for tertiary services to the general hospitals that are still a majority of the members. It is the only Children's Hospital that remains a subscribing member. Ahrne and Brunsson (2008) note that when a meta-organization and its members become too similar, there is no need for the meta-organization. AR10 reports that the Children's Hospital *"approached PiP with a proposal to use their membership to work collaboratively in developing regional specialist networks. They plan to use the independence of the PiP Board to ensure that developments are prioritised and owned by providers . . . .and that the requirements of all members are accounted for at the planning stage. In order to take this on the main change for PiP will be the requirement to accept new members from across the region. PiP members are currently considering this proposal."* (AR10, p. 2). AR11 reports *"we have continued to work more closely with [the Children's Hospital] in the work around developing a strategy for specialist clinical networks"* and, significantly, *"establishing clear governance arrangements . . . will be achieved through creating a Board and two sub-committees; one focusing on acute service networks and the other focusing on integrated community pathways."* (AR11, p. 3). This 'internal jolt'—the division of activity and of member interests into wide area networks and local service projects—was reported as proceeding. However, AR12 also reports two external 'jolts'. The new government, elected in 2010, passed the Health and Social Care Act 2012. Despite promises not to pursue more structural change, it does so, creating still more fragmentary and numerous commissioning organizations—now called Clinical Commissioning Groups (CCGs). AR12 also notes the *'establishment of the [regional] Strategic Clinical Network [SCN] (Maternity and Children) and the Clinical Senate."* Whilst an official endorsement of the clinical network as a core mode of organizing by the NHS, the report of the annual conference for 2012 notes challenges to the Partnership's role, stating that *"We need to bring existing local/informal networks into the work of the SCN ... and involve all stakeholders."* For a Partnership that had been recognized for the depth and richness of clinical engagement, and for its work to develop and support informal and formal clinical networks, this was a significant threat. Nevertheless, AR12 remains optimistic:

> *"PiP has continued to be a stable and influencing advocate for children and young people. The focus on improving health outcomes ... across the region remains as strong as it did when the organization started in 1997. The organization has actively responded to the 'external' challenges—whilst also reviewing itself as an organization and strengthening its governance arrangements."* (AR12, Chair's Foreword, p. 2)

The focus for the future (AR12, p. 13) sets out activities that are less about change through the redesign of services as networks—representation of members, facilitation of interaction and support to informal networks, education and sharing good practice, developing and monitoring standards, guidelines and quality improvement measures, and engagement with children and young people as service users. These match more closely to the functions of a meta-organization discussed by Ahrne and Brunsson (2008). In terms of the Partnership's membership, there is a broadening of the appeal: The Report advises *"All NHS and social care organizations involved in, or concerned with the provision, commissioning or regulation of services for children and young people are eligible to become a member."* (AR12, p. 15). Yet, the membership profile shows a clear return to the general hospital as the dominant member type.

Table 1, as shown below, provides a more systematic enumeration of the membership of the Partnership, and change in membership composition year by year. It also notes the degree to which the policy environment is conducive to attention and action on children's services and to collaborative approaches to service provision and improvement. Both affect the Partnership's ability to attract membership and to influence, through work with external organizations, the environment to the members' advantage.

Table 1. Membership of the Partnership: Composition and changes 1997–2014.

Partnership Phase	Date	Annual Report	Membership			Conducive Environment	
			Number of Members	Similarity	Change/Continuity and Composition	Policy on Collaboration & Networks	Policy Emphasis on Children
Initiation and formalization	1997	AR1	9	Very high	9 general hospitals	No	No
	1998	AR1	11	High	**2 new:** 2 community service trusts → 9 general; 2 community	No	No
	1999	AR2	11	High	No change	No	No
	2000	AR2/3	13	High	**2 new:** 1 general hospital; 1 community services provider → 10 general; 3 community	No	No
Wide Area Managed Clinical Networks	2001	AR3/4	18	Varied	**5 new:** 3 specialized Children's Hospitals, 1 community services trust, 1 Primary Care Trust (PCT) → 10 general; 4 community, 3 specialized, 1 PCT	Supportive within market	Very positive
	2002	AR5	19	Varied	**5 new:** 4 PCTs; 1 community services trust **4 loss:** 3 community services trusts assimilated into PCTs; 1 PCT → 10 general; 2 community; 3 specialized, 4 PCT	Supportive, within market	Yes
	2003	AR6	19	Varied	No change	Supportive within market	Yes
Wide Area Networks Stalling	2004	AR6	17	Varied	**2 loss:** 1 specialized Children's Hospital (out of main region); 1 general hospital (2 members merge) → 9 general; 2 community, 2 specialized, 4 PCT	Disturbed	Yes
	2005	AR7	17	Varied	No change	Disturbed	Yes
	2006	AR7	17	Varied	No change	Disturbed	Yes
	2007	AR8	15	Varied	**2 loss:** 1 general hospital, 1 community services trust → 8 general; 1 community, 2 specialized, 4 PCT	Yes	Yes
	2008	AR8/AR9	16	Varied	**2 new:** 2 PCT **1 loss:** 1 PCT (out of main region) → 8 general; 1 community, 2 specialized, 5 PCT	Yes	Yes

Table 1. *Cont.*

Partnership Phase	Date	Annual Report	Number of Members	Similarity	Membership	Conducive Environment	
					Change/Continuity and Composition	Policy on Collaboration & Networks	Policy Emphasis on Children
	2009	AR9	16	Varied	No change	Yes	Yes
	2010	AR10	17	Varied	**1 new:** 1 PCT → 8 general; 1 community, 2 specialized, 6 PCT	Disturbed	Unknown
Split Agenda and Competition for Field (Meta-) Organization	2011	AR11	16	Varied	**1 loss:** 1 specialized Children's Hospital (out of main region) → 8 general; 1 community, 1 specialized, 6 PCT	Yes	No
	2012–2014	AR12	18	High	Geographical extension of Partnership boundary. **8 new:** 5 general; 2 community; 1 new style commissioner—Clinical Commissioning Group (CCG) **6 loss:** 6 PCTs (abolition of PCTs) → 13 general; 3 community; 1 specialized; 1 CCG	Yes	Yes

4.2. Membership and the Consequences of Compositional Change

In this section, we consider how the composition of the Partnership, set out in Table 1, has changed, why it may have done so, and with what consequences. We focus here on membership composition and change, and, particularly, on the criterion of 'member similarity', since this is the principal point of reference in meta-organization theory.

First, we note that the Partnership has survived. The Partnership is 'of', but not 'in', the NHS. Members are exclusively drawn from the NHS and the composition of the Partnership has been heavily influenced by the embeddedness of its membership in that structure, which dominates the field of children's health care. However, the Partnership itself is not subject directly to the policy decisions that shape it and its local organizational structure. It has survived because its overall membership has been sustained at or above a critical mass.

Second, however, the Partnership's membership has changed. The question of similarity and variety in membership is not addressed directly in the Annual Reports, although there are a number of points we can infer. Membership grew rapidly in the three years following the Partnership's inception and then stabilized. It is not a large membership (19 members are listed at the maximum), and so the admission of a new partner or the loss of even one member is of some significance—these events are indicated in the Annual Reports. There has been a high degree of continuity of membership of the founder members—a group of general hospitals and one of the Children's Hospitals has remained a member since it joined in 2001 as has one Primary Care Trust (PCT), also joining in 2001. This year is the point at which the criterion of 'similarity', that Ahrne and Brunsson (2008) suggest is characteristic of the meta-organization, becomes a question of significance. Whilst these two new members may share an interest in 'improving the quality and accessibility of children's services', (taken from the Partnership's statement of purpose, this being the declared criterion by which to judge an organization's suitability to join), they are quite different types of organization.

In its first phase, the membership of the Partnership is at its most coherent or homogeneous, dominated by general hospitals concerned to improve access to specialized services, potentially by developing their own, collaboratively. The Annual Reports use a self-referential term, *"in the geographical area covered by the participating organisations"*, but there are also references in later Reports to an extension of the geographical field to cover fully a region served by the long-standing Children's Hospital member. The majority of new members listed in the final Annual Report reviewed (AR12) are general hospitals, these identifying with the Partnership and with the Children's Hospital, and admitted following a decision by the Partnership to extend its geographical area to match the service catchment of the Children's Hospital. This, and the loss of the PCTs as members (abolished in a further NHS reorganization), shifts the balance of membership decisively back towards the general hospitals category.

Between these two periods, Table 1 indicates how variety has increased and how the membership has become spread, indeed split, between members of several types: First, the admission of the community service trusts, then, the organizations of primary interest to the Partnership founders, the Children's Hospitals; and the commissioning organizations also identified as essential in the objectives of the Partnership. In its most inclusive statement of eligibility to join, AR 11 (p3) has, within the Partnership's prospectus, a further broadening of intent: " ... *not only in continuing to support the current network of health care staff across the [region] but also developing new networks across the healthcare and well-being sectors.*" The final appeal in AR12 is to the widest set of organizations interested in children's health and social care to join the partnership. The criterion of similarity, spelt out in membership decisions, has, at this moment, significantly broadened, although there is no evidence in the Annual Reports of this in the new members admitted to the Partnership—rather, the converse.

Ahrne and Brunsson (2008) note that meta-organizations may define their membership in well-established terms or establish new categories of organization to influence the organizational field. In the case of the Partnership, the criterion for membership cuts across established ways of distinguishing NHS organizations and joins them in terms of their interest and responsibility for the quality of children's' services.

The (changing) mix of members is a significant factor in understanding the character of this meta-organization. The trajectory, or series of transitions in composition and activity, moved the Partnership to a point where there was sufficient variety in member identity, and in activity, to lead to proposals for internal division. Thus, AR11 announces *"PiP looks forward to expanding its networks, and further involvement of healthcare partners, by establishing clear governance arrangements. This will be achieved through creating a Board and two sub-committees; one focusing on acute service networks and the other focusing on integrated community pathways . . . ."* (p. 3). It is also important to note, in the complexity of identity and affiliation, the changes to the geography of the Partnership. This has come gradually, through member withdrawals and new affiliations, to align more fully with the NHS 'regions'—institutional or administrative identities. In a rich institutional context, where the meta-organization is inevitably highly embedded, there will be many competing ways of defining similarity, and tensions arising, then, in the definition of membership: Leaving the primary criterion of similarity broadly-defined invites a continuing, or recurrent, negotiation of the essential character of the meta-organization.

Third, there are some questions raised by the case about the terms in which member organizations understand the implications of membership. Ahrne and Brunsson (2008) account places the greatest emphasis on the formality of the meta-organization as an organization, and on the status of admission to membership of the meta-organization: The organization is admitted as a member and that carries with it a defined set of responsibilities and rights. Ahrne and Brunsson's conception leads them to the position that meta-organizations will be able to access all the necessary 'interests and resources' of their members. The Annual Reports indicate that the commitment of the whole organization cannot simply be assumed. This is exactly Ahrne and Brunsson's point—that the meta-organization turns the environmental order into organization—it is an intervention within a field. Members' autonomy and own governance is potentially affected by membership of the meta-organization and this may be uncomfortable and even resisted. Ahrne and Brunsson (2008, p. 65) observe *"Whether or not, and to what degree, organizations that were once part of the environment are more easily influenced and more predictable will vary from case to case. . . . The world will not necessarily be an easier place in a meta-organization than in an environment; rather it will tend to be more complex in many respects. From an environment that is often cumbersome may emerge an organization that is often cumbersome . . . "*. Stringer (1967) account of the multi-organization is less demanding: He conceives this arrangement as *"the union of parts of several organisations, each part being a subset of the interests of its own organisation"* (p. 107), and variability in members' responses is then a practical and empirical question rather than a matter for definition. The key point is that variability might be expected, especially where the meta-organization is both more inclusive in its membership and less powerful in terms of its capacity to direct members and to monitor and sanction member behavior. To allow for an understanding of the variation and dynamics in meta-organizations, we suggest it is necessary to consider carefully the 'internal' boundaries of the meta-organization—that is, the extent to which the meta-organization can call upon the membership of its individual constituents for the collective purpose. In the Partnership, all members have an interest in, and responsibility for, children's care. However, that interest and identity are more or less central to each organization. For the Children's Hospital, it is all. For the general hospital, community services trust, or the commissioner, it is one of many sources of identity and one of many responsibilities. Such understandings, embedded historically in the NHS and the wider care sector, cross-cut the Partnership's defining characteristic. In forming, the Partnership has sought to strengthen the identity and status of children's' services, and the potential of the Partnership to enact this purpose becomes defined and redefined, in part, in its membership.

Changes in policy can also disturb such understandings and thinking about membership. Two examples reveal the complexities of identity and the tensions between similarity and difference that Ahrne and Brunsson (2008, especially Chapter 5) suggest characterise meta-organizations. First, the Partnership, consisting of children's health service providers, had set out to engage with NHS commissioners. Successive Annual Reports comment on the difficulties in achieving such a bridging role between the Partnership and commissioners in its immediate environment. National policy and changes to the local organization of the NHS created a new 'hybrid' organisation—the Primary Care Trust. The Foreword to Annual Report 5 made comment on the possibilities this opened:

> "The year 2002–2003 marked the beginning of a whole new set of challenges . . . .Not least . . . the fundamental change to the commissioning environment in which we now all operate. It has always been an issue for PiP how most effectively to engage with multiple commissioners . . . . [Now] . . . PCTs are not solely commissioners but also significant providers of services to children. The latter point represents an opportunity for PiP . . . to see the PCTs not solely as commissioners but as full partners in the provision of seamless care for children. If we all begin to use this vision as a means to inform our thinking about how PiP might develop in the future, then the year 2002/2003 may come to be seen as the dawn of a new phase in the evolving story of Partners in Paediatrics."

Table 1 shows that PCTs did indeed become members of the Partnership, though relationships between the Partnership and NHS commissioning functions continued to be pursued formally in a forum which brought together all commissioners—non-member PCTs as well as member PCTs—but only for a part of the Partnership's geographical area. This lack of 'fit' between the structures and territories of the NHS commissioning and the Partnership has been a recurrent theme in the Annual Reports.

The second example concerns the attempt to affiliate organizations, newly-created by policy, during a later phase of the Partnership. Annual Report 7 (pp. 7, 9) talks of the new structures called 'Children's Trusts' to which the Partnership should relate. There is no record of any Children's Trust joining the Partnership. A shared concern with the quality of children's services was not a sufficiently strong source of attraction. Directly related to children's services, these organisations identified with—indeed, incorporated—the formal organisations of not only the health service and public health, but also social care, education, and criminal justice. More competitors to the Partnership than likely members, these organisations were, in any event, soon dissolved by a further round of policy change. Ahrne and Brunsson (2008, p. 105) explain this by talking of 'wrong similarities', where the primary identifications do not coincide. The Partnership attaches to the NHS and to health services for children—later attempts to extend beyond this primary identification—the child protection project, invitational messages, etc.—produced participants but did not attract new members.

Fourthly, nevertheless, we note the emphasis placed in the Annual Reports on the value of participation by non-members on the character and productive work of the Partnership. Huxham and Vangen (2000) account of the ambiguities and complexities of participation in collaborative arrangements in general helps to check and enrich the formalized sense of the meta-organization set out by Ahrne and Brunsson. In this light, it may draw too strong a boundary around the meta-organization, and place too heavy an emphasis on the principle of 'decided order'. Although the Partnership has formalities, and members have certain privileges of governance, nevertheless, the boundaries are less definite than Ahrne and Brunsson suggest. We make two points here. First, as Barnett et al. (2000) argue, the growth dynamics of collective action systems—R&D consortia in their case—is where the generalist meta-organization would have an advantage over those with narrower bases—their reference point is the range of functions and activities rather than member identities, but our case narrative suggests these may be closely related. They propose 'contagion' as the mechanism by which meta-organizations would recruit new members. From the annual reports, it might be understood that the ethos of openness has attracted interest and participation rather than membership from the wider identity group—all those concerned with children's services—rather than the narrower heartland of pediatric services. This may not be 'free-riding' behavior, but rather discrimination between associational opportunities: The Partnership has used 'participation' as a source of legitimacy and as a means of influence over external stakeholders. In addition, the extension of the Partnership into its environment is a response to membership composition. The changing relationships the Partnership has with the environment arise as membership composition changes.

The salience of the Police and of Social Services as elements of the environment arose, as the growth in membership by community service organizations demanded a strand of activity that would engage those members and justify their continuing membership. Second, in their account of the 'external control' of organizations, Pfeffer and Salancik (1978) suggest that it is helpful to consider organizations not simply in terms of the 'formal boundaries' defined by membership and structure, but to consider behavior and activity as the in vivo points at which to cut the web of organization. In this sense, the analysis not just of affiliation and support, but also of activity, is of importance. The formalities of Partnership governance are given attention: AR12 starts with a statement from the Chair that *"The organization has actively responded to the 'external' challenges—whilst also reviewing itself as an organization and strengthening its governance arrangements."* (p. 2). However, the dominant message is that the boundaries of significance to the members are set by the meaningful and productive activity of the Partnership rather than the niceties of its formal constitution. Outcomes are not wholly in the Partnership's control and there is frequent reference to the need and desirability of close connection to the health service commissioners, to the Strategic Health Authority, to Children's Trusts and the Directors of Children's Services, and so on. The external work is also 'internal work', and the Partnership is, consequently, emergent as much as decided, dependent, at the least, on decisions of others about how to manage their environment, including the Partnership.

5. Conclusions

There is much in Ahrne and Brunsson's account of meta-organizations that is recognizable in our case study. We note the formalized character of the Partnership and the effort made to produce a 'decided order', and the Partnership as 'an attempt' to reshape and influence the field of interest; and we note the work of the Partnership both to structure the contributions of and interactions among members, and to promote collective presence, voice, and action. The theory of meta-organization has validity as a means of asking questions of, 'seeing' and describing, analytically, the character and dynamics of the Partnership as a meta-organization. However, our analysis of the accounts of the Partnership nevertheless raises questions for the theory of meta-organization.

First, the theory of meta-organization takes a strong position on the characteristics that define the form, and Ahrne and Brunsson (2008, p. 92) suggest that where difference and complementarity are the basis for engagement an associational form would not be a natural choice; rather, they would expect a network. The case study of PiP suggests two possibilities for consideration. Either the partnership, both in its varied membership composition and in its pursuit, as a primary aim of collective action might be a hybrid, for example, a 'whole network' in Provan et al. (2007) terms, formally constituted and bounded, but with accepted variety. Alternatively, the Partnership may have evolved through phases from association to network and back towards association, in response to experience in and signals from its environment, but also seeking to follow the will of its members and to distinguish the Partnership clearly from its members' capabilities. This would be the explanation of co-evolutionary scholars. A third possibility looks to the theory: Meta-organization theory may find it important to respond to empirical studies and to other, relevant theoretical traditions. In doing so, it might 'unbound' itself from its more stringent assumptions, and tolerate a more diverse set of characteristics of the form. Berkowitz and Dumez (2016) also suggest the criterion of similarity may need further thought.

Second, since the theory of meta-organization focuses largely on internal dynamics, it makes sharp distinction between what is inside—the member organizations—and what is outside—all other organizations. Our case study, however, suggests that beyond this 'governance boundary' of formal membership, the environment remains highly salient. In Rodrigues and Child (2008) terms, co-evolution continues: Indeed, the differences between institutional environment and internal organization are often less readily discernible and are more closely intertwined than Ahrne and Brunsson suggest. Pfeffer and Salancik point out, " ... *the boundary is where the discretion of the organization to control an activity is less than the discretion of another organization or individual to control that activity"* (Pfeffer and Salancik 1978, p. 32). The Partnership is a decided order, but it is also an emergent

Adm. Sci. **2018**, *8*, 42

order. It is associational in form and practice; however, it also promotes and is understood by members as catalyzing and delivery changes to the production systems of members, and, by implication too, of non-members who form part of the system of children's services. Ahrne and Brunsson admit such 'collaboration' to the list of reasons for creating meta-organization, but they are pessimistic about its success.

This paper has examined the changing membership composition of a Partnership, which has many of the characteristics of a meta-organization as set out by Ahrne and Brunsson (2008, 2011). It traces the growth and stabilization of membership, enabling and limiting factors, and focuses on the pattern of membership composition over time—we term this 'compositional dynamics'. Ahrne and Brunsson's account stipulates an essential similarity of identity of members as a defining characteristic of a meta-organization. The paper explores what similarity might mean, how that criterion might break down, and what consequences compositional diversity might have for the meta-organization. Following the membership of the case study, Partnership, over some considerable time (17 years), we have been able to explore some effects of membership change on the focus and structure of the meta-organization, what it hopes to reach, and what it does. The paper has also suggested that the boundaries between the meta-organization and its environment and between members and non-members needs further attention in meta-organization theory. We note that the institutional environment remains of significance as a system of meanings that help to define similarity or difference between existing and potential members. Further, active non-members could be recognized as playing a potentially important role, if not in the governance, then in the energy and action radius of the meta-organization. Both questions about the boundaries of meta-organization in theory and practice would merit further case and comparative case research. The relationship between membership composition and the pattern of meta-organization activity over time is also an important area in the assessment and continuing elaboration of this novel and intriguing theory. Such detailed empirical studies will also help in appraising the arguments in theory about the distinctive character in meta-organization and its relationship to other (adjacent) types of inter-organizational entity.

Author Contributions: The authors contributed equally to this work.

Funding: The Strategic Research Council at the Academy of Finland, project CORE (313013 + 313017), made the contribution by Sanne Bor to the writing of the paper possible.

Conflicts of Interest: Sanne Bor declares no conflict of interest. Steve Cropper is Academic Advisor to Partners in Paediatrics and has been since 1998. He is a member of the Core Group of the Partnership and attends the Board of Members as Academic Advisor. He received an annual fee from Partners in Paediatrics from 2000-2011, but since 2011 has undertaken the role *gratis*. He has published about the Partnership and its work on Managed Clinical Networks before, naming the Partnership with its consent, and will be preparing a history of the Partnership for publication, with past officers of the Partnership, again with the Partnership's approval and support.

List of Annual Reports Partners in Paediatrics. (www.partnersinpaediatrics.org):

AR1   Partners in Paediatrics (undated) Report of Year 1 of the Partnership. 60p
AR2   Partners in Paediatrics (undated) Report of Year 2 of the Partnership. 50p
AR3   Partners in Paediatrics (undated) Report of Year 3 of the Partnership. 39p
AR4   Partners in Paediatrics (undated) Report of Year 4 of the Partnership. 10p
AR5   Partners in Paediatrics (undated) Year five of the Partnership: Working to implement the National Service Framework. 12p
AR6   Partners in Paediatrics (undated) Year six of the Partnership: Working to implement change. 16p
AR7   Partners in Paediatrics (undated) Year seven of the Partnership: Competing priorities: What should ours be? 20pp
AR8   Partners in Paediatrics (2007/2008) Year eight of the Partnership: Working to implement the National Service Framework. 12p
AR9   Partners in Paediatrics (2008/09) Partners in Paediatrics Annual Report 2008/09. 12p
AR10   Partners in Paediatrics (2010) Annual Report 2010: Taking care of quality. 12p
AR11   Partners in Paediatrics (2011) Annual Report 2011: Helping to maintain and improve the quality of services for children and young people. 12p
AR12   Partners in Paediatrics (2014) PiP Report 2012–2014. Partners in Paediatrics. Solihull, West Midlands, 16p

References

Ahrne, Göran, and Nils Brunsson. 2005. Organizations and meta-organizations. *Scandinavian Journal of Management* 21: 429–49. [CrossRef]

Ahrne, Göran, and Nils Brunsson. 2008. *Meta-Organizations*. Cheltenham: Edward Elgar Publishing.

Ahrne, Göran, and Nils Brunsson. 2011. Organization outside organizations: The significance of partial organization. *Organization* 18: 83–104. [CrossRef]

Ahrne, Göran, Nils Brunsson, and David Seidl. 2016. Resurrecting organization by going beyond organizations. *European Management Journal* 34: 93–101. [CrossRef]

Aynsley-Green, Albert, Maggie Barker, Sue Burr, Aidan Macfarlane, John Morgan, Jo Sibert, Tom Turner, Russell Viner, Tony Waterston, and David Hall. 2000. Who is speaking for children and adolescents and for their health at the policy level? *BMJ (Clinical Research Ed.)* 321: 229–32. [CrossRef]

Baker, Chris D., and A. R. Lorimer. 2000. Cardiology: The development of a managed clinical network. *BMJ (Clinical Research Ed.)* 321: 1152–3. [CrossRef]

Barnett, William P., Gary A. Mischke, and William Ocasio. 2000. The evolution of collective strategies among organizations. *Organization Studies* 21: 325–54. [CrossRef]

Bell, John, Brian Den Ouden, and Gerrit Willem Ziggers. 2006. Dynamics of Cooperation: At the Brink of Irrelevance. *Journal of Management Studies* 43: 1607–19. [CrossRef]

Berkowitz, Héloïse, and Sanne Bor. 2018. Why Meta-Organizations Matter: A Response to Lawton et al. and Spillman. *Journal of Management Inquiry* 27: 204–11. [CrossRef]

Berkowitz, Héloïse, and Hervé Dumez. 2016. The Concept of Meta-Organization: Issues for Management Studies. *European Management Review* 13: 149–56. [CrossRef]

Browning, Larry D., Janice M. Beyer, and Judy C. Shetler. 1995. Building Cooperation in a Competitive Industry: Sematech and the Semiconductor Industry. *Academy of Management Journal* 38: 113–51.

NHS Confederation. 2001. *Clinical Networks: A Discussion Paper*. London: NHS Confederation.

Cropper, Steve. 2001. Changing Institutional Frameworks: Formalisation as a Means of Institutionalising Collaborative Activity. In *Organisational Behaviour in Health Care: Reflections on the Future*. Edited by Lynn Ashburner. Basingstoke: MacMillan Business, pp. 82–106.

Cropper, Steve, Mark Ebers, Chris Huxham, and Peter Smith Ring. 2008. Introducing Inter-organizational Relations. In *The Oxford Handbook of Inter-Organizational Relations*. Edited by Steve Cropper, Mark Ebers, Chris Huxham and Peter Smith Ring. Oxford: Oxford University Press, pp. 1–25.

Cropper, Steve, and Ian Palmer. 2008. Change, Dynamics, and Temporality in Inter-organizational Relationships. In *The Oxford Handbook of Inter-Organizational Relations*. Edited by Steve Cropper, Mark Ebers, Chris Huxham and Peter Smith Ring. Oxford: Oxford University Press, pp. 635–63.

Das, Tushar Kanti, and Bing-Sheng Teng. 2000. Instabilities of Strategic Alliances: An Internal Tensions Perspective. *Organization Science* 11: 77–101. [CrossRef]

De Rond, Mark, and Hamid Bouchikhi. 2004. On the Dialectics of Strategic Alliances. *Organization Science* 15: 56–69. [CrossRef]

Department of Health. 2003. *Getting the Right Start: National Service Framework for Children*; Standard for Hospital Services; London: Department of Health.

Duriau, Vincent J., Rhonda K. Reger, and Michael D. Pfarrer. 2007. A Content Analysis of the Content Analysis Literature in Organization Studies: Research Themes, Data Sources, and Methodological Refinements. *Organizational Research Methods* 10: 5–34. [CrossRef]

Eisenhardt, Kathleen M., and Melissa E. Graebner. 2007. Theory Building from Cases: Opportunities and Challenges. *Academy of Management Journal* 50: 25–32. [CrossRef]

Human, Sherrie E., and Keith G. Provan. 2000. Legitimacy Building in the Evolution of Small-Firm Multilateral Networks: A Comparative Study of Success and Demise. *Administrative Science Quarterly* 45: 327. [CrossRef]

Huxham, Chris, and Siv Vangen. 2000. Ambiguity, complexity and dynamics in the membership of collaboration. *Human Relations* 53: 771–806. [CrossRef]

Langley, Ann. 2010. Temporal bracketing. In *Encyclopedia of Case Study Research*. Edited by Albert J. Mills, Gabrielle Durepos and Elden Wiebe. Thousand Oaks: Sage Publications, vol. 2, pp. 919–21.

Lowndes, Vivien, and Chris Skelcher. 1998. The Dynamics of Multi-organizational Partnerships: An Analysis of Changing Modes of Governance. *Public Administration* 76: 313–33. [CrossRef]

Majchrzak, Ann, Sirkka L. Jarvenpaa, and Mehdi Bagherzadeh. 2015. A Review of Interorganizational Collaboration Dynamics. *Journal of Management* 41: 1338–60. [CrossRef]

Paton, Calum. 2014. At What Cost? Paying the Price for the Market in the English NHS. Available online: https://chpi.org.uk/wp-content/uploads/2014/02/At-what-cost-paying-the-price-for-the-market-in-the-English-NHS-by-Calum-Paton.pdf (accessed on 23 June 2018).

Pfeffer, Jeffrey, and Gerald R. Salancik. 1978. *The External Control of Organziations: A Resource Dependence Perspective.* New York: Harper & Row.

Provan, Keith G., Amy Fish, and Joerg Sydow. 2007. Interorganizational Networks at the Network Level: A Review of the Empirical Literature on Whole Networks. *Journal of Management* 33: 479–516. [CrossRef]

Rodrigues, Suzana B., and John Child. 2003. Co-evolution in an Institutionalized Environment. *Journal of Management Studies* 40: 2137–62. [CrossRef]

Rodrigues, Suzana B., and John Child. 2008. *Corporate Co-Evolution: A Political Perspective.* Chichester: John Wiley & Sons.

Selsky, John W. 1998. Developmental Dynamics in Nonprofit-Sector Federations. *Voluntas: International Journal of Voluntary and Nonprofit Organizations* 9: 283–303. [CrossRef]

Selznick, Philip. 1957. *Leadership in Administration: A Sociological Interpretation.* New York: Harper & Row.

Stringer, John. 1967. Operational Research for "Multi-organizations". *Journal of the Operational Research Society* 18: 105–20.

Traxler, Franz. 2002. Associations: Different Dynamics in Associational Governance? In *The Effectiveness of EU Business Associations.* Edited by Justin Greenwood. Hampshire: Palgrave Macmillan, pp. 157–70.

Vlaar, Paul W.L., Frans A.J. Van den Bosch, and Henk W. Volberda. 2006. Coping with problems of understanding in interorganizational relationships: Using formalization as a means to make sense. *Organization Studies* 27: 1617–38. [CrossRef]

administrative
sciences

Article

Emotional Dimensions in Integrated Care for People with Multiple Complex Problems

Anneli Hujala [1,*] and Erja Oksman [2]

[1] Department of Health and Social Management, University of Eastern Finland, FI-70211 Kuopio, Finland
[2] Päijät-Häme Welfare Group, FI-15850 Lahti, Finland; erja.oksman@phhyky.fi
*   Correspondence: anneli.hujala@uef.fi

Received: 27 August 2018; Accepted: 4 October 2018; Published: 8 October 2018

Abstract: Cross-boundary collaboration, both multiprofessional and interorganizational, is needed when providing integrated care for people with multiple problems, who need services at the same time from diverse care providers. Multiple problems of clients also pose extra challenges for interaction between care professionals and clients. Emotional dynamics are always present in everyday interaction between human beings, but seldom explicitly addressed in research on integrated care. The aim of this reflective paper is to illustrate the emotional dimensions of integrated care in light of the experiences of care professionals in the context of care for people with multiple complex problems. The paper draws on a Finnish study on integrated care reflecting its findings from the perspective of emotional labor. The difficult life situations of people with multiple complex problems form an emotional burden, which is mirrored in the interaction between clients and professionals and affects relational dynamics among professionals. Professionals' fear of emotions and the different 'feeling rules' of care professions and sectors pose extra challenges to professionals' collaboration in this emotionally loaded context. Alongside the structural and functional aspects of integrated care, it is important that emotions embedded in everyday cross-boundary collaboration are recognized and taken into account in order to ensure the success of integrated care.

Keywords: integrated care; emotions; emotional labor; cross-boundary collaboration; care professional; patient; client; people with multiple complex problems; health and social care

---

1. Introduction

Integrated care is a concept used extensively to refer to advanced collaboration in the context of health and social care. To put it simply, integration means 'bringing together different actors or activities' (Axelsson and Axelsson 2009). Cross-sectoral collaboration, referring here to both multi-professional and inter-organizational collaboration of professionals and collaboration between clients and professionals, is needed to make care services for people more co-ordinated, flexible and continuous within the care systems, in order to produce better care for people. Person-centeredness is at the center of integrated care (World Health Organization 2016) and a holistic professional-client relationship forms a salient basis for cross-boundary collaboration. Multiprofessional refers here to collaboration between professionals (doctors, nurses, social workers) and interorganizational to collaboration over sectoral boundaries (primary health care, specialized health care, and social care).

Integrated care is expected to be of particular benefit for people with multiple complex health and social care problems who need services from several care providers in both health and social care (Goodwin 2015; Rijken et al. 2017). These people, from a collaboration perspective also called 'shared clients' (Oksman 2017), consist of somewhat different groups, such as those with multimorbidity, older persons regularly needing acute health services for several reasons, families with children who have special problems, drug users, young people or adults who suffer from mental problems. What these client groups have in common is that they need services from several care providers at the same time: from hospitals, from health centers or general practitioners in primary health care and also from social care. The existing disease-based and fragmented care systems do not meet the needs of people with multiple complex problems (Hujala et al. 2017). Collaboration between clients and professionals and among various professionals and between the sectors of care–specialized care, primary care and social care–is crucial.

Person-centered integrated care has been offered as a solution to solve the problems described above regarding care for people with multiple complex problems (Ahgren 2012; Van der Heide et al. 2018). This reflective paper draws on experiences and insights from a Finnish study addressing care professionals developing integrated care pathways for 'shared clients'. The emotional and other relational dynamics that the study participants highlighted in relation to these clients inspired us to take a closer look at the emotional side of integrated care and to consider if an approach addressing emotions could give any added value to the concept and approach of integrated care.

Collaboration among care professionals has been studied extensively (Cameron et al. 2014; D'Amour et al. 2008; Schepman et al. 2015), often specifically addressing the barriers and difficulties of multi-professional collaboration (see Axelsson and Axelsson 2009). Previous research has shown that successful collaboration between professionals requires a shared goal, commitment, trust and respect between the participants (e.g., Willumsen et al. 2012; see also Schruijer 2008). These issues may sound quite familiar, but it is not always so easy to realize this ideal in practice. The reasons why cross-boundary collaboration is so challenging may be better understood by also paying attention to emotional tensions, which tend to pervade all interaction between human beings.

In the context of integrated care, challenges related to interaction between human beings, such as emotional dynamics, are seldom explicitly addressed. This is not exceptional given that emotions have long been 'the neglected side' of organizational research in general (Fox and Spector 2002). At least, integrated care is most often described as a phenomenon taking place at system, organizational, professional and clinical levels, including functional and normative dimensions (Valentijn et al. 2013). Although numerous approaches and models of integrated care are available (see, e.g., World Health Organization 2016), the focus of research on integrated care is often on the structures, processes and tools of integration. Processes of integrated care refer to collaborative processes, but the main focus of integrated care is functional addressing the concrete ways in which collaboration should be organized and paying less attention to the human side of integrated care. Normative integration, which perhaps has the closest relationship to emotional dimensions, does indeed address the different values and cultures of professionals. These aspects have recently been emphasized by an approach highlighting value-based integration (see Minkman 2016), aiming at a better understanding of the values underpinning integrated care. In addition, person-centeredness has become a core aim of integrated care, emphasizing the importance of taking into account patients' needs and wishes and focusing more on person-relevant outcomes of integrated care (Van der Heide et al. 2018).

However, in spite of the recent diversification of the perspectives on integrated care we venture to claim that mainstream research and practice focus on the conventional points of views of rationality, where human beings tend to be rendered as rational actors in a technical and practical framework. Less attention is paid to the social, emotional and affective dimensions of integrated care. As in planning processes in general, these may even be considered irrational and irrelevant (see Osborne and Grant-Smith 2015). Emotional and other relational dynamics are present in particular when implementing integrated care, because ultimate implementation takes place at grass-root level in interaction between human beings.

As a phenomenon, emotions can be approached from a variety of perspectives. Traditionally emotions have been considered to be individual and internal phenomena (Osborne and Grant-Smith 2015). Psychodynamics emphasize the nonconscious nature of emotions at individual level; systems psychodynamics (developed by the Tavistock Institute of Human Relations) link nonconsciouos dynamics with organizational structures and see that routines and practices can serve as a social defence to manage the emotions of organizational members (Pratt and Crosina 2016). According to the constructionist approach, emotions do not exist inside us; they are not only an individual or internal phenomenon, but emerge from social interaction (Harré 1986; see also Gergen 1999). Our emotions are very closely connected to our relationships to other people (Burkitt 2014, p. 2); Brotheridge and Lee (2008, p. 109) claim that emotions are 'at the heart of all working relationships'. Further, emotions can be considered as emotional intelligence (e.g., Morrison 2007) or emotional competencies (e.g., Kinman and Grant 2011).

In this paper, we apply a broad understanding of emotions, recognizing both the individual and social dimensions related to them. One potential option to approach theoretically the presence of emotions in integrated care is the concept of emotional labor (Hochschild 1983; see also Zapf 2002; Zapf and Holz 2006). The concept was originally introduced by Arlie Hochschild in 1983 and has since also been applied in the field of health and social care (Mann 2005), especially in nursing (e.g., Gray 2009; Hunter and Smith 2007). Hochschild's 'sociology of emotions' reveals the taken-for-granted nature of interaction between people. It pays attention to what people feel, how they make sense of their feelings and how people have to regulate and manage their feelings not only in their individual lives (emotion work) but also at work (emotional labor) (Hochschild 1983; Garey and Hansen 2011).

In the emotional labor approach (Hochschild 1983), the client-employee relationship is emphasized, which matches well with the nature of person-centered integrated care. In this paper we do not focus so much on the ways care professionals display the appropriate feelings in given (face-to-face) situations with clients. Instead, the focus here is on the assumption that feelings related to the multiple complex problems of clients affect professionals' actions in any case—whether they are aware of them or not—in all their doings, not only in interaction with clients but also with other professionals. In emotional labor research, the original concepts of surface acting (faking emotions) and deep acting (trying to feel actual emotions required in the situation) have been complemented by a third form of emotional labor, natural and genuine emotional labor (Humphrey et al. 2015), which we think suits well in the context of care. A fruitful concept matching with care for people with multiple complex problems is emotional dissonance. Further, so-called feeling rules (display rules), i.e., organizational norms of feeling (Hochschild 1983; see also Diefendorff et al. 2011; Humphrey et al. 2015; Grandey and Melloy 2017) link the approach interestingly to cross-boundary collaboration in the context of shared clients.

This reflective paper is based on a Finnish study on integrated care. The aim here is to describe and illustrate the emotional and other relational dimensions of integrated care in light of the experiences of care professionals in the context of care for people with multiple complex problems. We hope that the insights presented here will raise further discussion on whether it is worth addressing 'the affective turn' (Burkitt 2014; Greco and Stenner 2008) and emotional dimensions more profoundly and in more detail in future research on integrated care.

2. Materials and Methods

The empirical material reflected here comes from a Finnish research project, Onnistu sote-integraatiossa/ Successful Integration of Health and Social Care (2016–2018), funded by the Finnish Foundation for Municipal Development (KAKS). The study was conducted in close collaboration with Parempi Arki/Better Everyday Life (BEL) development project (2015–2017), funded by the Ministry of Social Affairs and Health (Finland). The aim of the BEL development project was to support clients with multiple problems in everyday life by developing a person-centered and integrated care approach including services in both health care and social care. The overall aim of the research project was to add to the understanding of the prerequisites for successful integration. The BEL project was a pilot project addressing implementation of integrated care, connected to Finland's national reform aiming at the complete integration of health and social care in 2021.

In total, 250 care professionals from primary health care, specialized health care, social care, and the education sector were involved in the BEL development project. These same professionals were also the participants in the research project. The study participants were professionals working in the field of health and social care: nurses, doctors, social workers, therapists, teachers etc. The BEL project was an intervention project in which the professionals from different sectors (primary health care, specialized health care, social care and the education sector) and organizations (health centers, hospitals, social care organizations, schools) were joined together into 37 local cross-boundary development teams. The aim of these teams was to develop integrated care pathways for clients with multiple complex problems and multiple care needs–pathways linking care professionals from different organizations and different sectors to work together for the good of the people with multiple problems. Each team developed care for a chosen target group, for example for older persons regularly needing health services or for families with children who have special problems. The work of the BEL teams was supported by project coaches and through seminars (applying the Breakthrough method and other Leanmethods, see Bhat et al. 2014). Theoretically the development work drew on the extended Chronic Care Model (Barr et al. 2003).

The close collaboration between the research project and the development project enabled access to all materials produced by the BEL development project. The researcher (first author) was present in the seminars and workshops of the BEL project and the project manager of it (second author) also worked as a researcher, taking part in some of the interviews and in the data analysis. Together with the professionals involved in the development project, these arrangements enabled a fruitful dialogue between research and practice.

This reflective paper draws on the overall material and findings of both projects, in particular on the following data: (1) Lean-based Fishbone problem analysis (see Bhat et al. 2014) regarding clients with multiple complex problems, done by 21 BEL project teams (about 100 professionals). In these fishbone analyses the professionals analyzed the critical points in providing care for people with multiple complex problems. The outputs of the teams' analyses were transcribed and Atlas.ti software was used for preliminary thematic analysis of the fishbone problem analysis; (2) Research interviews with professionals and managers. Three cross-boundary BEL project teams were interviewed. Altogether, 14 care professionals (nurses, social workers, physiotherapists and doctors) from primary health care, social care and specialized health care participated these group interviews. In addition, individual interviews with nine managers connected to the BEL project, representing primary and specialized health care and social care were interviewed. Interviews were conducted by the authors of this paper (the researcher and the BEL project manager).

The interview themes concerned the professionals' experiences with clients with multiple complex problems, the challenges in providing and developing care for them, experiences of cross-boundary collaboration related to these clients, expectations of the collaboration outcomes, and management issues related to cross-boundary collaboration. The research material was analyzed by means of inductive content analysis and the original findings are presented in the research report (Hujala and Lammintakanen 2018). For the purposes of this reflective paper, the findings of the original analyses are used selectively to highlight the emotional and other relational aspects of the research material. The themes described below (1) emotional burden; (2) professionals' fear of emotions and (3) 'emotional territories' are based on the holistic reflection of the whole research material and illustrated here by purposefully selected quotations from the data.

3. Findings

3.1. Emotional Burden

The general and initial orientation of the whole research project was quite conventionally to address the prerequisites and challenges for a successful integration of care for people with multiple complex problems. During the development project and the related research process it became obvious—somewhat unexpectedly in a quite rational and functional framework of integrated care—how strongly care professional related emotions to integrated care for people with multiple complex problems. The findings of the study showed that the emotional burden of multiple complex health and social problems affects not only clients, but also the care professionals who deal with these people in their work.

The lives of people with multiple complex problems are often very difficult for themselves and for their next-of-kin. The existing disease-based and fragmented care systems do not meet the needs of these clients. This incompatibility causes clients serious difficulties: physical and/or mental illnesses, social and other related problems are a burden as such, and problems experienced with the health and social care system are felt to cause additional burden. In the following, we first describe the experiences of professionals, how and why they often felt these clients to be a burden and the effects they felt this burden to cause—not only to clients, but also to the professionals themselves.[1]

Both in the fishbone analyses and in the interviews, the professionals reported that clients with multiple problems get lost, become exhausted and wear themselves out in poorly coordinated service systems. In the fragmented care systems, clients are sent from one professional to another. Nobody is responsible for the coordination of their care, and clients have to repeat their problems over and over again to new professionals, who are not aware of a client's medical history.

> He had been sent from one place to another . . . and now he is a client in very many places . . . and the process continues and continues . . . it wears out the resources of the client and professionals are also coming to feel the lack of resources. (Care professional Px, not identified from the recording)

The professionals also recognized that people with multiple needs very often feel shame because of their problems. They are ashamed because they feel they lack the ability to cope with their lives. Shame is connected with a fear of being doomed, looked down on or being stigmatized by professionals. It is understandable that it is not easy to discuss difficult or sensitive problems with outsiders. Even asking for help occasionally may be felt to be difficult and degrading. The burden of such feelings multiplies when people have to confront these problems for a long time and explain them over and over again to new care professionals.

All this also leaves professionals feeling frustrated, inadequate and helpless. When clients' problems are complex, especially because this situation goes on and on, an individual professional feels that s/he just does not have solutions for the situation.

> . . . and the feeling of frustration for doctors and nurses . . . again . . . that very same client is here again and we cannot offer her anything and we are not able to help her. (Manager M4)

> Then both parties are exhausted and tired and do not know what to do. (Care professional Px, not identified from the recording)

Alongside the picture of the client who is worn out and ashamed about her or his situation, professionals also outlined another kind of image of this client group. They recounted that sometimes clients with multiple problems are evasive and do not tell about their actual problems, they downplay or deny the problem or the real reason behind the problem. Sometimes clients seem to tell a different version to different professionals.

> . . . the client . . . sugar-coats the truth or does not tell everything . . . it is terribly difficult to really help that kind of client. (Care professional P2)

> . . . The client is able to play any role whatsoever, if s/he wants to do so. (Care professional P3)

---

[1]   The experiences of the clients interviewed in the study are described in the original research report (Hujala and Lammintakanen 2018).

Professionals even spoke about clients as 'exploiters' of the system. Clients may require services, but they do not want to commit themselves to the care they are provided. They are passive, do not keep appointments with professionals and contribute nothing to their self-management. Some clients appeared to professionals as manipulators, who have endless needs. The professionals reported that nothing is enough for such clients.

> ... then we have this extreme, we have the clients who want everything. And they, they are ready to take everything and they demand everything, and nothing is enough for them. It is that kind of extreme, we have that kind of 'slough' there, that we have to restrict [giving services] ... (Care professional P2)

Emotional labor (emotional work) (Hochschild 1983) applied to this context means that care professionals have to be sensitive to clients' emotional burden and at the same time regulate their–often contradictory–feelings and emotions which arise when they confront clients with continuous complex problems. Feeling empathy and feeling compassion were examples of positive emotions, frustration and exhaustion of negative ones. In addition, in particular the 'exploiters' or 'manipulators' evoked quite extreme feelings such as mistrust, annoyance, cynicism and even anger. The findings of the study suggested that this kind of 'emotional dissonance', conflict between expected and experienced emotions, is not restricted to single face-to-face encounters, but the emotional burden may become a permanent state of mind. This not only results in a poorer quality of care for clients but causes stress and affects professionals' well-being; an impact of emotional labor identified extensively in previous research (see e.g., Zapf and Holz 2006).

3.2. Pandora's Box: Professionals' Fear of Emotions

In caring for people with multiple complex problems, one of the critical challenges for professionals is to identify 'shared' clients needing help and support from several care providers and therefore likely to benefit from cross-boundary collaboration among professionals. The professionals emphasized that even if they see that a client seems to have a problem which would require involving other professionals to be solved, it is not easy for the professional to bring the difficult issues to the fore if the client herself/himself is not willing (or is afraid) to talk about them. The fear of emotions creates a barrier between a professional and a client. The professionals described these encounters, for example, as follows.

> We do not have the courage and we don't have ways to confront a person, if s/he seems to have a social problem, which is behind everything else. There may be 50 visits [to a doctor or a professional] just because the real reason is loneliness. (Care professional P3)

A lack of time and lack of the 'right' questions are not the only reasons to pass on this kind of situation. One of the professionals interviewed described how she feels when seeing a client in this kind of situation:

> It is partly connected to it, that I think that I have only 20 min time [for the client]. What if s/he says something that I should really intervene in? And I do not have time now, because the next patient is already waiting at the door. So how could I do it in a smart way, so that somebody else could talk with her/him later, or call her/him, or something. (Care professional P3)

Thus, the fear of an emotional reaction inhibits the courage to ask the client about the underlying, wider problems. According to the interviewees, a professional may be afraid that the whole situation will break open. It is worth noting, that the professional is not only worried about the client's emotional reaction, but also about his or her own emotional reaction.

> ... [A] doctor or a nurse working in a practice does not dare to ask–because s/he is afraid that the issue is so sensitive, that the emotional reaction may be anything–either the client's or your own reaction. (Care professional P5)

The BEL project manager confirmed how it became quite clear during the BEL project that even though professionals identify a client with multiple problems, they may avoid asking about those problems.

... [W]e do know the people who traipse to the health center again and again. In a way, we are afraid of opening Pandora's box with the client, because there is no way to go forward. (The BEL project manager in a team interview)

The problem of Pandora's box concerns not only health care professionals and their concerns about patients' social problems. The interviewees explained that also social work professionals, too, may sometimes be too cautious to address 'deeper' problems of clients. They cited an example of a client who comes to see a social worker because of financial problems. It may take time and several visits before both parties are ready to say the underlying reason aloud, which may be, for example, use of alcohol or drugs. The problem of avoiding problematic issues is also recognized in the context of supervising care professionals. Revell and Burton (2016) emphasize the importance of supervision for social workers who confront significant emotional burden in their work, for example in child protection practice. Revell and Burton (Revell and Burton 2016, p. 1596) state, however, that in the same way as professionals also their supervisors may likewise fail to ask about emotionally difficult issues, for fear that they may raise too heavy concerns for discussion.

Difficult matters are tricky to bring out into the open: a professional may doubt his or her own ability to confront the problem. Avoiding an issue is easier, and sending the client to another professional may be a solution—and for the client the vicious circle continues. Integrated care–fixed procedures for multiprofessional collaboration–could be a solution: rather than choosing to avoid emotions by referral of clients, professionals could share the emotional burden by facing the client together.

Professionals may thus lack the courage to ask what is really the matter with the client. However, in the encounters there are always two participants. What hinders the client from bringing problems into the open?

... I think that it is partly because patients are also socialized to act like this ... They know the time is limited, you have to get to the most important point ... the issue you think is important from the professional's point of view, and it is obviously diseases. It cannot be that the professional would be interested in ... this kind of a social problem. (Care professional P6)

... [T]he client thinks that this is such a trivial issue, not worth mentioning. Then neither of them says a word about the most important issue. (Care professional P5)

The identification of the underlying problems is thus based on reciprocal behavior. The care professional focuses only on the issue the client raises and what she assumes the client expects. And the client behaves as she supposes the professional expects her to behave. They may be unsure, shy or even feel fear of professionals. Both lack the courage to get to the point and 'Pandora's box' is left unopened. The professionals called this 'half-way interaction': people do not wholly reach the other party in the interaction.

In emotional labor terminology (Hochschild 1983; Grandey and Melloy 2017), instead of so called surface acting (e.g., expressing emotions which are not genuinely felt) or deep acting (e.g., overcoming negative acting, trying to force oneself to feel positive or other appropriate emotions), the fear of emotions resulted in entirely avoiding and ignoring emotions. This is a very interesting point of view from the perspective of integrated care, while in this kind of situation it would be beneficial for all to ask help from other colleagues. As mentioned earlier, the professionals stated that one of the key problems is that clients are sent from one professional to another, which is just the opposite with the goal of integrated care. Here the professionals explicitly addressed emotional aspects as one reason for doing so–because it is easier than confronting the emotions related to problems. During the BEL development project, the professionals practiced concrete cross-boundary collaboration with clients in multiparty teams. A widely shared experience was that collaboration is an efficient way to share the emotional burden due to multiproblem clients. Integrated care arrangements should thus involve practices which encourage professionals to collaborate with other professionals and sectors to share the burden resulting from the demands of emotional labor.

3.3. Emotional Territories?

Axelsson and Axelsson (2009) use the word 'territoriality' to refer to the problems of cross-boundary collaboration. They claim that not only animals but also human beings tend to defend their 'own areas'; in the case of integrated care for people with multiple complex problems professional (doctor, nurse, social worker) and sectoral (primary care, specialized care and social care) territories.

It is natural that specialization has resulted in boundaries between care professions and sectors. An interesting question here is now, whether (and if so, how) emotions are related to the differences between professions and sectors. Emotional burden due to complexity of client's problems may be shared by collaboration, but it may also cause additional tensions and challenges in the interaction, if the ways of dealing with emotions differ.

The findings of the study reflected here did not directly address emotional differences between the professions and sectors. However, the professionals felt that there is still a clear distinction between the territories of care professions and sectors. Extreme (but quite general) stereotypes and prejudices underlying cross-sectoral collaboration regarding the three sectors persist and were described in the BEL project seminars by professionals as follows: Primary health care thinks it is omnipotent. Specialized health care isolates itself (due its allegedly superior know-how compared to others). The professionals in social care believe they are the only ones who are able to take a holistic view of a client, but at the same time the health sector wonders whether social care is actually needed. A certain kind of territorial defence seems to be embedded in these stereotypical summaries evidenced by the professionals.

The holistic person-centered view of patients and clients is one potential way to approach the 'emotion-related differences' between professions and sectors. Holistic person-centeredness (patient-centeredness, client-centeredness) is a vital part of integrated care (World Health Organization 2016). Further, the emotional dimension is an explicitly stated part of person-centeredness (Scholl et al. 2014; see also Van der Heide et al. 2018). In the integrative model of patient-centeredness by Scholl et al. (2014, p. 5) 'emotional support' is described as part of patient-centeredness as follows: "Recognition of the patient's emotional state and a set of behavior that ensures emotional support for the patient." In addition, the model states other related dimensions such as 'patient as a unique person' and 'patient empowerment'—while also emphasizing the dimensions addressing collaboration between diverse professionals.

According to the professionals interviewed in this study, in the health sector a patient is often still seen as a 'disease' and in the social sector client is seen 'a holistic person'. This (naturally highly simplified) distinction outlined below is mirrored in the stereotypes of doctors and social workers. A nurse working in the primary care reported as follows:

> ... I am working at a health care center ... and from the perspective of health care, we are there not able to think, or we have not been able to think of a person as a whole ... we take care of the disease, and we take care of that single thing. (Care professional P3)

The same professional described the role of the doctor as follows:

> ... [W]hen patients come to a health center, or come to see a doctor, very many of them still think ... they regard a doctor as an authority, an awfully big authority. You go as you were going to see the Almighty ... this is what you have picked up at your mother's knee: you have to [have] a fear of the Lord when you go to see a doctor. And you go to get a

solution to one problem only … When one goes to social work professional, the attitude is totally different. (Care professional P3)

Another professional confirmed this and claimed that this hierarchical status is maintained by other actors:

… [A]lso when other people, when they look at the doctor, they look upwards. Like nurses, and especially clients. So, the doctor stays up there if everyone looks up to her/him. (Care professional P5)

A totally different picture of social work and social workers was outlined by two of the managers interviewed in the study. They emphasized the importance of the relationship and a holistic view of a client.

Altogether, about support work and the basic principles of social work: it is still salient here that you [as a client] form a bond with someone [professional]. That you have a care professional with whom you have some kind of a relationship. And that [relationship] opens up the world for collaboration [between a client and professional] or otherwise that world stays closed. (Manager M1)

I would say like this, in a rather caricatured way, that in a way social services start from the holistic wellbeing of human beings. In health care there is more that old thing, that one has a medical problem which has to be solved and got rid and that's it. But this is, I would claim, it has changed and is changing and it has to be changed. But surely it is still like this. (Manager M9)

The differences between health and social sector are not only boundaries, there also seems to be a distinction between specialized health care and primary health care in how to orient toward holistic patient-centeredness, as shown in the following extract.

Whereas we think that it is not the task of the specialized care this continuous life-long support. It has to be built in the primary care, nearer … where people live. (Manager M7)

The different basic tasks of the sectors are mirrored naturally in the work of professionals. Especially when dealing with people with complex problems, the competencies of a professional may be challenged because they may be required to collaborate with professionals with completely different expertise and from sectors with completely different orientation towards patient-centeredness. In addition, power embedded in diverse sectors and professions is of course present: for example, it may be more difficult for a social worker to get her voice heard in the context of specialized health care. The uneven power relations embedded in the hierarchy and bureaucracy of the health and social system reinforce territorial thinking and increase mutual suspicion (Axelsson and Axelsson 2009).

If we extend the idea of territorial differences and tensions, through holistic patient-centeredness thinking, to emotional orientation, we could perhaps suggest something like 'emotional territories' embedded in other kinds of professional territories. From the point of view of emotional labor (Hochschild 1983), these emotional territories would refer to the different feeling rules (display rules) (Diefendorff et al. 2011; Humphrey et al. 2015) that different care sectors and different care professionals have. Each territory has to defend its own ways of acting, based on their education, role, status, ethical principles etc. on which their professionality in general is based on (Axelsson and Axelsson 2009)–also in an emotional sense. Diefendorff et al. (2011) define emotional display rules as shared norms, or emotion norms, governing the expression and regulation of emotion at work and claim these can differ depending e.g., on occupational requirements. It is quite understandable that these rules or norms vary across different professions, organizations and sectors. The professional hierarchy in health and social care further reasserts these differences.

For example, although emotion work is generally considered as part of nursing work, in Gray's study (Gray 2009, p. 171) on emotional labor among nurses the respondents felt–in addition to gender stereotypes–that emotions were seen as 'weaknesses' by other staff members, such as senior nurses and doctors. Conventionally, social work in particular is considered to be emotionally demanding work, in which paying attention to emotions is seen as a critical aspect (Morrison 2007). In spite of this, even in social work sharing feelings and asking for help may be seen as a weakness and lack of professional capacity (Revell and Burton 2016, p. 1595). The differences between professions are, however, changing, while patient-centered care is also getting more attention in medicine. Epstein (2000), for example, includes identification and responding to patient's ideas and emotions regarding their illness as an important component of physicians' behavior.

In integrated care, different feeling rules are encountered when professionals representing different sets of feeling rules work together in cross-boundary teams. In the context of people with multiple complex problems, the emotional burden described above constitutes an extra underlying challenge and complicates collaboration among professionals. We may ask if in such a situation a social worker, for example, dares or is otherwise able to act according the feeling rules of her/his own profession or sector, giving that a medical specialist may be socialized to a very different set of rules. Conversely, for a highly specialized doctor it may be against the conventional work role status and role expectations to become involved in emotional issues. Ashforth and Kreiner (2002, p. 230) refer to problems of 'collective face work' and 'emotional comparison', which may also be of relevance in cross-boundary collaboration between professionals in health and social care. Feeling rules related either to professions, organizations or sectors could also be called emotional climates or emotional cultures (see Grandey and Melloy 2017, p. 412) and merit special attention in the context of implementing integrated care.

4. Discussion

The aim of this reflective paper was to highlight the presence of emotions in the context of integrated care regarding, in particular, care for people with multiple complex problems. Although we as the authors of this paper are not experts in research on emotions, we hope this contribution could serve to raise more discussion on why–or if–emotional dimensions also deserve more attention regarding integrated care.

This paper was based on a study conducted only in one country, Finland, and elsewhere its findings can only be indicative. In the whole study, a total of 250 care professionals were involved through the workshops and material they produced in the course of a development project, based on close partnership with the research and development project. However, only a limited number of professionals and managers were interviewed. It is also noteworthy that the original aim of the study was concerned with integrated care in general and not specifically emotional aspects.

Nevertheless, the context of the study adds to its value: Finland's extensive national-level reform, which is expected to take place in 2021, is aiming at full integration of both health and social care (Regional Government 2018), which is still quite a rare effort internationally. Because of increasing interest and need to integrate care services in many other European countries as well (Goodwin 2015), experiences of how to combine rational and technical system level integration with the interactive level of human beings may be of interest to a larger audience. We claim specifically that the human side of integrated care should be taken into account when dealing with people whose life situations are complex and whose needs for care services from different care providers are high and complicated.

Based on the study reflected in this paper the following issues were highlighted:

- People with multiple complex problems are a salient and challenging client group in integrated care, and the emotional burden connected to them needs to be taken seriously. The emotional burden affects not only clients themselves but also professionals.
- Care professionals providing integrated care for this client group perform emotional labor: they have to balance with contradictory emotions and cope with emotional dissonance. Fear of

emotions may result in avoiding confronting clients' problems. By integrated care arrangements, through cross-boundary collaboration, the temptation to just send a complicated client on to the next professional could be avoided.

- Emotional burden may have a negative effect on the wellbeing of professionals, which is an important consideration when aiming at sustainable and effective health and care systems (see Bodenheimer and Sinsky 2014).

- Cross-boundary collaboration among professionals has potential to share the emotional burden. However, the different 'feeling rules' or 'emotional cultures' (Hochschild 1983; Diefendorff et al. 2011) of care professions and sectors may be a challenge to the implementation in practice of integrated care.

To sum up, according to the research findings reflected here, integrated care is not only rational action. As Griffith and Glasby (2015) state, public policies on integrated care focus mainly on structural issues. However, although macro- and meso-level integration form the grounds for cross-boundary collaboration, the ultimate implementation of integration is accomplished at micro level by grassroots actors in interaction between care professionals and clients. There is no need to exaggerate the significance of emotional dimensions of integrated care, but no reason to avoid or neglect them, either. The aim should perhaps be to 'normalize' emotions (Ashforth and Kreiner 2002) and emotion labor (Hochschild 1983) as part of the implementation of integrated care. This means 'making the extraordinary seem ordinary' (Ashforth and Kreiner 2002) so that both the identification and sharing of the emotional burden among care professionals would be an accepted and routine way of working in cross-boundary collaboration. As stated in systems psychodynamics (Pratt and Crosina 2016), organizational structures may be established to protect individuals from emotions; structural arrangements enhancing collaboration may thus also serve as arenas for professionals to share the burden of emotions. In addition, training for professionals in confronting emotional situations and emotional pressures in cross-boundary collaboration is needed (Diefendorff et al. 2011). We believe that the emotional dimensions present in everyday life interactions (Jacobsen 2019; Williams 2001) deserve more attention—hopefully from multidisciplinary perspectives—in the future research of integrated care, in particular in the context of cross-boundary collaboration among care professionals needed by people with multiple complex problems.

Author Contributions: The authors contributed equally to this paper.

Funding: The research project Onnistu sote-integraatiossa (Successful Integration of Health and Social Care) was funded by the Finnish Foundation for Municipal Development (KAKS) and the development project Parempi Arki (Better Everyday Life) by the Ministry of Social Affairs and Health (Finland).

Conflicts of Interest: The authors declare no conflicts of interest.

References

Ahgren, Bengt. 2012. The Art of Integrating Care: Theories Revisited. *The Open Public Health Journal* 5: 36–9. [CrossRef]
Ashforth, Blake E., and Glen E. Kreiner. 2002. Normalizing emotion in organizations: Making the extraordinary seem ordinary. *Human Resource Management Review* 12: 215–35. [CrossRef]
Axelsson, Susanna Bihari, and Runo Axelsson. 2009. From territoriality to altruism in interprofessional collaboration and leadership. *Journal of Interprofessional Care* 23: 320–30. [CrossRef] [PubMed]
Barr, Victoria J., Sylvia Robinson, Brenda Marin-Link, Lisa Underhill, Anita Dotts, Darlene Ravensdale, and Sandy Salivaras. 2003. The expanded Chronic Care Model: An integration of concepts and strategies from population health promotion and the Chronic Care Model. *Healthcare Quarterly* 7: 73–82. [CrossRef]
Bhat, Shreeranga, E.V. Gijo, and N.A. Jnanesh. 2014. Application of Lean Six Sigma methodology in the registration process of a hospital. *International Journal of Productivity and Performance Management* 63: 613–43. [CrossRef]
Bodenheimer, Thomas, and Christine Sinsky. 2014. From Triple to Quadruple Aim: Care of the Patient Requires Care of the Provider. *Annals of Family Medicine* 12: 573–76. [CrossRef] [PubMed]

Brotheridge, Céleste M., and Raymond T. Lee. 2008. The emotions of managing: An introduction to the special issue. *Journal of Managerial Psychology* 23: 108–17. [CrossRef]

Burkitt, Ian. 2014. *Emotions and Social Relations*. London: Sage.

Cameron, Ailsa, Rachel Lart, Lisa Bostock, and Caroline Coomber. 2014. Factors that promote and hinder joint and integrated working between health and social care services: A review of literature. *Health and Social Care in the Community* 22: 225–33. [CrossRef] [PubMed]

Diefendorff, James M., Rebecca J. Erickson, Alicia A. Grandey, and Jason J. Dahling. 2011. Emotional Display Rules as Work Unit Norms: A Multilevel Analysis of Emotional Labor among Nurses. *Journal of Occupational Health Psychology* 16: 170–86. [CrossRef] [PubMed]

D'Amour, Danielle, Lise Goulet, Jean-François Labadie, Leticia San Martín-Rodriguez, and Raynald Pineault. 2008. A Model and typology of collaboration between professionals in healthcare organizations. *BMC Health Services Research* 8: 188. [CrossRef] [PubMed]

Epstein, Ronald M. 2000. The Science of Patient-Centered Care. *Journal of Family Practice* 49: 805–10. [PubMed]

Fox, Suzy, and Paul E. Spector. 2002. Emotions in the workplace. The neglected side of organizational life. Introduction. *Human Resource Management Review* 2: 167–71. [CrossRef]

Garey, Anita Ilta, and Karen V. Hansen. 2011. *At the Heart of Work and Family: Engaging the Ideas of Arlie Hochschild*. eBook. ProQuest Ebook Central. New Brunswick: Rutgers University Press, Available online: https://ebookcentral.proquest.com/lib/uef-ebooks/detail.action?docID=817176 (accessed on 7 October 2018).

Gergen, Kenneth. 1999. *An Invitation to Social Construction*. London: Sage Publication Ltd.

Goodwin, Nick. 2015. How should integrated care address the challenge of people with complex health and social care needs? Emerging lessons from international case studies. *International Journal of Integrated Care* 15. [CrossRef]

Greco, Monica, and Paul Stenner, eds. 2008. *Emotions, A Social Science Reader*. London and New York: Routledge.

Grandey, Alicia A., and Robert C. Melloy. 2017. The state of the heart: Emotional labor as emotion regulation reviewed and revised. *Journal of Occupational Health Psychology* 22: 407–22. [CrossRef] [PubMed]

Gray, Benjamin. 2009. The emotional labour of nursing—Defining and managing emotions in nursing work. *Nurse Education Today* 29: 168–75. [CrossRef] [PubMed]

Griffith, Laura, and Jon Glasby. 2015. "When we say 'urgent' it means now … " Health and social care leaders' perceptions of each other's roles and ways of working. *Journal of Integrated Care* 23: 143–52. [CrossRef]

Harré, Ron. 1986. *The Social Construction of Emotions*. Oxford: Basil Blackwell.

Hochschild, Arlie R. 1983. *The Managed Heart: Commercialization of Human Feeling*. ProQuest Ebook Central. Berkeley, Los Angeles and London: University of California Press, Available online: https://ebookcentral.proquest.com/lib/uef-ebooks/detail.action?docID=870020 (accessed on 7 October 2018).

Hujala, Anneli, and Johanna Lammintakanen. 2018. Paljon sote-palveluja tarvitsevat asiakkaat keskiöön. Onnistu sote-integraatiossa -tutkimushankkeen raportti. (Clients Needing Multiple Services in the Centre of Integrated Health and Social Care. A Research Project Report). Available online: https://kaks.fi/wp-content/uploads/2018/01/paljon-sote-palveluja-tarvitsevat-ihmiset-keskioon.pdf (accessed on 14 August 2018). (In Finnish)

Hujala, Anneli, Helena Taskinen, and Sari Rissanen. 2017. *How to Support Integration to Promote Care for People with Multimorbidity in Europe? Policy Brief 26, Health Systems and Policy Analysis.* Brussels: European Observatory on Health Systems and Policies. Available online: http://www.euro.who.int/en/about-us/partners/observatory/publications/policy-briefs-and-summaries/how-to-support-integration-to-promote-care-for-people-with-multimorbidity-in-europe (accessed on 11 November 2017).

Humphrey, Ronald H., Blake E. Ashforth, and James M. Diefendorff. 2015. The bright side of emotional labor. *Journal of Organizational Behavior* 36: 749–69. [CrossRef]

Hunter, Billie, and Pam Smith. 2007. Emotional Labour: Just another buzz word. *International Journal of Nursing Studies* 44: 859–61. [CrossRef] [PubMed]

Jacobsen, Michael H. 2019. Introduction. In *Emotions, Everyday Life and Sociology*. Edited by Jacobsen Michael H. London and New York: Routledge, pp. 1–12.

Kinman, Gail, and Louise Grant. 2011. Exploring Stress Resilience in Trainee Social Workers: The Role of Emotional and Social Competencies. *British Journal of Social Work* 41: 261–75. [CrossRef]

Mann, Sandi. 2005. A health-care model of emotional labour. An evaluation of the literature and development of a model. *Journal of Health Organization and Management* 19: 304–17. [CrossRef] [PubMed]

Minkman, Mirella. 2016. Values and Principles of Integrated Care. *International Journal of Integrated Care* 16: 1–3. [CrossRef]

Morrison, Tony. 2007. Emotional Intelligence, Emotion and Social Work: Context, Characteristics, Complications and Contribution. *British Journal of Social Work* 37: 245–64. [CrossRef]

Oksman, Erja. 2017. Parempi Arki -Hankkeen Loppuraportti. (The Report of the Better Everyday Life Project). Available online: https://www.innokyla.fi/web/hanke1911098 (accessed on 14 November 2017). (In Finnish)

Osborne, Natalie, and Deanna Grant-Smith. 2015. Supporting mindful planners in a mindless system: Limitations to the emotional turn in planning practice. *Town Planning Review* 86: 677–98. [CrossRef]

Pratt, Michael G., and Eliana Crosina. 2016. The Nonconscious at Work. *Annual Review of Organizational Psychology and Organizational Behavior* 3: 321–47. [CrossRef]

Regional Government. 2018. Integration of Social and Health Services. Available online: http://alueuudistus.fi/en/integration-of-social-and-health-services (accessed on 28 March 2018). (In Finland)

Revell, Lisa, and Victoria Burton. 2016. Supervision and the Dynamics of Collusion: A Rule of Optimism? *British Journal of Social Work* 46: 1587–601. [CrossRef]

Rijken, Mieke, Verena Struckmann, Iris van der Heide, Anneli Hujala, Francesco Barbabella, Ewout van Ginneken, and François Schellevis. 2017. On Behalf of the ICARE4EU Consortium. In *How to Improve Care for People with Multimorbidity in Europe?* Policy Brief 23, Health Systems and Policy Analysis. Brussels: European Observatory on Health Systems and Policies. Available online: http://www.euro.who.int/en/about-us/partners/observatory/publications/policy-briefs-and-summaries/how-to-improve-care-for-people-with-multimorbidity-in-europe (accessed on 11 November 2017).

Schepman, Sanneke, Johan Hansen, Iris de Putter, Ronald Batenburg, and Dinny de Bakker. 2015. The common characteristics and outcomes of multidisciplinary collaboration in primary health care: A systematic literature review. *International Journal of Integrated Care* 15: e027. [CrossRef] [PubMed]

Scholl, Isabelle, Jördis M. Zill, Martin Härter, and Jörg Dirmaier. 2014. An Integrative Model of Patient-Centredness—A Systematic Review and Concept Analysis. *PLoS ONE* 9: e107828. [CrossRef] [PubMed]

Schruijer, Sandra. 2008. The Social Psychology of Inter-organizational Relations. In *The Oxford Handbook of Inter-Organizational Relations*. Edited by Cropper Steve, Huxham Chris, Ebers Mark and Smith Ring Peter. Oxford: Oxford University Press. Available online: http://www.oxfordhandbooks.com/view/10.1093/oxfordhb/9780199282944.001.0001/oxfordhb-9780199282944-e-16 (accessed on 11 November 2017).

Valentijn, Pim, Sanneke Schepman, Wilfrid Opheij, and Marc Bruijnzeels. 2013. Understanding integrated care: A comprehensive conceptual framework based on the integrative functions of primary care. *International Journal of Integrated Care* 13: e010. [CrossRef] [PubMed]

Van der Heide, Iris, Sanne Snoeijs, Sabrina Quattrini, Verena Struckmann, Anneli Hujala, François Schellevis, and Mieke Rijken. 2018. Patient-centredness of integrated care programmes for people with multimorbidity. Results from the European ICARE4EU project. *Health Policy* 122: 36–43. [CrossRef] [PubMed]

World Health Organization. 2016. Framework on Integrated, People-Centered Health Services. Report by the Secretariat. Available online: http://apps.who.int/gb/ebwha/pdf_files/WHA69/A69_39-en.pdf?ua=1 (accessed on 29 March 2018).

Williams, Simon J. 2001. *Emotion and Social Theory:Corporeal Reflections on the (Ir) Rational*. eBook. ProQuest Ebook Central. London, Thousand Oaks and Calif.: Sage Publications, Available online: https://ebookcentral.proquest.com/lib/uef-ebooks/detail.action?docID=870020 (accessed on 7 October 2018).

Willumsen, Elisabeth, Bengt Ahgren, and Atle Ødegård. 2012. A conceptual framework for assessing interorganizational integration and interprofessional collaboration. *Journal of Interprofessional Care* 26: 198–204. [CrossRef] [PubMed]

Zapf, Dieter, and Melanie Holz. 2006. On the positive and negative effects of emotion work in organizations. *European Journal of Work and Organizational Psychology* 15: 1–28. [CrossRef]

Zapf, Dieter. 2002. Emotion work and psychological well-being. A review of the literature and some conceptual considerations. *Human Resource Management Review* 12: 237–68. [CrossRef]

Article

Developing Effective Collaborations: Learning from Our Practice

Jo Kennedy *, Ian McKenzie and Joette Thomas

Animate Consulting, Glasgow G12 9BG, UK
* Correspondence: jo@animateconsulting.org.uk

Received: 25 October 2018; Accepted: 3 September 2019; Published: 9 September 2019

Abstract: In this article we explore the challenges inherent in developing effective interorganizational relationships in the context of supporting the integration of health and social care in Scotland. We begin by outlining the context of health and social care integration and the nature of the program. We then describe the theories that underpinned our approach and outline in detail how the approach worked in practice in one area. We go on to discuss our reflections on six practices participants found helpful in creating the conditions necessary for effective collaboration. Finally, we end by reflecting on our learning.

Keywords: collaboration; leadership; integration; shared purpose; accountability

1. Introduction

Health and social care integration has been underway across Scotland for the past 3 years. It involves a wide range of large and small, public sector and voluntary organizations working together in ways which are completely new for them and throws up a wide range of interorganizational dynamics. The authors are partners in a small business (Animate) specializing in supporting interorganizational and intraorganizational work. In this article we have chosen to focus on a large contract supporting health and social care integration across Scotland. We start by exploring the context, then describe our overall approach, focusing in detail on how we worked in one area as illustrative of our practice across the whole. Finally we clarify our learning about six practices, which we have found to be at the heart of developing the kind of interorganizational relationships which enable organizations to truly collaborate. We know that collaborating is not easy; by exploring the learning from our own practice, we hope to support other collaborations to achieve their potential more easily.

2. The Context

In 2016 the Scottish Government legislated to bring together health and social care in to a single, integrated system, joining up services and thereby improving the experience for those using support. An ageing population and the impact of austerity on health and social care budgets introduced another driver for collaboration—a decline in financial resources, which looks set to continue.

Although new integrated boards were created in 31 areas across Scotland with responsibility for large parts of the health and social care budget, the original National Health Service (NHS) Boards and local authorities, with statutory responsibility for social care, remained, and most staff are still employed by them. So, health and social care 'integration' is in fact mostly a process of (multi-party) collaboration by which two large organizations, made up of many different departments, and large numbers of smaller organizations, attempt to work together to provide a better and more seamless service to people with health issues; in effect, almost the whole population.

The Scottish Government realized that developing interorganizational relationships to enable such collaboration would need support, and as part of that support, funded three national health and social care organizations, NHS Education for Scotland (NES), the Scottish Social Services Council (SSSC) and the Royal Scottish College of General Practitioners (RSCGP), to design a support and development program, Collaborative Leadership in Practice (CLiP) which drew heavily on their own experience of dialogue, coaching and action research methodologies and practice. They contracted with Animate, and another consultancy organization, similar in size and approach, to deliver it.

Through CLiP, we were commissioned to support collaboration in 10 partnership areas. Two members of our team, Jo Kennedy and Ian McKenzie, and one associate, delivered the interventions, whilst the third member of our team, Joette Thomas, supported our learning. The exact nature of the interventions we delivered was determined in collaboration with the partnership itself but it always involved either team coaching or facilitation.

3. Using an Action Research Approach

The program was managed by leadership development practitioners or project managers from the three national agencies, to whom we reported regularly in action research meetings, facilitated by a 'learning partner', who supported us to use an action research approach[1]. The idea was that we could encourage those who were part of CLiP to see what changes they were experiencing in themselves and their teams as they began to develop interorganizational relationships, which then resulted in changes across the wider organization(s) or system resulting in improvements for people in communities.

This action research approach meant that as we took action, we sought to understand the impact of that action together. It also worked on a number of levels. Firstly, and most importantly, it helped us to articulate a theory of change. This was that working on one's own attitudes, behaviors and assumptions about the other, and subsequently on our relationships with our fellow practitioners from other agencies, spreads better practice in our teams, changes the relationships between our organizations and ultimately can lead to positive outcomes for those using services. This theory of change made sense to practitioners. We used graphic tools to map it quite specifically, and practitioners then felt more legitimized in spending time exploring their own assumptions, their own understanding of collaboration and their role in relation to it, rather than immediately rushing to action. Secondly, it helped us to define a sense of common purpose, identify the changes we were seeking and evaluate whether we were achieving them. Furthermore, it helped us to track small changes over time in relation to the overall change we were seeking.

4. Developing Our Interventions

In all honesty, before writing this article, we had never considered in any depth, how our intra-organizational approach differed from our inter-organizational approach. We just knew from feedback from our clients, and from evaluating the impact, that the approach worked in both contexts.

Writing this article forced us to ask the question: how do we determine the interventions we use to support interorganizational collaboration? We also revisited the theoretical underpinning of our practice, which could best be described as eclectic. We draw on a range of organizational development theories and have trained in systems, psychodynamic and gestalt approaches to working with groups and organizations. When we began working interorganizationally we drew on many of the same theories and approaches we used in our intraorganizational work. We learned over time that there were three sources which made most sense to our clients, in the interorganizational collaborations in which they are currently working. The work of Heifetz (2009) on adaptive leadership helps us to support people to: navigate complexity by taking the time to stand back and look at the whole; be more comfortable with not knowing the answer straight away and understand the value of bringing different views and different approaches to an issue and indeed the absolute imperative to do that

---

[1] For further information on the approach we used to learn and on action research more generally c.f. www.research-for-real. co.uk.

when faced with 'adaptive challenges' (Heifetz et al. 2009). Interorganizational collaborations, like health and social care integration, are set up to address 'adaptive challenges', like how do we improve the health and wellbeing of Scotland's population; the answer to which is not within the 'gift' of any single organization. We find that making the distinction between a technical fix and an adaptive challenge, language pioneered by Heifetz, is very useful for the practitioners we work with, who are extremely familiar with the pressure to provide quick solutions to complex issues, without taking the time to consider who needs to be involved, and how, in developing a new approach.

We have found Wilber's Integral Theory equally useful. The simple four quadrant diagram which we discovered originally in an article on Resistance Free Change (Klein 2009) supports us to explain the aspects of intraorganizational and interorganizational working, systemically. In his book on Integral Psychology (Wilber 2000), Ken Wilber defines Network Logic as follows: "A dialectic (dialogue) of whole and part. As many details as possible are checked; then a tentative 'big picture' is assembled; it is checked against further details, and the big picture is readjusted. And so on, indefinitely with ever more details constantly altering the big picture—and vice versa. The 'whole' discloses new meanings not available to the 'parts', and thus the big picture will give new meaning to the details that compose it." We do not go into such depth in working with practitioners, but we do highlight how easy it is to pay attention to the 'objective' and tangible systems, processes and competencies within an organization or between organizations, and ignore the 'subjective' aspects which are less easy to see, such as values and beliefs, individual hopes and aspirations, culture, informal working practices and unwritten rules. When explaining it we often cite the old adage 'culture eats strategy for breakfast' attributed to Peter Drucker. This often elicits a weary laugh from the practitioners we work with, who are used to multiple strategies, plans and protocols which are never embraced or enacted. Explaining how paying attention to the 'whole system' including individual aspirations, values and beliefs and the cultures which have grown up in teams as well as the more familiar external process in organizations, can provide a way to move forward and makes sense to practitioners in both intraorganizational as well as inter-organizational contexts. However, in interorganizational contexts it is even more meaningful. Practitioners are used to starting with developing new structures, new roles and new job descriptions, to promote interorganizational working, rather than seeking at the same time to explore how to make it possible for individuals and teams to work in completely new ways, ways which often threaten their sense of identity; and to understand and value the approach taken by another organization, without feeling threatened by that difference.

Finally, Kegan and Lahey's (Kegan and Lahey 2009) work on Immunity to Change, enabled us to provide practitioners with a way of seeing resistance as something to be understood rather than something to be overcome. The Immunity to Change process introduces the idea of the 'hidden competing commitment' which could be underlying the resistance to change and needs to be both honored and understood. It also challenges practitioners to explore the assumptions they make about what might happen as a result of making a change and encourages the testing of such assumptions. This process, again is useful in a wide range of contexts, not just interorganizational working, but we have found it particularly useful in that context, because interorganizational working always necessitates change and often provokes fear, which leads to untested assumptions about what might happen as a result of that change. The Kegan and Lahey approach gives practitioners a simple process to help them really understand their own and others' resistance, rather than deny it, ignore it or fight it.

Being eclectic in our theoretical approach sometimes makes it hard to explain exactly how we work in both an intraorganizational and interorganizational context. So, over the past two years we have done some internal work to try to clarify and define our distinctive approach, and have come up with a working approach, which we are calling 'Stretch'. Stretch is not based on our understanding of Heifetz, Kegan and Lahey and Wilber. Instead it draws on a whole range of theory which has influenced us and is firmly rooted in the learning we are generating from our current practice. As such, it is a work in progress rather than a finished product. Currently, it has six elements (or imperatives) which as consultants we try to adopt ourselves and to use to support the development of intraorganizational and interorganizational relationships. The elements are be curious, be appreciative, be proactive, be courageous, be thinkers and be communicators.

We use Stretch when working within organizations and between organizations; but we find that in our work on interorganizational collaboration, particular elements come to the fore namely: curiosity, courage and communication.

Working interorganizationally necessitates being able to tolerate a high level of difference without finding it threatening or overwhelming. We know that from our own experience and from our coaching practice, that raising individual's levels of awareness and insight into the impact of their own behavior, particularly when fearful or under threat, can have a transformative impact on groups and organizations. We know from our psychodynamic training that, as individuals and groups we are naturally threatened by 'the other' and often find ways of excluding them. We seek to raise awareness of this in our interorganizational work by exploring the assumptions which naturally arise about 'the other' and examining the ways in which we both consciously and unconsciously exclude. Encouraging curiosity is one of the most accessible ways we have found to express this. To support curiosity, we use 'light' psychometric processes in the room to enable people from different organizations to gain more insight into themselves and others, and to grow in understanding of their own 'working style'. Sometimes, we consider the 'working style' which might be dominant in their own organization and encourage them to be curious about the working style that might be dominant in other organizations too.

Drawing on our understanding of the work of Kegan and Lahey in particular, we encourage individuals and groups to identify their assumptions about others and about the work they are doing, and to ask more questions of themselves and one another. Some of these questions involve taking risks. We acknowledge and support differences and potential conflicts to emerge, drawing attention to them in the room and opening up the space for conversations about them. These conversations often take courage on all sides. Clearly courageous conversations are necessary within organizations as well as between organizations, but we find that interorganizational working requires a particular kind of courage, which often means people stepping outside their 'comfort zone', being willing to question their own professional identity, taking the risk to share resources and sometimes giving up working practices or aspirations which have been dearly held.

Finally, we spend a lot of time exploring how and what to communicate both within and outside the room. Again, this is as necessary within organizations as it is between organizations, but it is even more complex interorganizationally. Organizations develop their own ways of communicating internally through formal and informal systems, which are often impenetrable to those from other organizations. The same words may be used to mean different things in different organizations. Rather than just examining communication systems, as we would when we work intraorganizationally, when we work interorganizationally we support both informal and formal communication processes to be dismantled and rebuilt to suit a new entity and a new purpose.

Running through all the Stretch elements is a relational, purposeful approach. This means that we work hard to get to know our clients as human beings, and we prioritize giving them the time to get to know one another too; believing this knowledge will support them to take up their roles more purposefully and effectively together. We focus on defining purpose at every stage, from every perspective, and try to keep the purpose at the forefront, seeking to clarify it throughout our intervention.

5. Interorganizational Working in Practice

As part of our work on one of the national programs mentioned earlier, our team has worked with ten health and social care partnerships across Scotland, over the past two years, all at different stages of integration. All face the same challenges, which can be summarized as: greater demand, which has to be met with fewer resources. The pressure just to 'get things done' is huge and mitigates against the time it takes to establish a common vision, clear roles and truly effective working practices.

Adm. Sci. **2019**, *9*, 68

To describe the context of all ten would mean getting into a level of detail, which is beyond the scope of this journal article. However, our approach, although tailored to the individual context, was broadly similar in all of them. So, the description of the one below gives an impression of our work across the whole. Names have been substituted to protect anonymity. The consultant working in the site was one of the three authors of the article.

Beston is a small town on the edge of a large city in Scotland. It was chosen by the Health and Social Care Partnership (HSC) as a site in which to launch an inquiry involving practitioners from across disciplines. George, the 'strategic program manager' asked Jo, a consultant with Animate Consulting, to attend a startup meeting with him, and several other senior health and social care managers, to scope out an approach to promote better joint working for the benefit of housebound elderly people. The initiative was seen as a way of trying out 'locality working' in practice, with the aim being that we could devise a process, which other localities could learn from.

General Practitioners (GPs) are the first point of contact for many patients; they are also the most likely to be working in isolation. The HSC partnership decided to focus the project around two GP practices. They invited the GPs to attend six meetings with other health and social care practitioners who were also supporting housebound elderly people. The intention was to see how together, the group could improve the lives of elderly housebound people by ensuring that they received more of the right kind of services at the right time. Crucially, the HSC gave Delia, the 'integration manager' time to support the initiative, inviting people, organizing rooms and following up actions in between meetings.

Meetings were held monthly over a six month period. Each meeting lasted three hours. Fifteen–twenty people attended each meeting. No one (except Jo) attended all six meetings, although most people were present for at least four out of the six meetings. They included: two GPs (from different practices), district nurses, a social worker, a day center manager, a mental health specialist, a community librarian, several people from voluntary sector organizations who were providing community support or support to carers, a pharmacist, an occupational therapist, an IT specialist and one or two senior managers. In all, 10–15 organizations were represented. Jo's role was to design, facilitate and support the inquiry process.

Setting up the first meeting required courage on the part of Delia, who issued the invitations. It was an unusual meeting because: it was long; there was no fixed agenda; it took place in a community setting and the practitioners had different levels of experience and of status within their own organizations. What they had in common was a clear intention to work together better to support housebound elderly people in their geographical area. The first meeting began with a focus on communication. Jo invited people to say who they were and why they were there. The GPs in particular found this useful. They had not met most of the other practitioners, and they were immediately curious about all the support that was available from the voluntary sector organizations. Already many people in the group were beginning to question the assumptions they made about those who worked in other organizations being in some way 'less skilled' or 'more informed'. Almost everyone found it strange: hardly anyone had had the 'luxury' of three hours to sit together and discuss how to tackle the issues they had in common. They started by considering what worked currently about the way they worked interorganizationally, taking time to get to know one another (rather than just read each other's name badges) and getting clear about the purpose of their work together.

They were invited to identify the kinds of changes they wanted to see as a result of this process. Aspirations included: more trust, stronger relationships, more community involvement, better use of technology and a stronger focus on personal outcomes. During the second half of the meeting we focused on four stories of real people who were using support in Beston. Four small groups worked to distil the learning from each of the stories. Several interesting conclusions emerged: Three out of the four people receiving services were overwhelmed and confused by the amount of support they received from different organizations; people were afraid to change their 'care packages' in case they could not get them back again if their needs increased and information recorded by one practitioner in one organization was inaccessible to others in a different organization.

Telling stories of the present engendered a desire for immediate action and practitioners highlighted things they wanted to do (like sharing information) or questions they wanted to ask (such as 'what is a wellbeing clinic and how might it work?') before they met the following month. During that first meeting one of the nurses was visibly angry and upset, fed up with the ever-increasing volume of work, and the inefficiency of the systems and structures. Jo encouraged her to speak out and the group members respected the courage this took by listening to her. By the end of the meeting she had agreed to take a lead on researching the wellbeing clinic. Although Jo did not explicitly use Wilber's integral theory she was encouraging people to think systemically, drawing on their own values and aspirations, considering the culture of their organizations, examining the systems they used and most importantly beginning to create a new interorganizational entity to support housebound elderly people better.

In between every meeting Jo met with Delia, to debrief, discuss progress and plan the next meeting. Delia communicated with individual group members between meetings and nudged actions. She was always able to keep Jo abreast of what was going on, highlighting underlying issues and ensuring that the agenda was really focused on moving forward. Jo and Delia quickly developed a format for the meetings, which encapsulated an action research approach. Each meeting began with a short recap, using a visual plan which was pinned on the wall, and an update on actions in the whole group, which took the best part of an hour. This was followed by an in-depth focus on two or three key areas, in smaller groups, which led to agreement on actions in the large group. They always finished by checking out how people were as they left.

The second meeting began with more introductions as new people joined. By this time the existing members of the group were able to explain that the group provided 'an opportunity for trial and error in a safe environment, a place to share enthusiasm and frustrations, energy and honesty, a place where we can learn, a chance to identify and talk about the big issues'. They caught up on progress in relation to the actions identified in the previous meeting. In addition, they focused on three areas: tapping into the lived experience of users and carers; medication and information sharing.

During the third meeting Jo used a visual scenario planning tool to identify the future they wanted to create, where they were now in relation to that future, and the key areas they wanted to work on. That provided them with six clear priorities to focus on. By this time the group was appreciating the distinction between technical fixes and adaptive challenges (Heifetz). They identified some 'quick wins' such as telling pharmacists which of their patients attended the day center so that they could drop off medicines there, to avoid getting overwhelmed by some of the more intractable issues, such as integrating different information systems. At the end, group members reported that the meeting generated 'lots of little things that will make a big difference' and provided 'a forum that works towards integration that we can't find in the day to day'.

And yet, Delia and Jo were beginning to get impatient themselves, and were sensing that group members might be too. Group attendance was irregular and actions agreed at the meeting were not always being carried out between meetings. They were struggling even to get started on developing integrated systems across agencies, because the individual systems were not functioning themselves. Some practitioners had competing priorities and were not able to give the work the attention they wanted to, and others, found the cross-sector approach threatening to their sense of identity and professionalism, and stopped attending. The GPs were attending but were still skeptical and although positive in meetings were struggling to prioritize taking action in between.

During the fourth meeting they talked about some of these difficulties, using the Kegan and Lahey insights on resistance to examine what was underneath some of the barriers. The group had still not managed to identify how many housebound elderly people the GP practices supported. Nor had they managed to coordinate support around them. Getting to the bottom of who was 'housebound' and considering how to surmount the legal obstacles to sharing information, was tedious and taxing work. Having had the courage to acknowledge this, they recharged their energy by turning their attention to making the best use of the voluntary sector day center. They developed ideas for 'small tests of change', expanding its use by statutory sector agencies. By the end of the meeting the GP was commenting: 'I am learning more about how other organizations work—these small tests of change are very important—I see my role as information sharing—I will ask the district nurses to pop into the day center'.

Delia and Jo were conscious that there were only two meetings left and during the fifth meeting they focused on what group members felt should become 'business as usual' in the HSC partnership, with a particular focus on developing flexible care packages for people (so that they did not feel the need to hang on to any support they were offered) and devising efficient ways of sharing information between agencies.

Delia and Jo met with senior managers to consider the results of the initiative before the final meeting. They were both anxious, aware of how slow progress had felt in relation to some of the key issues they had identified at the outset; however, the managers were very positive. They recognized a strong foundation for future collaboration. They saw that giving staff time away from the frontline had been valuable. Four ways to continue the work were identified: monthly multi-disciplinary team meetings in each GP practice, focusing on particular patients; continuing to work on far more flexible review process which really put the person at the center; developing the role of the voluntary sector day center and continuing to tackle the obstacles to information sharing.

During the sixth and final meeting they agreed plans to take forward the four initiatives. We ended by checking back against the outcomes agreed at the beginning. Group members identified that they had improved communication and understanding of each other's roles, made new partnerships and found out how to help one another to provide better services. They spoke of practical integration on the frontline. One member said 'we have gained traction' whilst another spoke of 'inspiration, enthusiasm and commitment'.

6. The Six Practices

The Beston story typifies our approach to supporting interorganizational collaboration. Using the three elements of Stretch: be curious, be courageous and be communicators, helped us design our interventions. We invited all the relevant partners to be in the room together; we took time to get to know one another, and one another's roles; we agreed a shared purpose, which mattered to all of us; we acknowledged diversity and recognized and worked on frustration; and we tried out small tests of change, building those that worked into 'business as usual'. Although it worked well enough, we only really scratched the surface in terms of being able to talk openly about some of the tensions and power imbalances between partners. This was largely because the group was fluid as most practitioners could only afford the time to attend some of the meetings. Prioritizing time to think remains very hard for practitioners delivering services, which means that developing adaptive solutions to complex issues is a real challenge.

However, Stretch really only defines our approach. The group created practices together which enabled their interorganizational relationships to develop and true collaboration to take place. These practices were facilitated by Stretch, in particular the support of courage, communication and curiosity and most importantly a clear and unequivocal focus on purpose and outcomes for people using services. In the rest of this article we explore the six practices, adopted in Beston, and in other areas, which for us have become the hallmarks of interorganizational collaboration. We identified the practices through reflection. Jo and Delia reflected first, in between each meeting in Beston, discussing what they had learned from the meeting, which interventions had worked well and what could be improved, and designed the approach to the next meeting together.

The authors also reflected as a team, telling stories from Beston and the nine other partnerships which made up our part of Collaborative Leadership in Practice, and drawing learning from our practice, using a reflection cycle and with the support of our learning partner.[2]

The practices are:

- Suspending disbelief;
- Defining a shared purpose which everyone can sign up to;
- Developing accountability to a shared purpose;
- Exploring diversity and building trust;
- Designing purposeful structural change;
- Supporting courageous and systemic leadership.

6.1. Suspending Disbelief

Many of those in health and social care have experienced a lot of change throughout their working lives. They have not initiated much of this change, and sometimes it has not led to better outcomes for themselves as practitioners or for those using services. Integration requires a suspension of disbelief. It means taking the risk to set up a new system in which professionals take up new roles and do things they are not accustomed to doing. It requires some give as well as some take, and it will take some time to see whether the risk will pay off.

> "Will our patients get a better service at the end of all this? I can see it is a massive amount of work to make it all join up." (GP)

We saw some practitioners willing to suspend disbelief and take the risk. We saw other practitioners, and particularly those who have little experience of interorganizational working, reluctant to take the risk, and quite deeply entrenched in their own system. Sometimes this related to power. Those with the most power, were often the most reluctant to collaborate, because it meant sharing it. Those with the least power, had little to lose by collaborating.

What we found helpful in encouraging people to suspend disbelief and take the risk to establish interorganizational relationships, was to foster a sense that something had to be done, both by looking at what worked currently, but also by exploring honestly the failings in the current system and how they impacted on particular people, both patients and practitioners. This created urgency.

What practitioners valued most in almost every workshop we ran or every event we facilitated was the chance to understand what each other did. As soon as they began to explore each other's roles and each other's organizations in any depth, they almost always found ways of helping one another in very practical ways. These turned into what are commonly known as 'small tests of change'. For instance, GPs began changing their prescribing practices so that home care staff did not have to visit so often, and housebound elderly people could go out to a local lunch club rather than stay in so that a worker could visit them and support them to take their medication. This meant the GP having to spend more of their budget on medications which could be given twice a day rather than four times a day, but they were willing to do it because they could see what a difference it made to the quality of life of their patients. These small practical experiments in doing things differently began to add up to a conviction that maybe things could be better through collaborating across and between organizations.

Suspending disbelief was facilitated by the three elements of the Stretch approach: curiosity, courage and communication.

---

2 We use a variety of reflection cycles but they all start with us individually telling stories of our experience and then going through a cycle which includes observing, reflecting, planning and identifying actions (ORPA designed by Research for Real and based on the work of Yolande Wandsworth).

6.2. Defining a Shared Purpose, and Getting Everyone to Sign Up to It

Health and social care integration aims to evidence high-level outcomes, which are achieved for society as a whole and not just for the participating organizations.

The pressure to produce these outcomes as a result of integration is intense and unrelenting. The Scottish Government are expecting more for patients and people who use services, at a lower cost. At a societal level, there is a real reluctance by politicians, and the general public, to accept that the present system is unaffordable and health and social care services will need to be rationed in some way.

In practice this means that difficult decisions about where to ration are left to local health and social care leaders and managers again requiring courage. As well as improving services, health and social care practitioners are tasked with improving public health overall (as a way of reducing demand), and mobilizing as yet undefined, community resources. Given this context it is no wonder that the task can feel overwhelming and produce both a sense of hopelessness and embattlement. This is compounded by media coverage, which is mostly hostile.

Within this context, we commonly found that people were inclined to 'get on with the job' without beginning with curiosity or communication which could lead to establishing meaningful tasks, roles and responsibilities. Developing a shared purpose enabled practitioners to explore their own role in relation to delivering that purpose and to explore what felt new, different and challenging about it. This makes it sound as if the purpose was fixed and immutable. In Beston it was not. As issues were explored, short term and medium term goals like encouraging the nurses to visit older people whilst they were at the lunch club, rather than in the homes, which meant they had to stay in all day, were constantly revisited and refined in the light of new knowledge. The long term goal of improving the wellbeing of housebound elderly people through improving their services, remained the same.

Ensuring that those who would be working towards the purpose were part of defining it was crucial. We saw several plans written by consultants or managers, which felt at best meaningless and at worst dishonest, to those working on the ground.

6.3. Developing Accountability to a Shared Purpose

Health and social care partnerships are accountable to the Scottish Government for delivering targets. These targets are often imposed from above, can be controversial, are often resented by practitioners on the ground and little understood by the general public. Instead we attempted to develop a sense of accountability to people who were using services and putting them at the heart of the shared purpose was fundamental to this. The ideal way to do this was to get them in the room as part of defining this purpose. However, this was not always possible. So, we encouraged practitioners to bring their stories into the room and started with those, trying to ensure that those closest to people using services had a strong voice. This worked well in Beston, where we started the process by focusing on 4 case studies of older 'housebound' people; creating in those in the room a sense of wonder, that people had so much unnecessary and conflicting support, a sense of frustration both at the waste of resources and the distress caused to the recipients of the services and an urgent desire for change and improvement.

6.4. Exploring Diversity and Building Trust

Schruijer points out that "successful collaboration means being able to work with diversity . . . diversity which in itself gives rise to distrust, stereotyping and conflict" (Schruijer 2006).

Providing health and social care services to the whole population naturally entails a huge range of diverse specialisms and skills. Interdisciplinary working adds another dimension to interorganizational working. It is at its most effective when these specialists can work well with one another across organizational boundaries. For instance, when a GP (who works within her own small partnership business) knows enough about an older person's support at home, that she can prescribe medication to be taken at a mealtime when a home carer (who works for the local authority) is likely to be there to administer it.

Exploring diversity could be both an affirming and exciting experience in groups when they began to realize the potential of what was on offer. However, they could also experience it as threatening, particularly when their own specialism was under threat and when their organizations were competing for scarce resources.

In several interorganizational groups we experienced a real reluctance to talk about the painful and threatening aspects of working together. This manifested itself in conflict avoidance, which resulted in simmering frustration, or at the other extreme a refusal to talk to or work with people from different organizations. Both these behaviors naturally enough resulted in unproductive collaborations in which a lot of time and effort was wasted in either avoiding difficult subjects or not being able to get the right people in the room to talk about them.

Good solid working relationships are at the heart of collaboration. Building these relationships across organizations takes time, commitment and a willingness to take a risk to notice areas of disagreement and explore difference.

We have noticed two attitudes to relationship building. The first is the assumption that they are already built, which made us wonder whether participants were 'colluding' in avoiding the discomfort and conflict, which might be inherent in going a bit deeper and working towards meaningful change.

We experienced this phenomenon strongly in one partnership in which we worked, where a real discussion of difference was seen as very threatening. We were constantly told that relationships were good and therefore coming together was a redundant activity; managers just needed to be left alone to get on with their work in their way. All difficulties were blamed on budget cuts and poor leadership.

This entrenched sense of powerlessness and being victims of forces beyond their control, was the view of a minority of group members, but they had a strong voice, and other members of the group found it impossible to challenge them. When we challenged them, we felt more like school-teachers, than facilitators or consultants.

Over time this changed. Two years later, those most resistant to change have moved on, managers have begun exercising their power in more constructive ways and difference is being confronted more openly. However, there is a deep-rooted power imbalance between the two main parties, health and social care. The split in the senior leadership team is acknowledged but entrenched, so progress is both slow and frustrating.

The second attitude we encountered was that it is not worth taking the time to build relationships because we need to get on with the work. What we have found is that taking the time to explore what matters to people, individually, what their work experience is, and what their values are, provides a strong foundation for developing a common endeavor, as is demonstrated in the Beston example detailed earlier. It enables people to overcome their instinctive fear of 'the other', and to challenge their assumptions about the other's motivations. It leads to the development of working relationships which are based on respect rather than assumptions; where each partner recognizes the value in, and the contribution of the other. It enables the development of trust, where each partner is confident that the other is committed to the same end; and will put that end before their own organizational or individual interests.

It does not avoid conflict but it does create the conditions in which difference can be addressed constructively, rather than explosively or covertly. Ultimately it leads to getting the job done quicker and more effectively because there is less chance of miscommunication and misunderstanding.

When people have the courage to name either their fears or their suspicions, it often had a transformational effect on the group, who were then able to work together in a far more meaningful way. Sometimes this could be as simple as someone saying they felt overwhelmed and unsupported, as the nurse did in the Beston example. That was an experience others could relate to, and it felt true enough that the group immediately understood that we were there to work on the real issues.

Creating safe enough conditions for groups to work in this way was often challenging. Trust takes time to develop and can only be sustained if all parties demonstrate through their actions as well as their words, that they are working towards the same goals. Open and transparent leadership, which modelled a strong collaborative approach was key and is discussed later.

6.5. Designing Purposeful Structural Change

"I might have had this almost mystical belief that the structures and processes we are putting in place will lead to integration, when the hallmark of integration will be relationships and dialogue. It needs to be built on that solid foundation, otherwise nothing else will work, whatever procedure you type up and circulate." (social work team manager)

New structures bridging organizations were often created, before purpose and working practices had been explored, before relationships had been developed and before a new culture had even been discussed let alone defined. The urge to act quickly and concretely without real forethought was strong. One practitioner commented:

"Health and social care integration is not about new structures, but about how we make services work locally. When you make it real and concrete through relationship and dialogue, it makes sense." (participant)

Part of the hopelessness and disaffection we encountered in our work in integration came from a mismatch between the aspiration and the reality epitomized by structures, which were impeding rather than facilitating collaboration (this was particularly true in IT where it is very difficult to share data). Structures were also failing to hold people to account for poor performance and to enable and reward good practice.

The most effective structural changes followed a clear agreement on what would support working to purpose and were facilitated by good relationships. This meant that even when structural change meant people either losing their jobs or being redeployed, they could see the rationale and justification for it in relation to the wider outcomes for those benefiting from the collaboration.

"We deliberately didn't focus on structural moves at the beginning—our focus was on working together . . . structure would come later and is still coming, we are trying to get the best fit at this point in time, structural changes create huge tension, leave all of us feeling insecure." (leader within a health and social care collaboration)

6.6. Courageous and Systemic Leadership

The biggest common denominator for successful collaborations was courageous and systemic leadership, at different levels of the organizations. This meant having leaders at the top who were willing to take the risk to challenge the targets imposed on them by government. It meant leaders who showed that they were willing to look beyond their own and their organization's interests to the wider interests of the collaboration.

It meant leaders who were willing to try new ways of working, knowing that they might fail. It meant leaders who took the time to listen and try to understand the whole picture rather than become immersed in one part of it. It meant leaders who were willing to create a structure for the long term rather than something which suited their interests in the short term. One leader spoke about this as designing a collaboration that would work for the next generation of leaders, rather than for himself or his colleagues.

It meant leaders who were willing to listen to the dissenting voices and acknowledge where they were right rather than trying to shut them down.

It meant leaders who were willing to give themselves and others the time needed to explore the underlying issues and complexity rather than reaching for immediate and short-term solutions.

We saw plenty of examples of this kind of leadership. It added up to systemic leadership, which moved from blaming one party or another to a real understanding of how the current conditions had been created and what needed to be done to address them.

We also saw plenty of examples of failures in leadership where leaders modelled putting themselves before the interests of the collaboration often in quite concrete ways. One leader sought a pay rise whilst arguing that he did not have the finance to set up permanent collaborative roles. Whilst there were undoubtedly good reasons for the pay rise it had a devastating effect on the morale and credibility of the collaborative venture.

Although modelling good leadership at the top of the collaboration is crucial, good leadership at every level is at the heart of making a difference on the ground and delivering positive outcomes for people in communities. One leader commented:

> "Empowerment of staff helps to get things happening from the bottom up. There are things happening that they don't tell me these days. It is not out of control but good innovation, it's a trust thing."

7. Final Reflections

Through reflection we came up with the six practices any interorganizational collaboration would do well to adopt. Taking the plunge and suspending disbelief was fundamental to getting started on collaboration in the context of health and social care integration. Defining a shared purpose and developing accountability to one another for working towards that purpose gave an impetus and a clear direction to the collaboration. Taking the time to build relationships, explore diversity and tackle the difficult dynamics inherent in difference, ultimately facilitated faster and more purposeful action. And finally, modelling courageous and systemic leadership at every level renewed energy and motivation.

What we have learned is that good intentions are not enough. For collaboration to be effective there needs to be a very clear purpose which is foreground and center all of the time. Even with that clear purpose, effective collaboration takes time, effort and commitment, so finding real ways to notice the difference it makes from the outset is crucial. These differences do not have to be large. For practitioners to commit themselves they just needed to see small improvements in the lives of their patients, which ignites their hope that working together could be far more productive than working on their own or in their own silo.

The work of Heifetz, Wilber and Kegan and Lahey has proved useful both to us in developing our thinking and our approach as facilitators and consultants, and to participants in interorganizational collaborations when we have used it directly. We are still discovering which elements of our Stretch approach work best in the interorganizational context. Encouraging curiosity, developing new ways of communicating and providing conditions in which people can be courageous have definitely worked, but undoubtedly there is more that we can learn about this. Senior leadership came to endorse the value of spending time together to work on developing relationships and exploring roles and purpose before plunging into action. It was not without frustration but it did allow us to explore pain and frustration in a meaningful and ultimately productive way.

The last words come from participants in the Beston collaboration who have continued to meet and address their common issues in smaller configurations:

> "I feel really energized, the openness has been really encouraging—this work could have such a big impact." (Occupational Therapist)

> "I am sensing real enthusiasm from our different roles—this work is really important— and it is about aligning needs with support rather than having an agenda about cutting services." (service manager)

Adm. Sci. **2019**, *9*, 68

Author Contributions: These authors contributed equally to this work.

Funding: This research received no external funding.

Conflicts of Interest: The authors declare no conflict of interest.

References

Heifetz, Ronald. 2009. The Nature of Adaptive Leadership. Available online: https://www.youtube.com/watch?v=QfLLDvn0pI8 (accessed on 20 March 2018).

Heifetz, Ronald Abadian, Ronald Heifetz, Alexander Grashow, and Martin Linsky. 2009. *The Practice of Adaptive Leadership: Tools and Tactics for Changing Your Organisation and the World.* Boston: Harvard Business Press.

Kegan, Robert, and Lisa Lahey. 2009. *Immunity to Change: How to Overcome It and Unlock the Potential in Yourself and Your Organisation (Leadership for the Common Good).* Boston: Harvard Business Review.

Klein, Eric. 2009. *Leading Resistance-Free Change: More Results. Less Struggle.* San Isidro: Dharma Consulting.

Schruijer, Sandra G. L. 2006. Research on Collaboration in Action. *International Journal of Action Research* 2: 222–42.

Wilber, Ken. 2000. *Integral Psychology: Consciousness, Spirit, Psychology, Therapy.* Boulder: Shambala Publications.

Article

Networks Originate in Minds: An Exploration of Trust Self-Enhancement and Network Centrality in Multiparty Systems

Oana C. Fodor [1], Alina M. Fleştea [1,*], Iulian Onija [1] and Petru L. Curşeu [1,2]

[1] Department of Psychology, Babeş-Bolyai University, Cluj-Napoca 400015, Romania;
oanafodor@psychology.ro (O.C.F.); iulianonija@yahoo.com (I.O.); petrucurseu@psychology.ro or
petru.curseu@ou.nl (P.L.C.)

[2] Department of Organization, Open University of the Netherlands, 6419 AT Heerlen, The Netherlands

* Correspondence: alinaflestea@psychology.ro; Tel.: +40-264-590-967

Received: 23 July 2018; Accepted: 4 October 2018; Published: 9 October 2018

Abstract: Multiparty systems (MPSs) are defined as collaborative task-systems composed of various stakeholders (organizations or their representatives) that deal with complex issues that cannot be addressed by a single group or organization. Our study uses a behavioral simulation in which six stakeholder groups engage in interactions in order to reach a set of agreements with respect to complex educational policies. We use a social network perspective to explore the dynamics of network centrality during intergroup interactions in the simulation and show that trust self-enhancement at the onset of the simulation has a positive impact on the evolution of network centrality throughout the simulation. Our results have important implications for the social networks dynamics in MPSs and point towards the benefit of using social network analytics as exploration and/or facilitating tools in MPSs.

Keywords: social networks; multiparty systems; trust; centrality

---

1. Introduction

Multiparty systems (MPSs) are social systems, composed of several organizations or their representatives that interact in order to make decisions or address complex issues with major social impact (Curşeu and Schruijer 2017). Such issues include sustainable urban development, natural resource management (including water use), or dealing with climate change. Therefore, MPSs bring together various stakeholder groups (typically more than three parties) that engage within, as well as between, group interactions in an attempt to find integrative solutions to these complex issues (Curşeu and Schruijer 2018). MPSs often face significant challenges in reaching the desired outcome, as they embed substantial diversity (e.g., interests, backgrounds, and power asymmetries) (Vansina and Taillieu 1997; Fleştea et al. 2017) on the one hand, and a great degree of interdependence on the other hand (e.g., the sustainable and comprehensive solutions can be reached only by building on integrative actions).

In some cases, MPSs can have a formal governance structure (especially in situations in which formal representatives of the state or government are part of the MPS), yet most of the times the governance of MPSs emerges from the interactions, joint practices, and efforts aimed at unraveling and working with the interdependencies among the stakeholders that compose the system (Bouwen and Taillieu 2004). Such an emergent governance is often hindered as the stakeholders that join the system may bring in frictional relational histories, misunderstandings, or false assumptions that lead to stereotyping and negative behaviors and impede the functioning of the whole system (Schruijer 2006). Due to the relational tensions, oftentimes, some of the stakeholders may get marginalized or even be excluded from the system. In such a case, these stakeholders cannot achieve their aims. Moreover, the system itself may lose its integrity and ultimately fails to achieve its purpose. Therefore, goal achievement motivates stakeholders to be actively engaged in the relational dynamics of the MPS. In social network terms, stakeholders seek to establish and maintain advantageous central positions in the social networks that capture the relational landscape of the MPS. A key question is: what makes a stakeholder central in the collaboration network of an MPS?

Popular business literature acclaims trust as a social lubricant and scholarly research shows that trust fosters collaboration in work teams (Costa et al. 2018), decreases conflict (Curşeu and Schruijer 2010) and facilitates the development of collaborative relations in MPSs (Vansina and Taillieu 1997). Organizational research shows that trust is more likely to emerge in decentralized (organic) rather than hierarchical organizational structures (Costa et al. 2018). Moreover, social network research claims that knowing who trusts whom accurately predicts who will interact with whom and in what way (Kilduff and Brass 2010). Trust however is a multifaceted (e.g., cognitive, affective, relational, etc.) and multilayered (e.g., interpersonal, intra-group, inter-group, etc.) phenomenon and its relationship with actors' structural positions in social networks is complex. Building on social interdependence theories (Deutsch 1949; Holmes 2002), we set out to explore the role of trust expectations as antecedents of network centrality in MPSs. We build on social comparison and self-enhancement arguments (Kwan et al. 2004) to argue that at the onset of social interactions in MPSs, stakeholders engage in social comparison (me versus others) and the emerging trust self-enhancement (trust in myself versus trust in others) ultimately shapes one's centrality in the collaboration network in MPSs. In other words, we claim that one's centrality in social networks originates from trust expectations based on the social comparison processes at the onset of social interactions.

In this paper, we build on the social network approach to argue that an MPS can be conceptualized as a network of groups that interact with each other in order to jointly define and solve the task at hand. We extend the research on MPSs in several ways. First, our exploration is among the first attempts to explore the dynamics of network centrality using sequential evaluations of network perceptions collected at four points during a behavioral simulation. We use a longitudinal data collection approach to test the effect of trust self-enhancement on the emergence and evolution of network centrality. Second, we employ a socio-structural view and a network aggregation procedure in which we combine individual perceptions of network centrality to obtain group level estimates that are representative for each stakeholder group. As such, our paper provides an empirical illustration of how social network procedures can be used to understand the dynamics of MPSs. Third, we explore trust self-enhancement as one of the cognitive antecedents of the structural position in the MPS network. Using this self-enhancement approach to trust, we move beyond the traditional view that trust is the property of an agent and we explore trust as emergent from social comparison processes in a context of social relations.

2. Theory and Hypothesis

2.1. A Social Network Approach to MPSs

MPSs bring together various stakeholder groups with the goal to address complex issues, oftentimes resulting in decisions with far-reaching implications (i.e., sustainability decisions, designing new laws, etc.) (Curşeu and Schruijer 2017). The decision tasks that such systems face are often vague at the onset of the stakeholders' interactions and the outcome is difficult to predict from the initial expectations and aspirations each stakeholder has. In order to be successful, the stakeholders in the MPS are compelled to engage in collaborative processes and are motivated to establish and maintain a central position in the relational landscape of the MPS. That is, each stakeholder is expected to actively participate and share its interests, views, and concerns regarding the topic at hand. Moreover, as the views and interests expressed during interactions are often diverse, the stakeholders are required to engage in and integrate the task disagreements, in search for the integrative potential of the situation

(Gray 1989; Curşeu and Schruijer 2017). In doing so, the stakeholders also need to handle the differences regarding their identities, status, and power (Schruijer 2006), and work with the various perceptions and behavioral expectations they hold regarding both one's own group and the other groups in the system (Curşeu and Schruijer 2018).

So far, the dynamics of MPSs was explored under a variety of frameworks, ranging from psychodynamics (Schruijer and Vansina 2008), to relational (Gray 1989; Schruijer 2008) and process-based approaches (Gray 1985). In this paper, we take a structural approach to MPSs and argue that MPSs are social networks, in which stakeholder groups are represented by nodes that are interconnected by an evolving web of social ties. In this framework, the MPS dynamics is captured by the structural changes that occur in the nodes and tie characteristics during social interactions (Snijders 2001). In other words, in a structural approach, the evolution of the social network structure in an MPS captures the dynamics of the relational landscape emerging in such a complex system.

Social capital research brought extensive evidence on the value of social ties, linking one's position in the network to various beneficial outcomes such as: power (Brass and Burkhardt 1993; Kilduff and Krackhardt 1994), leadership (Brass and Krackhardt 1999; Pastor et al. 2002), or performance (Hansen 1999; Tsai 2001). Out of the various metrics that describe an actor's structural position in the system, centrality refers to the degree to which a node (a stakeholder group in this case) is connected to all the other nodes in the network (Westbay et al. 2014). Collaboration centrality, in particular, indicates the number of collaborative relations between a stakeholder group and the other groups in the system. We used two indicators of network centrality, namely betweenness and closeness. Betweenness centrality refers to the number of times that a stakeholder in the system connects other stakeholders (pairwise) that are not directly in contact in the network (Freeman 1979). It is a measure of a bridging role in the MPS. On the other hand, closeness centrality refers to how close a node is from all the other nodes in the system (Freeman 1979). A stakeholder with high closeness centrality is situated in the middle of the MPS network and well connected with the rest of the stakeholders.

A stakeholder group that has a central position in an MPS is likely to be more influential and efficient in working at the multiparty and own agenda, as compared to a peripheral actor. It benefits from the multiple exchanges with other groups within the system such that it has greater access to information, support, and other resources received through the social ties (Oh et al. 2004). A stakeholder that is on average closer to the other stakeholders in the system (i.e., it has a high level of closeness centrality) can gather useful information more easily, while it can also more readily communicate its interests throughout the network and work on its agenda. Similarly, a stakeholder with high betweenness centrality plays the role of a broker, facilitating the information flow between other unconnected nodes in the MPS (Burt 1995). As previously discussed, openly discussing vested interests and concerns (i.e., handling task disagreements) among all stakeholders in the system, as well as solving relational conflicts, is a requirement for a successful collaboration (Curşeu and Schruijer 2017). On the other hand such a stakeholder can also act as a gatekeeper, blocking the information flow in the network (Burt 1995). Due to the dependency of others, on the stakeholders with high betweenness centrality, the latter is often considered an indicator of the power and influence these actors have in an MPS (Krackhardt 1996). In other words, given the high degree of interdependence experienced by stakeholders in MPSs, seeking a central position in the collaborative process is an advantageous strategy for maintaining one's status, power, and influence in such systems.

2.2. Trust Self-Enhancement and Centrality in MPS Systems

Trust or perceptions of trustworthiness refer to an individual or shared group belief that another stakeholder (individual or group) is honest, reliable (i.e., makes efforts to uphold commitments), and fair i.e., will not take advantage given the opportunity) (Cummings and Bromiley 1996; Zaheer et al. 1998). Whether within-group or between groups, trust is therefore a lubricant for social relations. Abundant research showed that trust increases cooperation (and cooperation further increases trust in a spiral effect (Ferrin et al. 2008), and it does so even in the absence of authority relations (Bradach and

Eccles 1989), itfosters information sharing and reduces the need to monitor others' behaviors (Curall and Judge 1995; Uzzi 1997).

To summarize, conventional theorizing of trust and social networks suggests that trust in others is a key ingredient for cooperation and communication (Rousseau et al. 1998). In other words, if stakeholders trust other stakeholders, they will be inclined to reach out, establish ties, cooperate, and ultimately increase their collaborative centrality. However, as argued by Edelenbos and van Meerkerk (2015), "the relations between connective capacity, trust and boundary spanning are not unproblematic" (p. 27) as generalized trust in others could also generate lock-in effects and ultimately isolate stakeholders in sparse ego-centric social networks and decrease their network centrality. In an exploration of social networks emerging in a water governance context (in the U.S. National Estuary Program), Berardo (2009) showed that if a particular stakeholder trusted another party, they did not seek to establish ties with additional parties in the system that were trusted by their trustee. However, if the initial level of trust towards a party was low, stakeholders made sure that they were accurately informed by seeking input from all parties in the system. Berardo (2009) suggests that the network behavior of stakeholders with a generalized lack of trust in others could be driven by self-defense and motivate these (non-trusting) stakeholders to acquire a central position in the network, in order to be well informed and establish (or maintain) a strategic advantage. We argue that trust self-enhancement is actually the driving mechanism explaining one's network centrality. Network behavior is driven by social comparison, and if a stakeholder has a substantial amount of self-trust and rather low trust in others (high trust self-enhancement and high group distinctiveness), they will tend to establish and maintain a large number of social ties and become a central actor in the network and acquire more power.

The role of trust self-enhancement in MPSs is grounded in the extension to the intergroup interactions of the expectation states theory (Berger et al. 1974; Berger et al. 1977). In line with this theory, the stakeholder groups form expectations about how much they trust themselves and the other stakeholders, as well as their collaborative intentions. Before the groups have the chance to interact with one another, they build a generalized anticipation related to the trustworthiness and collaborativeness of the other stakeholders in the system (Curşeu and Schruijer 2018). Trust self-enhancement, as we argued before, increases group distinctiveness and the motivation to establish and maintain an advantageous position in the MPS social network. Therefore, trust self-enhancement becomes a basis for expected and real status and prestige differences among stakeholders (Berger et al. 1974; Berger et al. 1977). Given the high interdependence experienced in MPSs, trusting oneself more than others may foster self-interest and motivate stakeholders to seek contact with as many stakeholders as possible in order to maintain a sense of control and a high group distinctiveness. We argue that trust self-enhancement increases stakeholders' expectations to achieve a central network position fosters their collaborative efforts and ultimately influences the real experienced centrality in the MPS (as indicated by betweenness and closeness centrality).

Social identity and social categorization theories (Tajfel and Turner 1979) state that social categorization ("us" versus "them") is associated with in-group valorization (i.e., ascribing positive intentions and qualities to in-group members) and out-group devaluation (i.e., assigning negative qualities and intentions to out-group members). We argue that trust self-enhancement (i.e., a difference in the level of perceived trustworthiness of "our" group versus the other groups operating in the system) is likely to arise and point towards a self-enhancement inter-group strategy (i.e., we perceive "our" group to be more trustworthy compared to the way we perceive the other groups in the system). In other words, trust self-enhancement motivates the groups to seek and maintain a central position in the collaboration network in order to maintain their distinctiveness.

Therefore, our study investigates the role of trust self-enhancement in stakeholders' centrality in the social network that emerges in MPSs as these stakeholders seek agreement in a decision situation. Moreover, ones' expectations of collaboration centrality will sequentially predict the centrality of that stakeholder in the social network as intergroup interactions progress. *We therefore hypothesize that:*

Hypothesis 1 (H1): *Trust self-enhancement has a positive influence on the perceived stakeholder centrality in the social networks across time.*

3. Methods

3.1. Sample and Procedure

This study used a participative learning experience developed based on the principles of a multiparty simulation described in Vansina et al. (1998). The simulation was developed as a learning tool to be used in educational settings in order to teach students about inter-organizational relationships and group dynamics. The data were collected during nine simulations with a total of 239 participants (198 females, average age 23.65 years), nested in 54 groups. The participants were bachelor's and master's degree students, enrolled in a Romanian University, and the simulation was part of their curricular activity. Each simulation included six groups acting as representatives of organizations that have a high stake in the Romanian education system: The Ministry of National Education, The Romanian Agency for Quality Assurance in Higher Education, The National Trade Unions Federation, The National Alliance of Student Organizations in Romania, The Romanian Association of Entrepreneurs, and The Civil Society. Their task was to reach consensus on a decision regarding two critical topics of Education Law. Specifically, the task was to decide (through consensus) whether two articles from the education law (related to university rankings and funding based on academic performance) should be immediately applied, postponed for a limited or unlimited period of time, or suspended. In other words, the simulation creates a multi-party decision context in which several stakeholders collaborate to make a decision in which they have vested interests.

Each simulation started with a briefing on the role that each of the six stakeholders has for the Romanian education system and on the structure of the simulation. The stakeholders interacted in real time and the simulation lasted one day. Therefore, during intergroup interactions, the stakeholders could not avail the passage of time beyond the amount of time allocated for the simulation (e.g., thus, they could not assume that several days/weeks have passed). Groups started with an initial within-group discussion (the first survey took place after this stage, at Time 1), followed by three iterations of 45 min between-group visits (where only a maximum of three stakeholders were allowed in the same room), and plenary sessions with delegates from each stakeholder in the system (subsequent evaluations took place after each plenary session at Times 2, 3, and 4). After the initial briefing, the participants were asked to express their preferences for a maximum of three stakeholders involved in the system or for taking an observer role. Based on their expressed preferences, each participant was assigned to a stakeholder group and instructed to study the booklets containing information about their interests, expertise, and access to resources, as well as general information about each of the remaining stakeholder in the MPS. All simulations ended with a debriefing session focused on reflecting on the within and between group dynamics.

3.2. Measures

Participants were asked to fill in a questionnaire at four time points: after the first in-group meeting (Time 1—planning the strategy, before interacting with the other groups), and after each of the three plenaries (Times 2, 3, and 4)—the round table meetings where delegates attempted to integrate the information they had collected during visiting times and to reach consensus. The questionnaire was based on a round robin procedure (each stakeholder evaluated all the other stakeholders in the system including self-ratings) and included measures of trust and collaborative relations. The questionnaire at Time 1 evaluated the expectations one had regarding the trustworthiness and collaboration of the stakeholders in the system, and at Times 2, 3, and 4, the items referred to perceptions regarding the experienced collaborativeness of each stakeholder.

At Time 1 we used a round robin procedure to evaluate the expected trustworthiness of one's own and the other groups, on a seven-point Likert scale (1 = "not at all" to 7 = "very much"). The item was worded as follows: *Based on the information you have gathered so far, how trustworthy is the organization "X"?* Trust self-enhancement was evaluated using a procedure described in Kwan et al. (2004) as the difference between self-rated trust and trust ascribed to all the other stakeholders in the system. According to Kwan et al. (2004), this self-enhancement index reflects (favorable) social comparison processes or the extent to which the members of a stakeholder group perceive their own group as more trustworthy than they perceive the other stakeholders in the system.

To compute network centrality, we used a matrix approach, and asked respondents to generate pairwise evaluations of the collaboration between the stakeholders in the system: *Based on the information you have gathered so far, please rate the quality of the relation between all the organizations.* Therefore, we asked participants to fill out a matrix containing all dyadic relations among stakeholders. The evaluations were made on a scale between −5 and +5 (where −5 refers to a very conflictual relation and +5 to a very collaborative relation, 0 represents the absence of conflict or the absence of collaboration). Therefore, to estimate the collaborative ties, we have recoded all negative values as zero. We have focused on the ties participants reported for their own group as these are most likely to be the accurate representations of the collaborative relations in MPSs (participants might have had misconceptions about the relations among other groups in the MPS) (Casciaro 1998). As such, the centrality indices were computed by aggregating individual perceptions of own group centrality in the context of the MPS network. Networks were generated for each group, in each session, at four time intervals. As indicators of network centrality, we have used two indices that estimate centrality for each stakeholder in the network relative to the rest of the network, namely closeness and betweenness centrality. Closeness centrality is a measure defined as the sum of geodesic distances from a node to all others in the network. Geodesic distance from a node to another node is the length of the shortest path connecting them (Freeman 1979). In other words, closeness centrality is an estimate of how central a particular stakeholder in the generic MPS network is. A stakeholder with high closeness centrality indicates that the members of the respective stakeholder group perceive it "in the middle" of the MPS network. Betweenness centrality is a measure of how often a given node falls along the shortest path between two other nodes, and is typically interpreted in terms of the potential for controlling flows through the network. The betweenness of a target stakeholder in the MPS network estimates the relative number of stakeholder pairs that can only communicate with each other via the target stakeholder. Therefore, a node with a high betweenness is very likely to have substantial power because it can control the possibility of other nodes reaching each other via efficient paths (Freeman 1979).

4. Results

Means, standard deviations, and correlations are presented in Table 1.

In order to perform the network analyses, data was processed in the open-source statistical programming language R (R Core Team 2013, Vienna, Austria). Networks were generated by aggregating individual perceptions within each group, in each simulation, at four points in time. Networks visualization was run using the qgraph package from R (Epskamp et al. 2012) and the igraph package (Csardi and Nepusz 2006). In order to weight the degree of collaboration for each stakeholder nested in each simulation, we used the scores ranging from 0 to +5 where 0 represents absence of collaboration and +5 a very collaborative relationship (scores between −5 and 0 were excluded as they were illustrative of conflictual relations and not collaboration.). The aggregated networks obtained were in the form of weighted undirected networks with multiple ties. Closeness and betweenness indices (Freeman 1979) were computed with the centrality function from qgraph packages. This function computes and returns betweenness and closeness indices between all pairs of nodes in the graph with a tuning parameter of $\alpha = 1$. When $\alpha = 1$, the outcome is the same as the one obtained with the classical Dijkstra's algorithm (Dijkstra 1959; Opsahl et al. 2010).

Table 1. Means, standard deviations, and correlations for the variables included in the study.

	Mean	SD	1	2	3	4	5	6	7	8	9	10	11
1. Group size	4.31	1.29											
2. TR Self T1	4.82	1.12	−0.108										
3. TR To T1	4.85	0.71	0.014	−0.021									
4. TRSE T1	−0.04	1.34	−0.098	0.847 **	−0.549 **								
5. CollBet T1	2.98	5.49	−0.288 *	0.456 **	0.069	0.345 *							
6. CollBet T2	2.22	3.64	−0.120	0.214	0.305 *	0.017	0.425 **						
7. CollBet T3	3.26	4.98	−0.146	0.228	0.318 *	0.022	0.404 **	0.614 **					
8. CollBet T4	1.93	4.74	−0.033	0.296 *	0.251	0.114	0.425 **	0.517 **	0.641 **				
9. CollClo T1	1.01	0.66	0.272 *	0.314 *	−0.010	0.268	0.264	0.196	0.090	−0.092			
10. CollClo T2	0.76	0.50	−0.212	−0.023	−0.024	−0.007	0.011	0.378 **	0.183	−0.028	0.568 **		
11. CollClo T3	0.67	0.49	−0.165	0.028	0.026	0.010	0.278 *	0.360 **	0.296 *	0.139	0.311 *	0.637 **	
12. CollClo T4	1.55	0.79	0.003	0.013	0.064	−0.023	0.230	0.395 **	0.411 **	0.313 *	0.382 **	0.415 **	0.546 **

Note: TR Self—trust self-rated, TR To—trust ascribed to others, TRSE—trust self-enhancement, CollBet = collaboration betweenness, CollClo = collaboration closeness, SD—standard deviation, T1 = Time 1, T2 = Time 2, etc., * $p < 0.05$; ** $p < 0.01$.

As we collected data in four successive waves during the simulation, we could explore sequential mediation models (model 6) using the Process Macro (Preacher and Hayes 2008, Preacher and Hayes 2008). As network indicators were computed based on aggregated networks at the group level, we entered group size as a covariate in the analyses. We then estimated sequential mediation paths from trust self-enhancement as evaluated at Time 1 (expectations) to subsequent centrality scores in the four time lags. The results of the mediation analysis for betweenness as an indicator of network centrality are presented in Table 2 and summarized in Figure 1.

Table 2. Overview of the mediation effects estimated in our analyses.

Estimated Mediation Chains	Betweenness Centrality		Closeness Centrality	
	Effect Size (SE)	95% CI	Effect Size (SE)	95% CI
TSE→CT1→CT4	0.25 (0.27)	[−0.07, 1.03]	0.03 (0.03)	[−0.01, 0.11]
TSE→CT1→CT2→CT4	0.09 (0.13)	[−0.03, 52]	−0.01 (0.01)	[−0.05, 0.01]
TSE→CT1→CT3→CT4	0.10 (0.17)	[−0.02, 0.78]	−0.01 (0.01)	[−0.04, 0.01]
TSE→CT1→CT2→CT3→CT4	0.13 (0.12)	[0.01, 0.70]	0.02 (0.01)	[0.01, 0.05]
TSE→CT2→CT4	−0.09 (0.13)	[−0.55, 0.04]	0.01 (0.02)	[−0.01, 0.08]
TSE→CT2→CT3→CT4	−0.12 (0.10)	[−0.55, −0.01]	−0.02 (0.02)	[−0.07, 0.01]
TSE→CT3→CT4	−0.09 (0.20)	[−0.67, 0.22]	0.01 (0.04)	[−0.05, 0.09]

Note: TSE—trust self-enhancement, CT1—centrality at Time 1, CT2—centrality at Time 2, CT3—centrality at Time 3, CT4—centrality at Time 4.

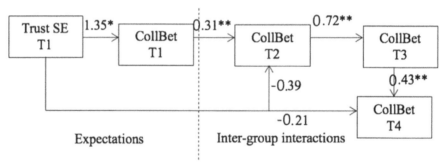

Figure 1. Results of the sequential mediation model for collaboration betweenness. Note: SE—self-enhancement, CollBet—collaboration betweenness, T1 = Time 1, T2 = Time 2, etc., * $p < 0.05$; ** $p < 0.01$; path coefficients are non-standardized coefficients reported from the most complete model, i.e., the model in which all previous variables in the mediation chain are included.

The full sequential mediation chain from trust self-enhancement expectations, to collaboration betweenness at Time 1, then at Times 2, 3, and 4 is significant. The indirect effect (trust self-enhancement → collaboration betweenness at T1 → collaboration betweenness at T2 → collaboration betweenness at T3 → collaboration betweenness at T4) was positive and significant, the effect size was 0.13 (SE = 0.12), with a 95% confidence interval (CI) of 0.01–0.70, and because the confidence interval did not contain zero, we can conclude that the indirect effect was positive and significant as hypothesized. In other words, trust self-enhancement had a positive influence on the perceived betweenness at the end of the simulation, by sequentially increasing betweenness at Time 1, then Time 2, then Time 3 and Time 4. However, the results of the sequential mediation revealed an additional significant indirect effect. This indirect effect led from trust self-enhancement expectations at Time 1 to betweenness at Time 2, then Time 3, then Time 4, thus estimating the effect of trust expectations on network centrality as estimated after the inter-group interactions commence. This indirect effect was, however, negative: −0.12 (SE = 0.10), 95% CI [−0.55, −0.01], and as the confidence interval did not include zero, the effect was considered significant. In other words, trust self-enhancement negatively predicted the betweenness at the end of the simulation, by sequentially decreasing betweenness at Times 2 and 3.

We used a similar bootstrapping procedure to estimate the sequential mediation effects from trust expectations to network closeness. The results of the mediation analysis for the closeness centrality indicator are presented in Table 2 and summarized in Figure 2.

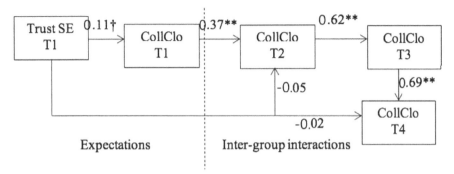

Figure 2. Results of the sequential mediation model for collaboration closeness. Note: SE—self-enhancement, CollClo—collaboration closeness, T1 = Time 1, T2 = Time 2, etc.; [†] $p < 0.10$, ** $p < 0.01$; path coefficients are non-standardized coefficients reported from the most complete model, i.e., the model in which all previous variables in the mediation chain are included.

As indicated by the path coefficients presented in Figure 2, the full sequential indirect effect (trust self-enhancement → collaboration closeness at T1 → collaboration closeness at T2 → collaboration closeness at T3 → collaboration closeness at T4) was positive. The indirect effect was 0.02 (SE = 0.01), 95% CI [0.01, 0.05], and as the confidence interval did not include zero, we can conclude that the effect was significant. The sequential mediation analysis for closeness did not reveal any other significant indirect effects; therefore, we can conclude that the indirect effect for closeness was aligned with our hypothesis. A full summary of all mediation effects estimated with model 6 in the Process Macro (Preacher and Hayes 2008) is presented in Table 2.

5. Discussion

This study explores the implications of trust self-enhancement (i.e., a group assigns more trust to oneself as compared to the trust assigned to the other stakeholder groups) for the evolution of perceived centrality (expected before the intergroup interactions and experienced during the intergroup interactions) in the MPSs. More exactly, we analyzed the impact of trust self-enhancement expectations on betweenness and closeness centrality indices as they evolved during the intergroup interactions in an MPS composed of six stakeholders dealing with a complex decision task.

As the results show, trust self-enhancement was a precursor of network centrality in the sense that trust self-enhancement at Time 1 (one's own group is perceived as more trustworthy as compared to the other stakeholders in the MPS) led to increased expectations regarding one's own betweenness and closeness centrality at Time 1 (prior to the interactions with other stakeholders). Then, these expectations sequentially increased the perceptions of experienced betweenness and closeness centrality at Times 2, 3, and 4.

Stakeholders that perceived themselves as being more trustworthy (i.e., more honest, reliable, and less likely to exploit the others), than the other stakeholders in the MPS, were motivated to seek and maintain a central position in the MPS network in order to maintain a high group distinctiveness and ultimately acquire more power. Central stakeholders could make useful contributions to the task at hand by sharing relevant information and by trying to integrate the differences stemming from the other stakeholder groups in the system that might not be otherwise connected through betweenness centrality (ultimately central actors may become more powerful this way). Moreover, expectations regarding one's own betweenness centrality in the collaboration network were further positively associated with perceptions regarding one's betweenness centrality observed in real inter-group interactions throughout the simulation. As previously argued, enacting such a bridging role within the MPS was an indicator of the stakeholder's power and influence within the system. Such a privileged position may have a beneficial impact for the success of the collaboration process, since, in order to achieve a comprehensive decision, the system is required to integrate the needs and concerns of all actors involved in the process (Schruijer 2006; Gray 2007; Curşeu and Schruijer 2017) and a stakeholder with high betweenness centrality can facilitate this process. However, such a stakeholder may also act as a gatekeeper, blocking the information flow and thus impeding the collaboration process (Burt 1995). In MPSs involved in decision-making tasks, as was the case in our study, such central stakeholders acting as gatekeepers may have prevented consensus to emerge.

Similarly, trust self-enhancement was positively associated with closeness centrality in the collaboration network throughout the simulation. Viewing one's own group as more trustworthy led first to an anticipation of having a more central position in the system, which, in turn, materialized in experienced closeness. The emergence of closeness centrality was relevant for the collaboration process, as the stakeholder groups that relationally are on average closer to the other stakeholders in the system (i.e., they have a high level of closeness centrality) could more easily gather useful information, communicate interests throughout the network, and help with integrating the diverse points of view. On the other hand, high levels of closeness centrality may also impede the potential for fruitful collaboration, as such central stakeholders may push forward their (hidden) agenda, by suppressing diversity and prevent participation, especially from less powerful stakeholders in the system (Curşeu and Schruijer 2017).

These results extend the expectations state theory (Berger et al. 1974; Berger et al. 1977) by showing that prior to engaging in intergroup interactions, self-enhanced perceptions of trust lead to expectations about a high centrality in the MPS network. These expectations are probably rooted in two mechanisms: self-esteem and self-defense. On the one hand, high self-trust mobilizes the stakeholder to actively engage in intergroup interactions, and on the other hand, rather low trust of others may stimulate the stakeholder to reach out to others in order to establish and maintain control over their actions in an MPS. Seeking and maintaining a high centrality in the MPS network is likely to be a mechanism that allows stakeholders to maintain their high distinctiveness as a group related to trust self-enhancement.

An important claim based on these results is that collaboration starts in the minds of those involved and it is later on shaped by the contextual dynamics and social complexities emerging in MPSs. This adds value to practice as well. The onset of interactions in MPSs seems to be crucial. Prior to any kind of interactions between the stakeholders, consultants and managers can guide the stakeholders to work with themselves and engage in reflective processes about the positive impact of their role in the system and empower them to create expectations about the contribution they can bring to the system.

Our findings also revealed an additional effect regarding the implications of trust self-enhancement for collaborative betweenness network centrality in interactions (not mediated by betweenness centrality expectations evaluated at Time 1). The indirect effect of trust self-enhancement via experienced collaboration betweenness at Time 2, and the sequentially at Time 3 and Time 4, was negative and significant (effect size -0.12, SE = 0.10, 95% CI [-0.55, -0.01]). Through this mediation path that excluded expectations of betweenness, trust self-enhancement actually decreased betweenness after the onset of intergroup interactions (although this effect was not significant). It was therefore likely that this negative significant indirect effect was explained by the sequential positive association between collaboration betweenness at Times 2, 3, and 4. A potential explanation is that initial trust self-enhancement may lead to overconfidence concerning one's centrality position in the MPS network. When the interactions begin, the stakeholders with high trust self-enhancement may discover that the other stakeholders do not perceive them as being so central in the system. Overconfidence could therefore be an alternative mechanism that explains the workings of trust self-enhancement in MPS.

This emergent result points towards a dual mechanism that connects trust self-enhancement with betweenness centrality. On the one hand, trust self-enhancement influences the expected network position and enhances one's centrality in the collaboration network. On the other hand, trust self-enhancement may generate overconfidence in one's position, that leads to a decrease in collaboration centrality after real between-group interactions start. We could fully explore the first mechanism through the sequential mediation analyses reported in Figures 1 and 2. However, we did not collect data on overconfidence that could elucidate the second mechanism likely to be involved here. Future research could further explore the co-existence of these two mechanisms linking trust self-enhancement expectations to centrality in the collaborative network.

To conclude, the main contribution of this study is the result concerning the sequential development of betweenness and closeness centrality, in line with the view of multiparty systems as dynamic entities (Curşeu and Schruijer 2017). In such a system, stakeholders with sometimes very different concerns and agendas interact in the hope of reaching a common goal that cannot be envisioned from the start of the interaction. In order to do so, the stakeholders are expected to share their interests and concerns and use their expertise to work through disagreements. Often, however, they start their interactions based on initial assumptions about each other, which they subsequently test and (re)shape according to the information gathered during intergroup interactions. In turn, the emerging cognitive structures (social networks in minds) will further influence the network centrality of the stakeholders. The structure of the collaboration network is thus subject to constant change, in line with the within and between group dynamics.

Our paper also points towards the relevance of using a social network analysis in the exploration of MPSs dynamics. Modern analytical approaches allow the integration of various network perceptions in aggregated social networks that capture the relational landscape of MPSs. Next to the benefit of using these approaches in research, one could envisage dynamic social network visualization tools used by facilitators of MPSs. MPS stakeholders are often trapped in the social dynamics of these systems and process interventions that may rely on social network visualization tools, which are needed in order to help the system overcome the hurdles of conflict and relational tensions and optimize the collaborative efforts.

Next to the contributions, our study has limitations as well. We have used a behavioral simulation, with a specific decision task and our results may not generalize to other tasks, inter-organizational settings, or MPSs. In order to ensure generalizability, our results need to be replicated in other settings and using other evaluation methods as well. Each of the simulations contained six stakeholder groups; therefore, the size of the social network was rather small, a fact that could have restricted the variance in our centrality measures. Moreover, our network analytic approach aggregated individual relational perceptions (or expectations at Time 1) within groups, and in doing so, we obtained a more accurate image of network centrality. However, we cannot claim that our measure of network centrality was based on objective, measurement-error free data. Rather we claim that due to the aggregation method used, we rely on intersubjective aggregation as an indicator of collaboration. Future research could extend these network approaches in MPSs and use more objective network indicators. Finally, our results focused on collaboration network centrality and no definite claims can be derived about the success of such collaborative relations. High betweenness and closeness may eventually be detrimental for the relational dynamics in multiparty collaboration. Stakeholders with high betweenness may act strategically and display dysfunctional inter-group behavior by filtering and distorting the information shared among the other stakeholders. Moreover, MPSs in which closeness is very high may eventually display collusive dynamics with negative implications for the outcomes of such MPSs (Gray and Schruijer 2010). Future research could investigate more directly the association between the two centrality indicators and collaborative goal achievement in MPSs.

6. Conclusions

Our study contributes to the literature on the dynamics of multiparty systems by using a relational, social-network approach to investigate how trust self-enhancement at the onset of inter-organizational relations impacts the evolution of collaboration centrality. Although the pivotal role of trust in collaboration was extensively explored so far, we show that collaboration network centrality displays a certain sequential development as it is only possible to predict centrality indicators from the ones evaluated in the previous time frame. This element is common to the social complex-adaptive systems that display such a sequential dynamic (Curşeu 2006). In other words, we show that a particular state of a multiparty system (e.g., collaboration centrality) can be predicted by using the previous state alone and not the more distant states. In order to understand the collaboration outcomes in such systems, one must understand the sequence of events in a comprehensive manner. It is therefore difficult to predict the outcomes of a multiparty system from compositional features or from its initial state alone. One needs to follow and comprehend the sequences of actions and interactions in such systems in order to grasp the complex nature of inter-organizational interactions.

Author Contributions: O.C.F., P.L.C. and A.M.F. designed and conducted the study; I.O. analyzed and aggregated the network data, P.L.C., O.C.F. and A.M.F. analyzed the data; O.C.F., A.M.F., P.L.C. and I.O. wrote and revised the paper. These authors contributed equally to this work.

Funding: P.L.C. and A.M.F. were supported by a grant of the Romanian National Authority for Scientific Research, CNCS—UEFISCDI, project number PN-III-P4-ID-ERC-2016-0008. The funders had no role in study design, data collection and analysis, decision to publish, or preparation of the manuscript.

Conflicts of Interest: The authors declare no conflicts of interest.

References

Berardo, Ramiro. 2009. Generalized trust in multi-organizational policy arenas: Studying its emergence from a network perspective. *Political Research Quarterly* 62: 178–89. [CrossRef]

Berger, Joseph, Thomas L. Conner, and M. Hamit Fisek. 1974. *Expectation States Theory: A Theoretical Research Program*. Cambridge: Winthrop.

Berger, Joseph, M. Hamit Fisek, and Robert Z. Norman. 1977. Status characteristics and Expectation States: A Graph-Theoretic Formulation. In *Status Characteristics and Social Interaction: An Expectation State's Approach*. Edited by Joseph Berger, M. Hamit Fisek, Robert Z. Norman and Morris Zelditch Jr. New York: Elsevier.

Bouwen, René, and Tharsi Taillieu. 2004. Multi-party collaboration as social learning for interdependence: Developing relational knowing for sustainable natural resource management. *Journal of Community and Applied Social Psychology* 14: 137–53. [CrossRef]

Bradach, Jeffrey L., and Robert G. Eccles. 1989. Price, authority, and trust: From ideals types to plural forms. *Annual Review of Sociology* 15: 97–118. [CrossRef]

Brass, Daniel J., and Marlene E. Burkhardt. 1993. Potential power and power use: An investigation of structure and behavior. *The Academy of Management Journal* 36: 441–70. [CrossRef]

Brass, Daniel J., and David Krackhardt. 1999. The social capital of 21st century leaders. In *Out-of-the-Box Leadership*. Edited by J. G. Hunt and R. L. Phillips. Stamford: JAI Press, pp. 179–94.

Burt, Ronald S. 1995. *Structural Holes: The Social Structure of Competition*. Cambridge: Harvard University Press.

Casciaro, Tiziana. 1998. Seeing things clearly: Social structure, personality, and accuracy in social network perception. *Social Networks* 20: 331–51. [CrossRef]

Costa, Ana Cristina, C. Ashley Fulmer, and Neil R. Anderson. 2018. Trust in work teams: An integrative review, multilevel model, and future directions. *The Journal of Organizational Behavior* 39: 169–84. [CrossRef]

Csardi, Gabor, and Tamas Nepusz. 2006. The igraph software package for complex network research. *Journal of Complex Systems* 1695: 1–10.

Cummings, Larry L., and Philip Bromiley. 1996. The organizational trust inventory: Development and validation. In *Trust in Organizations: Frontiers of Theory and Research*. Edited by Roderick Kramer and Tom Tyler. Thousand Oaks: Sage Publications, Inc.

Curall, Steven C., and Timothy A. Judge. 1995. Measuring trust between organizational boundaries role persons. *Organizational Behavior & Human Decision Processes* 64: 151–70. [CrossRef]

Curşeu, Petru Lucian. 2006. Emergent states in virtual teams: A complex adaptive systems perspective. *Journal of Information Technology* 21: 249–61. [CrossRef]

Curşeu, Petru Lucian, and Sandra Schruijer. 2010. Does conflict shatter trust or does trust obliterate conflict? Revisiting the relationships between team diversity, conflict, and trust. *Group Dynamics: Theory, Research and Practice* 14: 66–79. [CrossRef]

Curşeu, Petru Lucian, and Sandra Schruijer. 2017. Stakeholder diversity and the comprehensiveness of sustainability decisions: The role of collaboration and conflict. *Current Opinion in Environmental Sustainability* 28: 114–20. [CrossRef]

Curşeu, Petru Lucian, and Sandra Schruijer. 2018. Cross-level dynamics of collaboration and conflict in multiparty systems: An empirical investigation using a behavioural simulation. *Administrative Sciences* 8: 26. [CrossRef]

Deutsch, Morton. 1949. A theory of co-operation and competition. *Human Relations* 2: 129–52. [CrossRef]

Dijkstra, Edsger Wybe. 1959. A note on two problems in connexion with graphs. *Numerische Mathematik* 1: 269–71. [CrossRef]

Edelenbos, Jurian, and Ingmar van Meerkerk. 2015. Connective capacity in water governance practices: The meaning of trust and boundary spanning for integrated performance. *Current Opinion in Environmental Sustainability* 12: 25–29. [CrossRef]

Epskamp, Sacha, Angelique O. J. Cramer, Lourens J. Waldorp, Verena D. Schmittmann, and Denny Borsboom. 2012. qgraph: Network Visualizations of Relationships in Psychometric Data. *Journal of Statistical Software* 48: 1–18. [CrossRef]

Ferrin, Donald L., Michelle C. Bligh, and Jeffrey C. Kohles. 2008. It Takes Two to Tango: An Interdependence Analysis of the Spiraling of Perceived Trustworthiness and Cooperation in Interpersonal and Intergroup Relationships. *Organizational Behavior and Human Decision Processes* 107: 161–78. [CrossRef]

Fleştea, Alina M., Petru L. Curşeu, and Oana C. Fodor. 2017. The bittersweet effect of power disparity: Implications for emergent states in collaborative multiparty systems. *Journal of Managerial Psychology* 32: 401–16. [CrossRef]

Freeman, Linton C. 1979. Centrality in social networks: Conceptual clarification. *Social Networks* 1: 251–39. [CrossRef]

Gray, Barbara. 1985. Conditions facilitating interorganizational collaboration. *Human Relations* 38: 911–36. [CrossRef]

Gray, Barbara. 1989. *Collaborating: Finding Common Ground for Multiparty Problems*. San Francisco: Jossey-Bass Publishers.

Gray, Barbara. 2007. Intervening to improve inter-organizational partnerships. In *The Oxford Handbook of Inter-Organizational Relations*. Edited by Steve Cropper, Chris Huxham and Peter Smith Ring. Oxford: Oxford University Press, pp. 664–90.

Gray, Barbara, and Sandra Schruijer. 2010. Integrating multiple voices: Working with collusion in multiparty collaborations. In *Relational Practices, Participative Organizing*. Edited by Chris Steyart and Bart van Looy. Bingley: Emerald Group Publishing Limited, pp. 121–35.

Hansen, Morten T. 1999. The search-transfer problem: The role of weak ties in sharing knowledge across organization subunits. *Administrative Science Quarterly* 44: 82–111. [CrossRef]

Holmes, John G. 2002. Interpersonal expectations as the building blocks of social cognition. An interdependence theory perspective. *Personal Relationships* 9: 1–26. [CrossRef]

Kilduff, Martin, and Daniel Brass. 2010. Organizational social network research: Core ideas and key debates. *The Academy of Management Annals* 4: 317–57. [CrossRef]

Kilduff, Martin, and David Krackhardt. 1994. Bringing the individual back in: A structural analysis of the internal market for reputation in organizations. *Academy of Management Journal* 37: 87–108. [CrossRef]

Krackhardt, David. 1996. Social networks and liability of newness for managers. In *Trends in Organizational Behavior*. Edited by Cary L. Copper and Denise M. Rousseau. New York: John Wiley & Sons, Ltd., pp. 159–73.

Kwan, Virginia S.Y., David A. Kenny, Oliver P. John, Michael H. Bond, and Richard W. Robins. 2004. Reconceptualizing individual differences in self-enhancement bias: An interpersonal approach. *Psychological Review* 111: 94. [CrossRef] [PubMed]

Oh, Hongseok, Myung-Ho Chung, and Giuseppe LaBianca. 2004. Group social capital and group effectiveness: The role of informal socializing ties. *Academy of Management* 47: 860–75. [CrossRef]

Opsahl, Tore, Filip Agneessens, and John Skvoretz. 2010. Node centrality in weighted networks: Generalizing degree and shortest paths. *Social Networks* 32: 245–51. [CrossRef]

Pastor, Juan-Carlos, James R. Meindl, and Margarita C. Mayo. 2002. A network effects model of charisma attributions. *The Academy of Management Journal* 45: 410–20.

Preacher, Kristopher J., and Andrew F. Hayes. 2008. Asymptotic and resampling strategies for assessing and comparing indirect effects in multiple mediator models. *Behavior Research Methods* 40: 879–91. [CrossRef] [PubMed]

R Core Team. 2013. *R: A Language and Environment for Statistical Computing*. Vienna: R Foundation for Statistical Computing, Available online: http://www.R-project.org/ (accessed on 22 December 2017).

Rousseau, Denise M., Sim B. Sitkin, Ronald S. Burt, and Colin Camerer. 1998. Not so different after all: A cross-discipline view of trust. *Academy of Management Review* 23: 393–404. [CrossRef]

Schruijer, Sandra. 2006. Research on collaboration in action. *International Journal of Action Research* 2: 222–42.

Schruijer, Sandra. 2008. The psychology of interorganizational relations. In *The Oxford Handbook of Interorganizational Relations*. Edited by Steve Cropper, Mark Ebers, Chris Huxham and Peter Smith Ring. New York and Oxford: Oxford University Press, pp. 417–40.

Schruijer, Sandra, and Leopold Vansina. 2008. Working across Organisational Boundaries: Understanding and working with the psychological dynamics. In *Psychodynamics for Consultants and Manager*. Edited by Leopold Vansina and Marie-Jeanne Vansina-Cobbaert. Hoboken: John Wiley & Sons, pp. 390–410.

Snijders, Tom A. 2001. The statistical evaluation of social network dynamics. *Sociological Methodology* 31: 361–95. [CrossRef]

Tajfel, Henri, and John C. Turner. 1979. The social identity theory of intergroup behavior. In *Psychology of Intergroup Relations*. Edited by Stephen Worchel and William G. Austin. Chicago: Nelson-Hall, pp. 7–24.

Tsai, Wenpin. 2001. Knowledge transfer in intraorganizational networks: Effects if network position and absorptive capacity on business unit innovation and performance. *The Academy of Management Journal* 44: 996–1004.

Uzzi, Brian. 1997. Social structure and competition in interfirm networks: The paradox of embeddedness. *Administrative Quarterly* 42: 35–67. [CrossRef]

Vansina, Leopold, and Tharsi Taillieu. 1997. Diversity in collaborative task-systems. *European Journal of Work and Organizational Psychology* 6: 183–99. [CrossRef]

Vansina, Leopold, Tharsi C. B. Taillieu, and Sandra G. L. Schruijer. 1998. Managing multiparty issues: Learning from experience. In *Research in Organizational Change and Development*. Edited by William Pasmore and Richard Woodman. Bingley: Emerald, vol. 11, pp. 159–83.

Westbay, James D., Danielle L. Pfaff, and Nicholas Redding. 2014. Psychology and Social Networks. A dynamic Perspective. *American Psychologist* 69: 269–84. [CrossRef] [PubMed]

Zaheer, Akbar, Bill McEvily, and Vincenzo Perrone. 1998. Does trust matter? Exploring the effects of interorganizational and interpersonal trust on performance. *Organization Science* 9: 141–59. Available online: http://nbn-resolving.de/urn:nbn:de:0168-ssoar-370051 (accessed on 21 March 2018). [CrossRef]

Article

Cross-Level Dynamics of Collaboration and Conflict in Multi-Party Systems: An Empirical Investigation Using a Behavioural Simulation

Petru Lucian Curseu [1,2,*] and Sandra Schruijer [3,4]

[1] Department of Psychology, Babeş-Bolyai University, Cluj-Napoca 400084, Romania
[2] Department of Organisation, Open University of the Netherlands, Valkenburgerweg 177,
    6419 AT Heerlen, The Netherlands
[3] Utrecht University School of Governance, Utrecht University, Bijlhouwerstraat 6, 3511 ZC Utrecht,
    The Netherlands; S.G.L.Schruijer@uu.nl
[4] TIAS School for Business and Society, Tilburg University, Warandelaan 2, 5037 AB Tilburg, The Netherlands
[*] Correspondence: petrucurseu@psychology.ro; Tel.: +40-264-590-967

Received: 2 April 2018; Accepted: 21 June 2018; Published: 28 June 2018

Abstract: Multiparty systems bring together various stakeholder parties and their representatives and offer a platform for sharing their diverse interests, knowledge and expertise in order to develop and realize joint goals. They display complex relational dynamics in which within-party interactions (interpersonal interactions within each stakeholder party) as well as between-party interactions (interactions between the stakeholder parties) intertwine to generate bottom-up and top-down influences. We investigate these influences in a behavioural simulation. Our results show that changes in task conflict at the stakeholder party level positively predict changes in perceived collaborativeness in the overall system, while changes in relationship conflict at the stakeholder party level positively predict changes in perceived conflictuality in the system. Moreover, we show that changes in perceived overall conflictuality leads to a proportional change in relationship conflict experienced within the stakeholder parties.

Keywords: collaboration; conflict; participation; multiparty systems; group dynamics; multilevel analysis

1. Introduction

Complex decisions with major social, environmental and economic consequences are often made by groups consisting of multiple organizations rather than by individuals alone (Curşeu and Schruijer 2017). In multiparty systems stakeholders explore their interdependencies and use their knowledge and expertise in order to integrate and develop their different perspectives and interests (Vansina et al. 1998; Schruijer and Vansina 2008; Schruijer 2016). The decision making in such systems is characterized by high complexity, given the complex nature of the problem domain, the various stakeholder parties involved and the diversities in interests, identities, perspectives and power positions. Relational dynamics in such multiparty collaborative systems shape the decision outcomes (Curşeu and Schruijer 2017; Schruijer 2008). Participants interact within their own stakeholder party to discuss their party's goals, aspirations and interests, while simultaneously they interact with the other stakeholders that have their own, often differing goals, aspirations and interests, so as to arrive at and realize a joint goal. Through this collective goal stakeholders can jointly address a problem which they cannot solve on their own, while through working towards the joint goal, stakeholders can serve their intra-organizational goals (Schruijer 2008).

In such multi-party systems, composed of several stakeholder parties, relational dynamics unfold at two levels: within stakeholder parties as well as between stakeholder parties. These two relational dimensions are not independent as the relational dynamics that arise from the stakeholder parties may influence the larger system as a whole (bottom-up influences) while system-level relational dynamics may spiral down from the larger system to influence the different stakeholder parties (top-down influences). So far, the literature on multi-party systems lacks systematic investigations of these jointly operating influences and it does not explore how task conflict and relational conflict experienced within the stakeholder parties have an impact on the relational dynamics of the system as a whole. Likewise, there is no direct empirical evidence on how changes in conflict and collaboration in the whole system influence the dynamics of task and relationship conflict within the participating stakeholder parties. We set out to explore the interplay of these bottom-up and top-down influences in multiparty systems, using a behavioural simulation.

In line with interdependence theory (Holmes 2002), when people foresee they will engage in social interactions, they build expectations about: (1) the nature of the situation and (2) the goals, motives and behaviours of the ones they will interact with. The expectations about others and the social situation will eventually shape behaviour in a variety of social contexts (Holmes 2002). In other words, in social situations, expectations and social behaviour are entwined.

In field theory and interdependence terms (Lewin 1936; Holmes 2002) two interdependence fields are generated in multiparty systems that explain the relational dynamics within as well as between parties. In the small parties (first interdependence field) people will build expectations about their own party (social situation) and their teammates (interaction partners), while in the larger multiparty system people will build expectations about the interests of other stakeholder parties and the general climate of the multiparty system as a whole. It is our contention that the expectation—behaviour entwinements at the two levels (party and multiparty system) are interdependent. More specifically our paper sets out to explore the extent to which the association between expectations and experienced social interactions within parties influences the expectation-behaviour entwinement in the larger system (bottom up influence) and the extent to which the entwinement between expectations and behaviours in the larger system is tied to the expectation-behaviour association within parties (top-down influence).

We consider the two forms of social interdependence described by Deutsch (1949), namely positive (as illustrated by collaborative intentions and behaviour) and negative (as illustrated by conflictual intentions and behaviours) interdependence. It follows that the entwinement between expectations for positive interdependence and realized collaboration within the stakeholder parties impacts the entwinement between expected collaborativeness and real collaborativeness in the larger multiparty system. Moreover, we also expect that the entwinement between expectations of negative interdependence and experienced (relationship) conflict within stakeholder parties is dependent on the same type of interdependence entwinement at the multiparty system level. We set out to explore the way in which the entwinement of expectations-experiences for positive and negative interdependence is transferred from the parties to the multiparty level (bottom-up influence) and the way in which the expectations-experiences entwinement for positive and negative interdependence at the multiparty level trickles down to impact the parties in the system (top-down influence). This interdependence dynamics and the bottom up and top down influences is depicted in Figure 1.

As the interplay between collaboration and conflict is essential for decision quality in multiparty systems (Curşeu and Schruijer 2017), our study has the potential to make several contributions to the literature. First, we answer the call for dynamic models of the interplay between emergent states in teams and multiparty systems (Costa et al. 2017; Shuffler et al. 2015; Waller et al. 2016) and we use a cross-lagged design to capture changes in collaborativeness and conflictuality. Second, we use a realistic behavioural simulation to tap into the complex dynamics of conflict and collaboration in multiparty systems and to explore the positive role of task conflict for collaboration in multiparty systems. Using a round robin method to evaluate collaborativeness and conflict, we capture both the top-down as well as the bottom-up interplay between collaboration and conflict in multiparty systems.

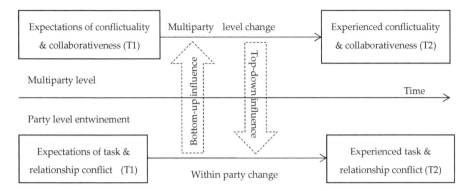

Figure 1. Bottom-up and top-down influences in multiparty systems. Note: T1 = time 1 (expectations before the interaction starts), T2 = time 2 (experienced dynamics at the party and multiparty level).

2. Theory and Hypotheses

Literature on multiparty collaboration is diverse and lacks integration (Vangen 2017). Theories of multiparty collaboration range from practice oriented theories of collaboration that theorize collaborative relations as ways in which stakeholders can achieve *collaborative advantage* (Huxham 2003; Vangen 2017) to more systemic approaches that distinguish between inputs, processes and outputs of collaborative relationships (Thomson and Perry 2006; Wood and Gray 1991). Multiparty systems are social systems composed of interdependent stakeholder parties that interact to discover ways of moving forward while dealing with existing contradictions (Vangen 2017). Collaborative relationships are inherently paradoxical as the stakeholders have to work with their similarities and their differences simultaneously in order to achieve collaborative advantage (Huxham 2003; Vangen 2017). In terms of organization, multiparty systems are formed of individuals, nested in stakeholder or interest parties that are ultimately nested in a larger system that strives for collaboration. Various interdependencies (both positive and negative) that exist among these systemic components are conceptualized as inputs for collaborative relationships (Wood and Gray 1991). These interdependencies are however not necessarily subject to formal or centralized control and members of multiparty systems have autonomy to discover viable ways of dealing with the paradoxes of collaboration (Thomson and Perry 2006). It is our contention that the paradoxes inherent to multiparty collaboration (Huxham 2003; Vangen 2017) reflect two co-existing forms of social interdependence. We further build on insights from Social Interdependence Theory (Deutsch 1949) to understand how interactions within the stakeholder parties (like conflict) influence the functioning of the whole system (bottom-up influences) while the interdependencies among the parties will shape the functioning of the individual stakeholder parties (top-down influences).

Social interdependence theory (Deutsch 1949; Johnson 2003) describes positive and negative forms of interdependence in social systems. Positive interdependence is reflected in so-called promotive or collaborative interactions in which an aggregate within the system achieves its goal only to the extent to which the other aggregates achieve their goals as well. The negative interdependence is reflected in contrient or conflictual interactions in which aggregates only achieve their goals at the expense of other aggregates in the system. In line with social interdependence theory we argue that collaborative and conflictual interactions in the system as a whole have an impact on the interactions that unfold within the aggregates.

2.1. Summary and Definitions

In our analysis, we focus on the entwinement between expectations and experienced interactions and the way in which this entwinement transfers in the system in a bottom-up versus top-down manner. We define *positive interdependence entwinement* as the association between expectations of positive interdependence and experienced collaboration (changes from expectations to what is really experienced after the interactions start) and *negative interdependence entwinement* as the association between expected negative interdependence and experienced conflict (changes from expected to experienced conflict). In what follows we will build on social interdependence theory to further specify the bottom-up and top-down influences in multiparty collaboration. Further on, we define *bottom-up influences* as the ways in which positive and negative entwinement transfers from stakeholder parties to the system as a whole. Finally, we define *top-down influences* as the ways in which the entwinement of positive and negative interdependence transfers from the large multiparty system to the stakeholder parties.

2.2. Bottom-Up Influences

Multiparty collaboration involves the exploration of various stakeholders' interests and working with the differences among the parties to identify or create common ground (Curşeu and Schruijer 2017; Schruijer and Vansina 2008). Collaboration does not imply the dissolution of stakeholders' boundaries, in other words, parties do not have to become the same, rather, they preserve their identity and find ways to achieve their own interests while working towards a joint goal. As parties develop relationships with other parties, they need to explore within their stakeholder party how to relate to the other stakeholder parties, where their points of connection are and where they could collaborate. Exploring possible collaboration with other parties is likely to stir up tensions within stakeholder parties as identities are challenged in confrontation with 'the other' and fears of being exploited, overruled or losing one's identity may be triggered. These tensions may result in frictions and conflict within the stakeholder parties. Relationship conflict refers to interpersonal frictions and has detrimental influences on group dynamics and group effectiveness while task conflict stands for addressing the different points of view openly and directly with the aim of arriving at a better way to deal with the task at hand based on an assessment and possible integration of these diverse views (Jehn 1995; Jehn et al. 1999; Curşeu and Schruijer 2017).

Bottom-up influences are the forces that originate in the relational dynamics experienced within the stakeholder parties while engaging in a collaborative process and have an impact on the intergroup dynamics at the multiparty system level. Conflict is a pervasive and multifaceted phenomenon in small groups (Jehn 1995), it is contagious and tends to spread among individuals and groups. For example, it has been shown that system-level conflicts around water use are often driven by social and cultural conflicts within stakeholder parties (Montaña et al. 2009). We therefore argue that changes in the relational frictions experienced within stakeholder parties tend to influence the conflictuality in the whole multiparty system. Likewise, changes in task conflict within stakeholder parties may have an impact on the collaborativeness in the whole system as positive experiences in constructively dealing with differences within one's stakeholder party may encourage representatives to engage in task conflict with representatives of the other stakeholder parties.

An illustrative example is presented in Bernard et al. (2014) related to sustainable agriculture. If farmers engage in continuous adaptation and change in order to meet their own needs they will be more likely to fulfil the expectations of their customers, investors and regulators and reduce the complaints of their neighbours. If, however farmers stick to the "old ways" of farming and resist change (lack of task conflict within the interest party) it is likely that their collaborativeness will decrease and the whole system will be composed of "loss-making investors, dissatisfied customers, angry neighbours and overacting regulators" (Bernard et al. 2014, p. 157). We posit a positive interplay between task conflict experienced within the stakeholder parties and the perceived collaborativeness of all other stakeholder parties in the multiparty system as a whole.

To summarize, we expect that the entwinement of positive and negative interdependence transfers from the individual stakeholder parties to the whole multiparty system (bottom-up influence). We therefore formulate the following specific hypotheses:

Hypothesis 1. *Changes from expected to experienced within-party relationship conflict lead to changes in the same direction from expected to experienced conflictuality among the parties in the system (bottom up transfer of negative interdependence entwinement).*

Hypothesis 2. *Changes from expected to experienced task conflict within parties lead to changes in the same direction from expected to experienced collaborativeness of all the other parties in the system (bottom up transfer of positive interdependence entwinement).*

2.3. Top-Down Influences

Top-down influences are created by the quality of the intergroup interactions that spiral down to influence the dynamics within the stakeholder parties. Based on open systems theory (Katz and Kahn 1978) and on a complex adaptive systems framework (Eidelson 1997) one can expect that forces at higher system levels limit the degrees of freedom at lower system levels.

Collaborativeness or promotive interactions reflect positive interdependence (Deutsch 1949; Johnson 2003). In the case of multiparty collaboration, promotive interactions are likely to exist when parties in the system realize that they need one another to realize their individual goals (Johnson 2003; Johnson and Johnson 2005). Through their individual actions, parties in the multiparty system promote the development and realization of collective and individual goals. As the collaborativeness of all stakeholder parties is perceived to increase, one may expect the tensions that are inherent to multiparty collaboration to decrease, which in turn may generate a positive relational climate within stakeholder parties. System collaborativeness creates more space for each stakeholder party to focus on the task and more courage may be shown to confront one another in the service of task accomplishment. As the tensions of multiparty interactions decrease and consume less time, more attention can be paid to the ideas and concerns of the individual members within parties (cf. Sherif and Sherif 1967); an increasing constructive climate at the system level may foster space to engage in constructive task conflict dealing with individual concerns at the party level. On the contrary, if the collaborativeness in the whole system decreases, the constructive engagement with the task at hand within stakeholder parties is likely to be jeopardized as anxieties regarding the other parties may distract the party members from the task at hand.

Conflictuality goes together with contrient or negative interdependence in multiparty systems. Negatively interdependent stakeholder parties realize their goals at the expense of goal realization of the other parties (Johnson 2003; Johnson and Johnson 2005). Parties engaging in conflictual interactions obstruct rather than support each other. Conflict is an emotionally laden experience (Pluut and Curşeu 2013) and tends to spiral down from the multiparty system level to the individual stakeholder parties. As stated in the social interdependence theory (Johnson and Johnson 2005) negative cathexis tends to spread among the participants in a system. Aligned with the emotional contagion model (Barsade and Gibson 1998), we expect that relational tensions experienced at the system level tend to induce relational frictions within stakeholder parties. One can imagine that when intergroup relational conflict is high, there is less attention to members' needs and concerns within a group (cf. Sherif and Sherif 1967), which in due time may cause frustration and friction internally.

We expect that the entwinement of positive and negative interdependence transfers from the multiparty system level to the stakeholder parties (top-down influence). We therefore hypothesize the following:

Hypothesis 3. *Changes from expected to experienced conflictuality perceived among the stakeholder parties in the multiparty system lead to changes in the same direction from expected to experienced relationship conflict within stakeholder parties.*

Hypothesis 4. *Changes from expected to experienced collaborativeness perceived among the stakeholder parties in the multiparty system lead to changes in the same direction from expected to experienced task conflict within the stakeholder parties.*

3. Methods

3.1. Simulation and Sample

One hundred and forty-five individuals (managers and consultants of which 54 women) with an average age of 43 years old participated in the study. Data was collected in five behavioural simulations that involved different participants. All participants were enrolled in postgraduate education at a business school or in a professional development program. We used a multi-party behavioural simulation (Schruijer and Vansina 2008; Vansina and Taillieu 1997; Vansina et al. 1998) in which seven or eight (depending on the number of participants) stakeholder parties engage in within-group as well as between-group interactions to deal with a complex regional development situation involving economic, social and environmental factors in the St Petersburg area, including the island Kotlin.

The participating parties were: a local authority (with an interest in the socio-economic situation on the island), a shipyard (the largest employer on the island facing a severe problem related to unemployment and decrease in business opportunities), an island-based yacht club (located on a scenic piece of land on the island and interested in developing their yacht club), a bank (interested in long-term investments), a group of young and rich entrepreneurs (with an emotional tie to the island), a Finnish yacht club (interested in new sailing routes for their members), a yacht club near St Petersburg (also wanting to expand their activities) and a technical school (associated with the Shipyard) (for more details see Vansina et al. 1998). Each party received the briefing describing their interests and had the freedom to develop their own strategy and approach.

At the onset of the simulation participants were allocated to a party based on their expressed preferences. Then each party received a booklet containing information concerning economic (e.g., risk of bankruptcy for the most important employer on the island), social (e.g., unemployment and social unrest) and environmental (e.g., water pollution) challenges in the region, as well as specific information concerning their own interests as a party.

The simulation proceeded in real time during a full day and few hours in the next morning and was followed by a joint debriefing. We allocated the first time slot of the simulation to the study of briefs within each party and develop their party strategy for interacting with the other stakeholder parties. No specific roles were assigned to the individual participants. After the within-party preparation, one-hour intergroup visiting and plenary meetings were alternated during the day. Intergroup visiting slots consisted of the possibilities to visit other parties (with a maximum of 3 parties being present at any particular time and place). During plenary meetings, all parties could be present and send their representative to the table, while the constituencies were allowed to sit behind their representatives and send notes.

The participating parties (36 groups having 3 to 4 members each over five simulations) were asked to fill out surveys concerning within-party (task and relationship conflict) as well as between-party dynamics (the perceived conflictuality and collaborativeness of all other stakeholder parties) three times during the simulation (before the interactions started, during interactions and after the simulation ended). In order to capture the entwinement between expectations and experienced social interactions, only the first and the second evaluations were used for further analyses as the intergroup interactions only started after filling out the first questionnaire.

3.2. Measures

Task conflict was evaluated with four items adapted from a conflict scale presented in Jehn (1995). For the first evaluation, at the onset of the simulation the content of the items were adapted to capture expectations ("To what extent do you expect disagreements in your interest party related to the task?", "To what extent do you expect differences of opinion in your stakeholder party?", "How often do you think the members of your interest party will disagree about how things should be done?", "How often do you think the members of your interest party will disagree about which procedure should be used to do your work?"), while for the subsequent evaluation, the items referred to experienced task disagreements within one's stakeholder party (e.g., "To what extent are there disagreements in your stakeholder party that are related to the task," etc.). The answers were recorded on a 5-point Likert scale (1 to 5) and Cronbach's alpha for this scale was 0.94 at time 1 and .88 at time 2 for the group level aggregated items. In order to support aggregation, we used computed RWG (James et al. 1984) that ranged between 0.82 and 0.98 supporting the aggregation of the scores at the group level of analysis. The change from expectations of task conflict as evaluated before the interactions started to the experienced task conflict will therefore reflect the entwinement of positive interdependence at the stakeholder party level.

Relationship conflict was evaluated with four items adapted from the same conflict scale (Jehn 1995) and, like with the task conflict scale, at time 1 referring to expectations ("How much jealousy or rivalry do you expect to see among the members of your interest party?", "How often do you expect to have personality conflicts in your interest party?", "How much tension do you think will exist among the members of your stakeholder party?", "How often do you think people will get angry while working in your interest party?"). At time 2 the items referred to experienced interpersonal frictions (e.g., "How much jealousy or rivalry is there among the members of your stakeholder party," etc.). The same 5-point Likert scale was used (1 to 5) to record the answers. Cronbach's alpha for this scale was 0.95 at time 1 and .85 at time 2 for the items aggregated at the group level. The RWG scores ranged from 0.73 to 1.00 supporting the aggregation of the scores at the group level. The change from expected relationship conflict to experienced relationship conflict will therefore be indicative of the entwinement of negative interdependence at the stakeholder party level.

Collaborativeness was evaluated using a round robin technique in which each participant was asked to evaluate the extent to which he or she perceived each of the participating stakeholder parties as being collaborative. At time 1 participants were asked to estimate the collaborativeness of each stakeholder party based on the reading of the briefing material ("Please evaluate how collaborative you think each stakeholder party will be." The evaluations range from 0 = not collaborative at all to 5 = very collaborative"), while at time 2 they were asked to evaluate the experienced collaborativeness ("Please evaluate the extent to which [each stakeholder party] is collaborative." The evaluations range from 0 = not collaborative at all to 5 = very collaborative"). To capture bottom-up influences (what individual parties bring into the larger system), we aggregated evaluations for each stakeholder party as a referent—how each stakeholder party is perceived by the other stakeholder parties in the system. As an index of collaborativeness for bottom-up influences, we used the average score for the collaborativeness of each stakeholder party as perceived by the other stakeholder parties (total system-level score excluding one's own party)—that is the average collaborativeness ascribed to a particular stakeholder party by the others in the system. To capture top-down processes (how the multiparty interactions impact the within-party climate), we have aggregated evaluations using the whole system as a referent—how each stakeholder party perceives all the other stakeholder parties. As an index of collaborativeness for the top-down influences we have used the average score for how collaborative each party sees all the other stakeholder parties in the system (again excluding one's own party)—that is the collaborativeness ascribed to all other stakeholders in the system by a particular party. In other words, we have use collaborativeness of each stakeholder party as evaluated BY others as an index in the bottom-up analyses and collaborativeness attributed TO all the others by each stakeholder party as an index in the top-down analyses. Change from the expected to the experienced collaborativeness reflects the entwinement of positive interdependence and the two indices will be separately used to capture the bottom-up and top-down influences.

Conflictuality was evaluated in a similar fashion as collaborativeness, using a single item that referred to expected conflictuality of each party at time 1 ("Please evaluate how conflictual you think each party will be. The evaluations range from 0 = not conflictual at all to 5 = very conflictual") and evaluated experienced conflictual relations at time 2 ("Please evaluate the conflictuality of . . . [each of the other stakeholder parties]". The evaluations range from 0 = not conflictual at all to 5 = very conflictual"). To capture the bottom-up influences, a conflictuality score was computed by averaging all scores received by each stakeholder party from all the other stakeholder parties (total system-level score, excluding one's own party)—that is, conflictuality ascribed to a particular stakeholder party by all other parties in the system. To capture the top-down influences, we have used the average score for how each stakeholder party perceived the conflictuality of all the other stakeholder parties in the system (excluding one's own party)—that is conflictuality ascribed by a particular party to all the other parties in the system. We have therefore used conflictuality as evaluated BY others as an index in the bottom-up analyses and conflictuality in the system (ascribed TO others) as a whole for the top-down analyses. As for collaborativeness, the change from expected to experienced conflictuality indicates the entwinement of negative interdependence and the two indices are used to capture bottom-up and top-down influences.

To summarize, in order to capture the top-down and bottom up influences, we have used different aggregation procedures of the data collected through the round-robin procedure for collaborativeness and conflictuality. For the bottom-up influences the aggregation reflects what each party brings into the system (collaborativeness and conflictuality of each party as seen by others), while for the top-down influences, the aggregation reflects what each party perceives in the system as a whole (collaborativeness and conflictuality ascribed to others in the system).

4. Results

Means, standard deviations and correlations are presented in Table 1. In order to test the dynamic interplay between the two forms of conflict and the changing intergroup perceptions we used the MEMORE macro in SPSS version 22 (Montoya and Hayes 2017). The macro allows mediation tests in repeated measures designs and the procedure does not focus on the effect of a particular independent variable but rather models the effect of change induced by a particular event in a variable (mediator) on change in another variable (dependent variable). In our design, between the two successive evaluations, parties engaged in within and between-group interactions. This systematic change is considered as main independent variable. As we argued before, interactions within one's stakeholder party are expected to trigger changes in the conflict experienced between stakeholder parties, which in turn influences the way in which other stakeholder parties are perceived during intergroup interactions and vice versa. The macro is based on a bootstrapping procedure and it includes terms that capture change as well as the average scores of the mediator variables. Overall, as interactions in the simulation unfold, stakeholder parties seem to experience less within-group relationship conflict than originally expected (effect size = -0.24, $SE = 0.10$, $CI_{low} = -0.45$; $CI_{high} = -0.04$) and they are rated as less conflictual by others than initially expected (effect size = -0.69, $SE = 0.10$, $CI_{low} = -0.90$; $CI_{high} = -0.49$). In Hypothesis 1 we stated that as parties start interacting, changes in relationship conflict within stakeholder parties positively coevolve with changes in perceived conflictuality in the whole system. The results support this hypothesis as the indirect effect size is significant and the 95% confidence interval does not contain zero (indirect effect size = -0.14; $SE = 0.06$; $CI_{low} = -0.24$; $CI_{high} = -0.01$). The results of the analyses carried out with MEMORE are summarized in Figure 2 following the example reported in Montoya and Hayes (2017). As we expected, change in relationship conflict within stakeholder parties has a significant positive influence on change in perceived system conflictuality (effect size = 0.58; $SE = 0.17$ $CI_{low} = 0.24$; $CI_{high} = 0.91$), in other words, as relationship conflict experienced within stakeholder parties change, this change triggers changes in the perceptions of conflictuality at the system level.

Table 1. Presents the means, standard deviations and correlations among the variables used in further analyses.

	Mean	SD	1	2	3	4	5	6	7	8	9	10	11
1. TC Time1	2.88	0.56											
2. TC Time 2	2.64	0.40	0.09										
3. RC Time 1	2.09	0.60	0.77 **	0.24									
4. RC Time 2	1.85	0.44	0.34 *	0.51 **	0.35 *								
5. CollBY Time 1	3.01	0.33	0.02	0.21	0.16	0.18							
6. CollBY Time 2	2.33	0.51	0.16	0.65 **	0.33 *	0.26	0.36 *						
7. ConflBY Time 1	2.57	0.58	0.45 **	0.12	0.60 **	−0.02	0.01	0.17					
8. ConflBY Time 2	1.74	0.36	−0.06	−0.39 *	−0.24	−0.09	−0.10	−0.58 **	−0.08				
9. CollTO Time 1	3.01	0.32	0.22	0.06	0.31	0.04	0.03	−0.02	−0.07	−0.17			
10. CollTO Time 2	2.33	0.39	0.17	0.46 **	0.12	0.18	0.37 *	0.40 *	0.07	−0.14	0.04		
11. ConflTO Time 1	2.57	0.65	0.49 **	0.12	0.55 **	−0.08	0.19	0.15	0.56 **	−0.13	0.30	0.31	
12. ConflTO Time 2	1.74	0.48	0.03	0.16	0.15	0.09	0.14	0.10	−0.12	−0.02	0.16	−0.06	0.16

Notes: * $p < 0.05$, ** $p < 0.01$; TC—task conflict within parties, RC—relationship conflict within parties, CollBY—collaborativeness ascribed by others, ConflBY—conflictuality ascribed by others, ColTO—collaborativeness ascribed to others, ConflTO—conflictuality ascribed to others.

Overall, as interactions unfold in the simulations, parties seem to experience less task conflict within stakeholder parties than originally expected (effect size = −0.23; $SE = 0.11$, $CI_{low} = -0.46$; $CI_{high} = -0.01$) and stakeholder parties are perceived as being less collaborative by others than initially expected (effect size = −0.61; $SE = 0.08$, $CI_{low} = -0.77$; $CI_{high} = -0.46$). Hypothesis 2 stated that as intergroup interactions begin, changes in task conflict within stakeholder parties positively coevolve with the changes in perceived system collaborativeness. Although the results do not directly support the mediation hypothesis as the 95% confidence intervals for the indirect effect include zero (indirect effect size = −0.06; $SE = 0.04$; $CI_{low} = -0.14$; $CI_{high} = 0.01$), the direct effect of change in task on conflict within stakeholder parties on change on perceived system collaborativeness is positive and significant (effect size = 0.26; $SE = 0.11$ $CI_{low} = 0.03$; $CI_{high} = 0.50$). In other words, change in perceived system collaborativeness is directly and positively triggered by changes in task conflict within stakeholder parties. Moreover, as also illustrated in Figure 3 the change in collaborativeness is also positively predicted by the average task conflict in the two evaluation points. We can therefore conclude that Hypothesis 2 received partial support.

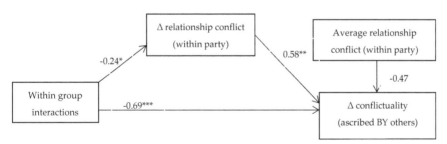

Figure 2. The overall mediation model for change in relationship conflict and conflictuality (bottom-up influence). Notes: * $p < 0.05$; ** $p < 0.01$, *** $p < 0.001$, Δrelationship conflict = relationship conflict at time 2 minus relationship conflict at time 1 and describes the negative interdependence entwinement at the stakeholder party level, Δconflictuality = conflictuality as perceived by others at time 2 minus conflictuality as perceived by others at time 1 and reflects the negative interdependence entwinement at the multiparty level.

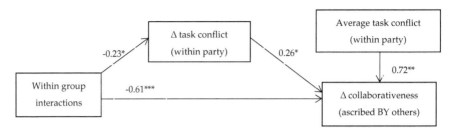

Figure 3. The overall mediation model for change in tach conflict and collaborativeness (bottom-up influence). Notes: * $p < 0.05$; ** $p < 0.01$, *** $p < 0.001$, Δtask conflict = task conflict at time 2 minus task conflict at time 1 (positive interdependence entwinement at the stakeholder party level), Δcollaborativeness = collaborativeness as perceived by others at time 2 minus collaborativeness as perceived by others at time 1 (positive interdependence entwinement at the multiparty level).

As interactions started during the simulation, parties seem to perceive the others as less conflictual than they expected initially (effect size = -0.83; $SE = 0.12$; $CI_{low} = -10.09$; $CI_{high} = -0.58$). Hypothesis 3 stated that changes in conflictuality at the system level are predictive of changes of changes in relationship conflict experienced within stakeholder parties. The mediation results support the mediation role for system conflictuality as the estimated confidence interval for the indirect effect does not include zero (indirect effect size = -0.23; $SE = 0.12$; $CI_{low} = -0.49$; $CI_{high} = -0.01$), the direct relation between change in conflictuality on change in experienced relationship conflict within parties is positive and significant (effect size = 0.28; $SE = 0.12$ $CI_{low} = 0.04$; $CI_{high} = 0.52$) supporting a top-down effect of system conflictuality on within party relationship conflict. The overall results supporting Hypothesis 3 are presented in Figure 4.

After interactions started during the simulation, parties perceive the others as less collaborative than expected (effect size = -0.67; $SE = 0.08$; $CI_{low} = -0.84$; $CI_{high} = 0.51$). Hypothesis 4 stated that the changes in collaborativeness at the system level co-evolve with changes in task conflict experienced within stakeholder parties. The results of this mediation analyses are presented in Figure 5 and reveal no significant indirect effect as the estimated confidence interval include zero (indirect effect size = -0.18; $SE = 0.18$; $CI_{low} = -0.60$; $CI_{high} = 0.11$) and the direct association between change in collaborativeness at the system level and task conflict experienced within parties is also not significant (effect size = 0.27; $SE = 0.23$ $CI_{low} = -0.20$; $CI_{high} = 0.75$).

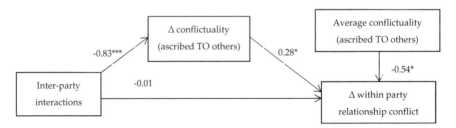

Figure 4. The overall mediation model for change in conflictuality and relationship conflict (top-down influence). Notes: * $p < 0.05$; *** $p < 0.001$, Δrelationship conflict = relationship conflict at time 2 minus relationship conflict at time 1, Δconflictuality = the conflictuality as perceived by each party for the system as a whole at time 2 minus conflictuality at the system level at time 1.

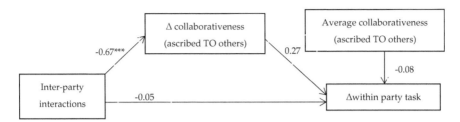

Figure 5. The overall mediation model for change in tach conflict and collaborativeness (top down influence). Notes: *** $p < 0.001$, Δtask conflict = task conflict at time 2 minus task conflict at time 1, Δcollaborativeness = collaborativeness as perceived by each party for the system as a whole at time 2 minus collaborativeness as for the system as a whole at time 1.

5. Discussion

Our paper addressed the interrelatedness of multiparty dynamics at different system levels. We focused on the entwinement between expectations and social interactions and analysed positive and negative interdependence (the interplay between collaboration and conflict). Moreover, we tested bottom-up and top-down influences, that is, how within- stakeholder party dynamics affect those at the system level, and, how system level dynamics affect dynamics at the stakeholder level, in a multiparty context. Building on social interdependence theory (Deutsch 1949; Johnson 2003) we argued that positive interdependence (facilitating collaborativeness) at the system level increase the degrees of freedom for elemental components of the system (allowing stakeholder parties to engage with the task and thus engage in within-group task conflict), while negative interdependence (facilitating conflictuality) decreases these degrees of freedom and stimulate relationship conflict within stakeholder parties.

As top-down influences we have tested the effect of the changes in collaborativeness and conflictuality perceived at the system level on the changes in task and relationship conflict experienced within stakeholder parties. Regarding bottom-up influences, we have tested the extent to which changes in task and relationship conflicts experienced within the stakeholder parties co-evolve with changes in collaborativeness and conflictuality at the system level. To disentangle the top-down and bottom-up influences we have used different referential models for collaboration and conflict. Overall, bottom-up processes received stronger support than top-down processes. Changes in task conflict within stakeholder parties are positively related to changes in perceived collaborativeness at the system level (that is, perceived collaborativeness of all stakeholder parties combined) while changes in within-group relationship conflict are positively associated with system conflictuality. From the two top-down influences investigated, only the effect of change in conflictuality at the system level on the changes in relationship conflict experienced within stakeholder parties was significant. This finding next to the significant bottom-up association between relationship conflict and perceived conflictuality supports the pervasive nature of especially relationship conflict in social systems (Van Bunderen et al. 2017; Pluut and Curşeu 2013). Conflict contagion or the transfer of negative cathexis (Johnson and Johnson 2005) seems to be an influential process in multiparty systems. Social interdependence theory (Deutsch 1949; Johnson and Johnson 2005) also claims that positive cathexis could be transferred among the parties engaged in the system. This claim warrants further empirical exploration as positive cathexis is claimed to be beneficial for collaboration (Johnson and Johnson 2005).

The cognitive synergy path (conceptually described in Curşeu and Schruijer 2017) and the positive interplay between changes in within-party task conflict and system collaborativeness are only supported for the bottom-up test. Changes in task related debates, in this case engaging in task conflict, within the stakeholder parties, are proportionally related to changes in parties' perceived collaborativeness. In other words, the more stakeholder parties engage internally with the different opinions regarding addressing the task, the more they have the potential to contribute to the overall collaboration in the system. Using the terms of social interdependence theory, task conflict seems to increase the perceived inducibility (openness to being influenced by others) of the parties. As inducibility increases, parties engage with the multiparty task at hand and promote the achievement of their collective goal (Johnson and Johnson 2005).

We call for more research integrating systems-psychodynamic theorizing (Schruijer 2016; Vansina and Vansina-Cobbaert 2008) and social interdependence theory (Johnson and Johnson 2005) as they both apply to multiparty systems. In social interdependence terms, for multiparty collaboration *substitutability* needs to be low (parties have unique competencies or resources that cannot be substituted by the other parties in the system), while *inducibility* is required (parties need to be open to social influence in the process of developing a collective goal) and *cathexis* is present (the transfer of positive and negative evaluations/emotions within and among parties). A key claim of social interdependence theory is that the structure of the individual goals in a given situation determines how participants interact. The structure of the stakeholder parties' goals in our simulation require collaboration or promotive interactions as parties cannot deal with the complex situation on their own. However, as our results show, parties often engage in conflictual (contrient) interactions and the emotional dynamics override the normative (cognitive and rational) need for collaboration. Exploring the (conscious and unconscious) emotional dynamics or the cathexis using a systems psychodynamic perspective could help us gain a deeper understanding of the dynamics of multiparty systems.

So far, we have offered a system interpretation of our results. In our simulation, different individuals engaged in interactions as representatives of the seven parties. They had to embark on these interactions without the restrictions of particular (individual) role prescriptions. As such, their interpersonal skills, personality and behavioural tendencies may have played an important role on how the interactions between group members unfolded. The aim of the simulation was not to attend to individual behaviours and no personal feedback was given to participants. Moreover, as the participants knew each other (they all took part in either a degree program lasting for 16 months or a professional development program), interpersonal histories may have been carried into the simulation and interpersonal conflicts from outside the simulation or interpersonal attraction for that matter, could have influenced the inter-group dynamics.

Our paper has several limitations. First, for the test of top down influences, data to test the models were collected from the same source for the mediator and dependent variables, therefore these analyses are susceptible to common source bias. However, given the fact that the evaluation of within-party conflict and the conflictuality and collaborativeness had different reference points and different rating intervals, we could argue that the common method bias concerns are attenuated. Second, in our study we only evaluated task and relationship conflict as experienced within the stakeholder parties and future research could also evaluate task and relationship conflict in the whole system and in this way test top-down and bottom-up influences in a different manner. Third, we have used aggregated individual scores to obtain evaluations of system collaborativeness and conflictuality. Future research could use global evaluations made by external observers for these two forms of social interdependence. Fourth, in terms of alternative interpretations, one could argue that the bottom-up influences as operationalized in our study actually reflect self-fulfilling prophecies (Merton 1948). Participants' expectations about positive and negative interdependence may lead them to behave in ways that are consistent with these expectations and as a consequence the way they are perceived by others in interactions is congruent with their own initial expectations. Moreover, the way we have operationalized the top-down influences may conflate false consensus effects (Ross et al. 1977). In other words, participants' experiences of positive or negative interdependence in their own parties may lead them to evaluate other parties as displaying the same forms of interdependence. Although, based on the data collected in this study we cannot refute these two alternative explanations, we argue that the aggregation of individual evaluations may have alleviated the self-fulfilling prophecy and false consensus influences. Finally, given the time-intensive nature of the behavioural simulations, our sample is small and future research could attempt to replicate our findings in larger samples and in different settings.

Practical Implications

Due to its pervasive negative influences, relationship conflict needs to be pro-actively managed in multiparty systems. Conflict reducing techniques both at the party as well as at the system level may help alleviate the detrimental influences of conflict escalation. Interventions aimed at generating task conflict within stakeholder parties will spur collaborativeness in the whole system. Simple normative interventions could help stakeholder parties to engage in healthy task debates as illustrated by research that used ground rules for collaboration to increase the quality of group debates and ultimately group rationality (Curşeu and Schruijer 2012). Moreover, process consultation may support multiparty collaboration by stimulating healthy task conflict and reducing the relationship conflict. Finally, behavioural simulations constitute experiential learning opportunities in which individuals can gain an understanding of multiparty dynamics and can develop their collaboration skills.

Author Contributions: S.S. and P.L.C. designed and conducted the study; P.L.C. analysed the data; S.S. provided the behavioural simulation materials and brochures; P.L.C. and S.S. wrote and revised the paper.

Funding: P.L.C. was supported by a grant of the Romanian National Authority for Scientific Research, CNCS—UEFISCDI, project number PN-III-P4-ID-ERC- 2016-0008. The funders had no role in study design, data collection and analysis, decision to publish, or preparation of the manuscript.

Conflicts of Interest: The authors declare no conflicts of interest.

References

Barsade, Sigal G., and Donald E. Gibson. 1998. Group emotion: A view from top and bottom. In *Research on Managing Groups and Teams*. Edited by Deborah Gruenfeld, Elizabeth Mannix and Margaret Neale. Stanford: JAI Press, pp. 81–102.

Bernard, Florence, Meinevan Noordwijk, Eike Luedeling, Grace B. Villamor, Gudeta W. Sileshi, and Sara Namirembe. 2014. Social actors and unsustainability of agriculture. *Current Opinion in Environmental Sustainability* 6: 155–61. [CrossRef]

Costa, Ana Cristina, C. Ashley Fulmer, and Neil R. Anderson. 2017. Trust in work teams: An integrative review, multilevel model and future directions. *Journal of Organizational Behavior* 39: 169–84. [CrossRef]

Curşeu, Petru, and Sandra Schruijer. 2012. Normative interventions, emergent cognition and decision rationality in ad-hoc and established groups. *Management Decision* 50: 1062–75. [CrossRef]

Curşeu, Petru Lucian, and Sandra G. L. Schruijer. 2017. Stakeholder diversity and the comprehensiveness of sustainability decisions: The role of collaboration and conflict. *Current Opinions in Sustainability Studies* 28: 114–20. [CrossRef]

Deutsch, Morton. 1949. A theory of co-operation and competition. *Human Relations* 2: 129–52. [CrossRef]

Eidelson, Roy J. 1997. Complex adaptive systems in the behavioral and social sciences. *Review of General Psychology* 1: 42–71. [CrossRef]

Holmes, John G. 2002. Interpersonal expectations as the building blocks of social cognition: An interdependence theory perspective. *Personal Relationships* 9: 1–26. [CrossRef]

Huxham, Chris. 2003. Theorizing collaboration practice. *Public Management Review* 5: 401–23. [CrossRef]

James, Lawrence R., Robert G. Demaree, and Gerrit Wolf. 1984. Estimating withingroup interrater reliability with and without response bias. *Journal of Applied Psychology* 69: 85–98. [CrossRef]

Jehn, Karen A. 1995. A multimethod examination of the benefits and detriments of intragroup conflict. *Administrative Science Quarterly* 40: 256–82. [CrossRef]

Jehn, Karen A., Gregory B. Northcraft, and Margaret A. Neale. 1999. Why differences make a difference: A field study of diversity, conflict and performance in workgroups. *Administrative Science Quarterly* 44: 741–63. [CrossRef]

Johnson, David W. 2003. Social interdependence: Interrelationships among theory, research and practice. *American Psychologist* 58: 934–45. [CrossRef] [PubMed]

Johnson, David W., and Roger T. Johnson. 2005. New developments in social interdependence theory. *Genetic, Social and General Psychology Monographs* 131: 285–358. [CrossRef] [PubMed]

Katz, Daniel, and Robert L. Kahn. 1978. *The Social Psychology of Organizations*. New York: Wiley.

Lewin, Kurt. 1936. *Principles of Topological Psychology*. New York: McGraw-Hill.

Merton, Robert. K. 1948. The self-fulfilling prophecy. *The Antioch Review* 8: 193–210. [CrossRef]

Montaña, Elma, Gabriela Pastor, and Laura Torres. 2009. Socioeconomic issues in irrigation literature: Approaches, concepts and meanings. *Chilean Journal of Agricultural Research* 69: 55–67. [CrossRef]

Montoya, Amanda K., and Andrew F. Hayes. 2017. Two-condition within-participant statistical mediation analysis: A path-analytic framework. *Psychological Methods* 22: 6–27. [CrossRef] [PubMed]

Pluut, Helen, and Petru Lucian Curşeu. 2013. Perceptions of intragroup conflict: The effect of coping strategies on conflict transformation and escalation. *Group Processes & Intergroup Relations* 16: 412–25.

Ross, Lee, David Greene, and Pamela House. 1977. The "false consensus effect": An egocentric bias in social perception and attribution processes. *Journal of Experimental Social Psychology* 13: 279–301. [CrossRef]

Schruijer, Sandra. 2008. The psychology of interorganizational relations. In *The Oxford Handbook of Interorganizational Relations*. Edited by Steve Cropper, Mark Ebers, Chris Huxham and Peter Smith Ring. New York and Oxford: Oxford University Press, pp. 417–40.

Schruijer, Sandra G. L. 2016. Working with group dynamics while teaching group dynamics in a traditional classroom setting: An illustration of a systems-psychodynamic point of view. *Team Performance Management* 22: 257–68. [CrossRef]

Schruijer, Sandra, and Leopold Vansina. 2008. Working across organizational boundaries: Understanding and working with the psychological dynamics. In *Psychodynamics for Consultants and Managers: From Understanding to Leading Meaningful Change*. Edited by Leopold Vansina and Marie-Jeanne Vansina-Cobbaert. London: Wiley, pp. 390–410.

Sherif, Carolyn W., and Muzafer Sherif. 1967. *Attitude, Ego-Involvement and Change*. New York: Wiley.

Shuffler, Marissa L., Miliani Jiménez-Rodríguez, and William S. Kramer. 2015. The science of multiteam systems: A review and future research agenda. *Small Group Research* 46: 659–99. [CrossRef]

Thomson, Ann Marie, and James L. Perry. 2006. Collaboration processes: Inside the black box. *Public Administration Review* 66: 20–32. [CrossRef]

Van Bunderen, Lisanne, Lindred Leura Greer, and Daan Van Knippenberg. 2017. When inter-team conflict spirals into intra-team power struggles: The pivotal role of team power structures. *Academy of Management Journal*. [CrossRef]

Vangen, Siv. 2017. Developing practice-oriented theory on collaboration: A paradox lens. *Public Administration Review* 77: 263–72. [CrossRef]

Vansina, Leopold, and Tharsi Taillieu. 1997. Diversity in collaborative task-systems. *European Journal of Work and Organizational Psychology* 6: 183–99. [CrossRef]

Vansina, Leopold S., and Marie-Jeanne Vansina-Cobbaert. 2008. *Psychodynamics for Consultants and Managers*. Hoboken: John Wiley & Sons.

Vansina, Leopold, Tharsi C. B. Taillieu, and Sandra G. L. Schruijer. 1998. Managing multiparty issues: Learning from experience. In *Research in Organizational Change and Development*. Edited by William Pasmore and Richard Woodman. Bingley: Emerald, vol. 11, pp. 159–83.

Waller, Mary J., Gerardo A. Okhuysen, and Marzieh Saghafian. 2016. Conceptualizing emergent states: A strategy to advance the study of group dynamics. *Academy of Management Annals* 10: 561–98. [CrossRef]

Wood, Donna J., and Barbara Gray. 1991. Toward a comprehensive theory of collaboration. *The Journal of Applied Behavioral Science* 27: 139–62. [CrossRef]

MDPI

St. Alban-Anlage 66

4052 Basel

Switzerland

Tel. +41 61 683 77 34

Fax +41 61 302 89 18

www.mdpi.com

Administrative Sciences Editorial Office

E-mail: admsci@mdpi.com

www.mdpi.com/journal/admsci

Lightning Source UK Ltd.
Milton Keynes UK
UKHW050030080922
408482UK00002B/94